More praise for
Live Your Dreams: Doctor's Orders

"Dr. Gerstein introduces us to 40 individuals who have accomplished the impossible to reach profound success. It is through the guidance of those who have traveled the path before us that we can learn to achieve our own life dreams. This book is a priceless treasure of tried-and-true wisdom for all ages."

Nido Qubein, President, High Point University, Chairman, Great Harvest Bread Co.

✦

"Dr. Gerstein has shown us, through many real examples, how we can convert dreams from aspiration to reality. If you have a dream, but have not realized it yet, read this book and inspire yourself to action!"

Dr. Lance Secretan, Author, *ONE: The Art and Practice of Conscious Leadership.*

✦

"The people in these stories will serve as role models for anyone who wants to live their dreams."

Robin Sharma, #1 Bestselling author of *The Greatness Guide.*

✦

"You can change your life or your attitude towards your life. We are all capable of change when we have the desire and intention to do so. This book can help coach and guide you and show you that reinventing yourself is possible."

Bernie Siegel, MD, Author of *365 Prescriptions For The Soul and Prescriptions For Living*

✦

"It's one thing to dream. It's another thing to have your doctor help you turn your dream into success. Read Live Your Dreams: Doctor's Orders *and your dreams may come true."*

W. Mitchell, C.P.A.E., Author of *It's Not What Happens to You, It's What You Do About It.*

Live
Your
Dreams:
Doctor's Orders

Samuel Gerstein, M.D.

Live Your Dreams:
Doctor's Orders

A GUIDE TO SELF-FULFILLMENT AND HAPPINESS

 Dreams For Real Inc.

ISBN 978-0-9781517-0-6

Library and Archives Canada Cataloguing in Publication

Gerstein, Samuel, 1957-
Live your dreams, doctor's orders : a guide to self-fulfilment
and happiness / Samuel Gerstein.

Includes bibiographical references and index.
ISBN 0-9781517-0-4

1. Self-actualization (Psychology). I. Title.

BF637.S4G476 2007
158.1
C2006-906408-3

Editorial, Style and Additional Research: Janet Matthews
www.janetmatthews.ca
Editing, Production, Cover Art and Book Design: Agnes Bellegris, Dianne Kehoe, The Big Think
www.thebigthink.ca

*This book is dedicated to my parents who
gave me the opportunity to explore my dream,
to my wife, Michelle, who believed in my dream
and supported me every step along the way,
and to my children, Ryan and Casey, so they
will know that their dreams are real.*

Contents

Part 2 – Your Outer World

Acknowledgements

First I'd like to thank all of the people who agreed to be interviewed by me for this book. Because they were all doing what they loved, they gave up some of their precious time to show me how they did it. All of those who participated in the intensive interviews are listed in the back of the book. To everyone else, I am grateful for indulging me in answering my queries.

I am grateful to my wife, Michelle Hoffer, for listening to my endless ideas that went into writing this book. Your enormous patience and insightful feedback greatly assisted me in completing this process, and I cannot thank you enough.

I'd like to thank my editors Janet Matthews and Agnes Bellegris. Thank you Janet for your positive enthusiasm, creativity and passion. Thank you Agnes for your hard work, trusting reliability and support. In addition, I am grateful to you, Dianne Kehoe for your innovative ideas and precise work in the book design. Their love for their work and their enthusiasm for this project has helped me make this a reality.

I greatly appreciate the tremendous feedback and support I received from members of my mastermind team, The Professional Infopreneurs Mastermind Group of Greater Toronto, notably Michael McGauley, Bahram Jam, Elizabeth Verwey, and Richard Seredynski.

I am very appreciative of Heidi Prosserman, Sam Hoffer and Bahram Jam, who reviewed early copies and gave tremendous feedback.

Finally, I'd like to thank all of the people and authors who have inspired me to pursue my own dream. A partial list includes Anthony Robbins, Barbara Sher, Bernie Siegel, Patch Adams, Ingrid Bredenberg, Mark Victor Hansen, Jack Canfield and Deepak Chopra.

Because of space limitations I was not able to include everyone I interviewed in *Live Your Dreams: Doctor's Orders*. However, I would like to acknowledge their kindness in taking the time to speak with me. I am indebted to each of them for being a living example of how to live your dreams at work. I learned so much from every one. The following is a list of all the people (listed in alphabetical order by their corresponding dream career) I formally interviewed:

Ronen Abergel – Hair Stylist; Bev Adcock – Administrative Assistant to the Mayor; Lynette Anthony – Customer Care Rep; Joan Barrington – "Bunky" – Therapeutic Clown; Allan Baum, President of a Security Systems Company; Brenda Barnes – Owner, Operator and Principal of Martingrove Montessori School; Nick Bartzis – Outsource Provider for Workplace Health and Safety solutions; Jennifer Beale – Publicist; Orlando Bowen – Professional Football Player; Normand Bouliane – Streetcar Operator; Stuart Brindle – Director of Golf Deer Creek Golf and Banquet Facility; Greg Brophy – President and Chairman of Shred It; Dorothy Brophy – Corporate Lawyer; Ian Buffett – Veterinarian; Brendan Calder – Professor, Rotman School of Management, University of Toronto; Dan Campitelli – Firefighter; Holly Champion – Owner Floral Company; Scott Channing – Millwright; Nadine Cyr – Naturopathic Doctor; Ginette D'Aigle – Early Childhood Educator; Luigi De Gasperis – Plumber; Mark Diamond – Camp Owner; Darryl Dueck – Video Producer and Actor; Susan Fennell – Mayor of Brampton; Cathleen Fillmore – Author, Speaker and Speaker's Bureau Owner; Mira Gandhi – Promotional Wear Developer; Mark Gelgor – Operations Director of Sportball™; Cary Gordon – Personal Trainer; Noel Gordon – Cook; Sharon Hampson – Singer For Children and Families; Brock Horton – Respiratory Therapist; Sherri Hunt-Serazin – Horse Trainer; Gregory Kaminsky – Founder & Owner of Sign Store; Gordon Kirke – Sports and Entertainment Lawyer & Sports Agent; Allan Koch, Farmer; Shirley Koch – Gardener; Laura Koot – News Presentation Editor; Shelley Kraus – Membership Director Fitness Club; Bill Laurin – Executive TV Producer of 1-800-Missing (Show Runner); Josh Lewis – Pharmaceutical Rep.; Janice Lindsay – Interior Colour Designer; Ed Lubberdink –

Health Coach (Chiropractor); Josette Luyckx – Artist – Clothing Designer; Declan Mackell – Carpenter – Sailboats; Charles Marcus – Professional Speaker; Brian Marks – Equipment Manager – Women's Hockey Team; Caroline Martin – Registered Massage Therapist – specialty in Athletic Therapy; John McAuley – President and CEO of Muskoka Woods; Scott McDiarmid – Home Renovator; Michael McGauley – Professional Speaker; Richard Mcleod – Owner of Interior Design Firm Montana & Associates; Bob Middleton – Geophysicist/Geologist; Dr. Gilbert Miller – Pediatrician; Lucas Miller – Power Skating and Hockey Coach; Kim Mitchell – Co-operative Education Instructor; Gloria Montesano – Villa Consultant; Elaine Morton – Owner and Operator of Aesthetic Salon; Carol Moxam – Event Planner; Rome Muia – Electrical Contractor; Kevin Mulhern – Project Manager at Financial Institution; Kimberley O'Brien – Corporate Communications Manager; John O'Dwyer – Business Coach & Management Consultant; Mara Ostby – Partner in HR Consulting Firm; Elaine Overholt – Vocal Coach and Singer; Avraham E. Plotkin – Rabbi; Goldie Plotkin – Rabbitzen; Ron Pollock – Diamond Importer and Wholesaler; Jeffrey Prosserman – Filmmaker; Dawn Ralph – Executive Director and Cofounder of The Peter F. Drucker Canadian Foundation; James Ralph – Pilot; Ricky Ramos – Sportball™ Coach; Dave Redinger – Owner Car Repair Shop; Susan Regenstreif – Music Specialist and Teacher; Heather Reisman – CEO Indigo Books and Music Inc.; John Robinson – Antique Chair Maker; Brent Rogers – Business Coach; Sheldon Rotman – Dentist; David Rudkin – Paleobiologist; Daniella Santana – Policewoman; Peri Shawn – Teacher; Penny Simmons – President and Founder of Penny Loafers Shoe Shine Company Inc.; Doug Sole – Drum Circle Facilitator, Professional Speaker, And retail Music Store Owner; Phil Solomon – Justice of the Peace; Manisha Solomon – Book Packager and Editor; Gary Stein – Architect; Tema Stein – Pediatric Physiotherapist and Osteopath; Tom Stoyan – Sales Coach; Pat Striewe – Representative for Workers Health & Safety Centre; Judy Suke – Motivational Humorist; Lesley Sullivan – Chef, and Catering Company Owner; Robin Tapley – Creator and Leader of Nature Tourism programs; Shavey Tishler – Director of Day Care; Tsufit – Singer/Actress and Coach; Ila Faye Turley – Actor; Mark Van Oene – Scientific Researcher; Elizabeth Verwey – Mentor in Time and Space Management; Mae Waese – Community Advocate; Jeff Wilson – Children's Camp Owner; Ray Winer – Chartered Accountant; Debby Winer – Photographer; John Wright – Executive Coach; John Zucs – Financial Analyst

Disclaimer

This book was written with the intent of expanding people's awareness of what is possible in the world of work. All of the stories of the people in the book are true accounts of their working lives up to the time of the interviews (from 2002 to 2004) that were used as the foundation for the research for the book. (To get an update of their career or to discover how to reach them, please refer to the contact information section in Appendices.)

The lessons that are related by the people in the book, as well as by Dr. Gerstein, are the opinions of the aforementioned authors. This book gives no guarantee of success or of reproducing any of the results achieved by the people interviewed for this book by following the lessons outlined in the text. In fact, one of the key concepts in the book is that people's life directions are as unique as the people themselves. No one can tell you what to do. That comes from within. Use this book to stimulate your own thought process of what may be right for you.

Every effort has been made to make this book as complete and accurate as possible. However, there may be mistakes both typographical and in content, therefore, the text should be used as a general guide and not as the ultimate source for career guidance.

The purpose of the book is to educate and entertain. The author and publisher assume no liability for any loss or damages alleged to be caused by the contents contained in the book. Please consult the appropriate professionals to obtain specific information regarding your personal situation.

Foreword
by Jack Canfield

In our first *Chicken Soup for the Soul* book, I tell a story of visiting the Temple of the Golden Buddha in Thailand. I was astounded to learn that this awesome solid-gold Buddha smiling down at us had been covered by a thick layer of clay for hundreds of years.

Historians believe that Siamese monks applied the clay to keep their precious treasure from being looted by an invading army. Unfortunately, it appears that all the monks were killed by the invaders, and the well-kept secret of the golden Buddha remained intact until 1957 when the statue had to be moved. To everyone's shock some clay fell off, and when the startled head monk applied a hammer and chisel, he discovered the sold-gold treasure underneath.

As we flew home I thought to myself, "We are all like that Buddha, covered with a shell of hardness created out of fear. Yet underneath, each of us is a 'golden Buddha; a 'golden Christ' or a 'golden essence' which is our real self. Somewhere between the ages of two and nine we begin to cover up our 'golden essence.' Much like the monk with the hammer and the chisel, our task now is to discover our true essence once again!"

In *"Live Your Dreams – Doctor's Orders"* - Dr. Gerstein does a superb job of exposing the true golden essence of forty ordinary people who all found a way to overcome their fear, chip off the clay and go for their dream. And after each story, he provides tips on how you, the reader can do it too.

There are many books out there today on how to achieve your dreams and find success. In this book Dr. Gerstein shows us what can happen when those principles are actually applied. By going beyond the tired theories of how to 'find a good job,' he opted to shoot for the moon and found example after example of people actually living their dreams at work. Based not on money, but on passion, joy and fulfillment - their dreams are no fantasy, but fully realized. Today, all of them are doing what they love, and their diverse and very individual stories show us all what living your dream can actually look like.

Too often in today's society we stop short of the dream. Instead, we focus on decreasing our pain, managing our stress and treating our illnesses. But why do we stop there? After all, good health is so much more than simply a lack of illness. It is a vitality for life, an abundance of energy that is our birth right. Good health is a good attitude, a strong body and a vibrant mind.

Dr. Samuel Gerstein walks his talk. As you will see from his personal story which begins the book, he was feeling the effects of work stress himself several years ago. His own journey of self discovery led him to his dream of helping others find theirs. I believe this book will inspire you to do the same. Read it if you are feeling lost, or if your work has little meaning. Read it if you are dissatisfied with or hate your job. Read it if you have given up hope that the majority of your adult life spent at work will ever be enjoyable or fulfilling.

One of the best ways to learn anything new is through the use of role models. Dr. Gerstein has provided us with forty powerful role models in people who overcame their fears and all the reasons why they 'couldn't,' and through dogged determination and creative resourceful-ness found a way to achieve their dream. And because we are all unique, the wisdom and inspiration in this book can be utilized as much by a confused young high school senior as a by disgruntled senior manager of a large downtown firm.

When Mark Victor Hansen and I created *Chicken Soup for the Soul,* our mission was to heal and change the world one story at a time. I am moved by the forty very special stories Dr. Gerstein has found and given to the world. They are an inspiration to all people who want to live their dream. It's a book that is meant to be read, absorbed and acted on. If you are tired of 'settling' in your life, see yourself doing what these people have done, and know that if they can do it, so can you.

Jack Canfield
Co-author of the Chicken Soup for the Soul® series and
Author of The Success Principles™

Introduction

The middle-aged man arrived at my Emergency Room with crushing chest pain. He was clutching his chest, sweating profusely and his skin colour was ashen gray. I saw him immediately and it did not take long to make the diagnosis of an acute heart attack.

We proceeded to give him medications to lessen the effect of the heart attack. When my shift was over, I went and sat with him. We talked about the stressors in his life and how they had contributed to his heart attack. I learned that he was a policeman, and that his career was the biggest source of stress he had to cope with daily. He told me the job had become just too intense and violent for him, and he had grown more and more frustrated over the last few years. He actually wanted to leave the force because it was just not who he was. We chatted about other issues in his life, and then just before I left him I looked him in the eyes and said;

"Now that you have experienced such a serious health effect of all the stress in your work life, it might be a good time to consider a career change." What he said next shocked me. I'll never forget his reply. He said, "Are you kidding? I only have eight more years until my pension."

I walked away astonished, hoping that he would live long enough to see that day. It was then that I realized how deep-seeded our beliefs and habits can become. Granted, having just suffered a heart attack he may have still been in denial as to what was really happening to him. But by the same token, if this crisis didn't shake him out of his slumbering state of awareness, I don't know what would. Over the years I have witnessed hundreds of cases of illnesses caused or precipitated by work stress. I was quite familiar with the pattern: Denial and passive acceptance of one's own fate.

It probably wouldn't have bothered me so much if the story I've just shared was a rare occurrence. However, after working in the ER for over twenty years and seeing over 65,000 patients, I have witnessed many such sad scenarios. People thinking and believing they are stuck doing something they hate, or tolerate at best. These same people must then cope with the resulting stresses and the resulting physical illnesses. People not realizing, or not believing they can do something about it.

I believe that too many people settle for lives way below their potential. I have found that many people have poor belief systems and very low self-esteem, and have, in effect, given up on themselves. When I have a few moments in the ER, usually while stitching up someone's cut, I sometimes ask my patients about their life direction, and what they really want to do. I have been surprised at how many people tell me that no one has ever bothered to ask them that before. Often, they simply had no one who believed in them.

I realized I wanted to help somehow, in a proactive way. I wanted to show them they had choices, and help them overcome their self-limiting beliefs. But the fast paced ER was not the right place.

I became increasingly frustrated knowing my patients were going to return to the same situation and habits that brought them to me in the first place. I knew their jobs were making them sick. But what was more astonishing was their belief that they were powerless to make any changes – they felt they couldn't do a darn thing about it.

Nowadays people have to work longer hours and more years just to maintain their lifestyles. They feel stressed at work, not because of the company they work for, but rather they say they are in a job that just doesn't fit them well. They don't love what they do, and simply tolerate it, or downright hate it. Studies show that unhappiness and work stress are more strongly associated with health problems than other life stressors, including financial and family problems.

Here's an interesting fact: Research has revealed a greater increase of heart attacks, abnormal heart rhythms and sudden death on Monday *than on any other day of the week*. And there is nothing special about Mondays except that for most people, it marks the beginning of their work week. The facts tell the story: long-term job strain is worse for your heart than gaining forty pounds in weight or aging thirty years!

Despite these known facts, work stress is more prevalent in society. Nearly half of all American and one quarter of Canadian workers suffer from symptoms of burnout, a disabling reaction to stress on the job. A whopping one million people per day in the United States are absent from work due to stress-related disorders.

Work stress affects people's health in so many ways. It can cause headaches and back pain, lead to more accidents at work and more infections. If left unchecked, it can progress to irritability and then to depression, which can lead to drug and alcohol abuse to alleviate the symptoms. Work performance suffers and blood pressure may increase or heartburn and chronic pain set in. After five to ten years of ignoring such continuous work stress, the most dangerous stage arises. Illnesses such as asthma, heart disease, high blood pressure, ulcers and stroke emerge. Emotionally and mentally, self-image is lowered and people become isolated from friends and family. Burnout follows, and in rare circumstances suicidal or even homicidal thoughts may set in. (Test your own level of work stress by looking at the **Work Stress Test** at **www.dreamsforreal.com** under "**Free Tools**".)

Work stress and its short and long term effects on your health are real. It may be the new millennium's silent killer. Like an iceberg, you may not notice how it is impacting your health as most of it is below the surface. Ironically, when people start to feel isolated and withdrawn from close contacts, they will actually work harder in an attempt to alleviate these feelings. This catapults them further down the proverbial vicious cycle of work stress.

When I ask my patients if they love what they are doing they often give the following responses. "My career isn't that bad. It could be a lot worse." "At least I have a job." "They pay me well. And what about those benefits?" "I like my co-workers." "No one bothers me at work." It always sounds like a lot of rationalization for a question that was not posed. Yes, those are all positives, but it doesn't answer the question: How much stress is your career causing you, and do you love your work?

Like many people when faced with an illness, especially one insidious in nature, we tend to deny, rationalize and ignore symptoms until they become serious. This is human nature. We all have an innate fear of change. Most would rather stick to the status quo and hope things turn out okay, rather than face the issue head on and admit we have to do something about it. That something almost always includes changes in behaviour or habits or both, and we all know how difficult it is to change our habits.

In addition to my Emergency work, I have a psychotherapy practice outside the hospital. One question I like to ask my clients there is, *"What service would they regret not doing when they are lying on their death bed?"* Because the truth is that this is all that work is – a service, to help other people in some way.

We all have unique talents, passions and purposes that many of us have never explored. For that matter, many people I speak with have never even been asked what their Dream Career might be, because that was not a priority or even reality for their parents, primary caregivers, teachers or other role models. Many of our parents were simply happy to be alive in the post-World War Two era, and living their dreams was the farthest thing from their minds. This way of thinking is passed from one generation to the next, and before mindsets can change, a couple of generations usually have to pass.

Here is another question I pose to my clients: What if a common bit of wisdom that has been passed down to you has been wrong, or of no value? Many families pass down values like they pass down their genes. They really believe they are facts, and must be accepted.

Here are just some of the common beliefs people have held as fact:

- Work has to be hard. If you enjoy it, it is not real work.

- Stop dreaming – this is the real world.

- Get a job with a good company and you'll be set for life.
- If you are uneducated you cannot be successful.
- Poor people can't change their financial situation.
- Small businesses can't compete with big companies.

These beliefs have all been proven to be false by the people interviewed for this book. They are not truths – they are myths. If you have carried any of these myths with you your whole life, you can now free yourself. They were not passed down with malice. The people who held these beliefs and passed them along really thought they were true. And some beliefs were more true generations ago, but today they just don't apply. You now have a choice. You no longer have to carry the weight of these false limitations like a chain around your neck. You can break free of them and adopt new, more appropriate beliefs to replace them.

Many people think dreamers are people who are trying to avoid reality. Nothing could be further from the truth – the proof is the people in this book. Granted it is certainly safer to be negative, and a cynic. "The world is falling apart." "We are polluting our earth." "Evil is pervasive." But in the midst of all of this doom and gloom, it takes real courage to be an optimist and follow your dreams. Go ahead; distract yourself with things you love. You are not avoiding reality – you are actually creating your own!

Work doesn't have to be a joyless struggle for a pay cheque. That is a myth probably propagated by the loud miserable majority that serious people (read joyless) are smarter and more productive. That is simply not true and there is mounting evidence to the contrary. Production often correlates directly with worker happiness and satisfaction, whether it is assembly line work or being a change manager in the financial services industry.

Some have referred to W. Timothy Gallwey as the father of the life coaching movement. He helped AT&T restructure its company and is the author of the best seller, *The Inner Game of Tennis*, (Random House, 1974). In his more recent book, *The Inner Game of Work*, (Random House, 2000; p. 85) he wrote:

"Too often we believe that enjoyment is what has to be sacrificed to the goal of excellence. The best performers in all fields provide much evidence to

the contrary. Most of us also know from personal experience that we perform better when we are enjoying ourselves."

As I continued to watch my patients' suffering, I became increasingly frustrated at work. I could relieve their suffering, but only on a temporary basis. I wanted to do more for them – I wanted to help them change their habits and prevent further work-stress related illness. It felt like I was doing only half a job – reacting to people after they became physically ill. I knew inside I could be doing more. As time passed, I began to feel empty. I became more irritable and had difficulty sleeping. Soon, I began to devalue what I was doing for my patients. All these feelings gnawed away at me for months. I grew quite restless and didn't know what to do. Then I realized the startling truth: I was suffering from work stress myself!

I began asking co-workers, friends, cousins and acquaintances about their satisfaction at work. To my surprise, many of them told me they were dissatisfied. When I asked what they were doing to change their situation, they often looked at me in disbelief thinking I must be naïve to even ask the question. "This is the real world," they said. "You can't live your dreams." I didn't have an answer for them – yet. I realized then the obstacles were just too big for many people.

The Search for Great Role Models

"To be yourself in a world that is constantly trying to make you something else is the greatest accomplishment."

Ralph Waldo Emerson

I finally began to see a pattern emerging. The same obstacles that people told me were holding them back would come up over and over again. I thought if I could find enough people who had overcome these obstacles and actually followed their dreams, then I wouldn't have to challenge my patients over the merits of their obstacles. I could just refer them to the person who had done it as proof that not only was it possible to overcome that obstacle, it was happening in our community today. Granted, just as no two people's Dream Career is the same, no two people's situation is identical. That is why I undertook to interview hundreds of people who were doing what they loved. I figured if I found enough people from different backgrounds and in different work situations, others would see themselves in these role models and would then be able to make the link to their own lives.

The task I set for myself was not easy. At first I began asking just about anyone to refer me to someone they knew who loved their job. Tragically, many people couldn't even give me one name; they said they didn't know anyone who was doing what they loved. But I was now on a mission, and there was no turning back. I was not going to stop until I had found people in every sector of society who were living their Dream Careers, and doing what they loved. I was sure they were out there – I just had to find them.

In addition, I reasoned there must be a common thread running through these people's lives that I could pass on to others seemingly stuck in unsatisfying careers. Eventually I found three people who were living their dreams. After each interview I asked that person to refer me to one other person they knew living their Dream Career. As my list began to grow, I realized I had found my first key:

People often associate with like-minded people.

People who were doing what they loved had a much better chance of knowing other people who were doing what they loved, than people who were not. I began weaving what I liked to call my Dream Career Blanket around the city of Toronto.

Toronto is a large metropolitan city in Canada, with a population of three million. People who live here are similar to people living in any large city in North America. If you were to take this research elsewhere, you would likely find a proportionate number of individuals living their dreams in your city too. In my experience, this research is not unique to Toronto. Each person I interviewed was another colourful thread in the blanket. I was on my way.

Not all referrals turned out to be the real deal. Some were what I called "false Dream Careers." They were successful in the way our society has hitherto defined success, meaning they had done well financially or were in positions of power. But these criteria have nothing to do with my book. One man I screened was the president of a furniture company. When I went over my **Dream Career Test©** with him, he kept telling me about the financial perks he reaped from his position. Take the **Dream Career Test©** yourself at *www.dreamsforreal.com* and see how you compare with the people in this book. Everyone I interviewed answered yes to at least nineteen of the twenty questions in the questionnaire. One woman I spoke with talked about the prestige she had attained by her position in a large downtown brokerage firm. A CEO tried to impress me with the power he had attained through his stock holdings. However, they didn't impress me because they weren't what I was looking for. I only had one criterion for success: **They had to love what they were doing.**

We all need money to live but I discovered that, for all the people I interviewed, money was not a prime motivator for doing what they were doing. That is not how they discovered happiness at work. I know this may sound like heresy, but it is the people whose stories are in this book who told me that. The annual income of the people interviewed range from $20,000 to $750,000 per year. I purposely asked the person with one of the lower incomes if he would change careers with the one earning $750,000. His reply was a swift and decisive, "no." I got the same reply from everyone in the book. They loved what they were *doing* not what they were *earning*, and were not willing to trade it for anything.

Studies show that money only serves as a temporary satisfier. People who receive a raise are happier, but that happiness is fleeting. Within a few months they are back at the same emotional level they were at before their raise. Rewards are important but not as satisfying in the long-term as finding your life purpose.

I intentionally did not interview many high profile entertainers, celebrities or professional sports figures because I know that some readers might cynically believe they were in it only for the money, power or fame. However, I had no problem including a professional football player who plays in the Canadian Football League. Anyone who knows anything about that league knows he is definitely not in it for the money.

All of the people in this book are ordinary people like you and me. They include men and women, self-employed business owners and employees, people in white and blue-collar careers. They also run the gamut in age from young to old, from very little formal education to others with PhDs. There are people in both religious and secular areas, as well as single, married and divorced people. Some owe a lot to the support supplied by their spouse, while others had to get a divorce to follow their dream.

Each story is as varied as the people themselves. Like you and me, they had something in common – they each had a dream. But, unlike so many people, they didn't just sit there wishing. They did something about their dream.

Overcoming All Obstacles

"Give me a lever long enough and strong enough and I will move the earth."

Archimedes

How did they do it? Somehow they managed to overcome all the obstacles in their path. They refused to allow anything or anyone to stop them from pursuing their dreams. And here's the thing: **If they can do it so can you.** They are not better than you or me. Instead, they have adopted an empowering set of thinking and behaviour patterns that anyone can choose to adopt.

Imitation is indeed the best form of flattery. When you were young you naturally and automatically imitated what you saw – generally from your parents. However, what you saw was not always the best role model of how to live your life. You now have a choice. The fact that you picked up this book is evidence that you already have one thing in common with the people in it – you are motivated to do something about your life. You are no longer satisfied with tolerating your situation. You want more and you deserve more. When you read this book you will discover that living your dreams is not a fantasy.

There were some themes that were common to all of the contributors. One notable theme was they were **focused on their path**, and what would keep them on their path, instead of being distracted by what could lead them off course. In other words, they kept their attention on the result they were after, rather than any obstacles that might be in their way. Many people I meet in the medical world are focused on what's wrong. After all, that is the Western paradigm – to look for the pathology and fix it.

Sadly, in all of my medical training and beyond I have rarely heard or read anything about the definition of health. So, I deduced that health was the absence of disease. Through the years I have learned that there is so much more to health. Factors such as quality of sleep, our energy level, and to a huge extent how we think are but a few examples of factors that contribute to real health. I have been trained to look for what's wrong with my patients instead of what's right. Even the primary reason for a patient's visit is labeled "chief complaint." That paradigm is slowly changing as people are becoming more proactive in their health care management, and primary care physicians are practicing more preventative medicine.

During each interview, I asked for examples of failures they'd had as they followed their path. I figured my readers would benefit from seeing how these mistakes and failures could be overcome. I was taken aback by the number of people who had a tough time citing even one failure. In the ER I am accustomed to hearing what's *wrong* with people. Many patients could go on forever listing their complaints, their mistakes, and their failures.

It is not the case that the people in this book didn't make their fair share of mistakes. I know that intuitively because they, and we, all share the same trait. They are human and we humans make mistakes. **The answer is in *what* they chose to focus on when something went wrong.** They chose to *learn* from their mistakes, forgive themselves quickly, make a new plan and then get the show back on the road. They are all individuals, but the trait they share is their refusal to waste time focusing on the negative because they want to get back to doing what they love.

I have come to believe this is not only a healthy attitude to have; it is also one of the key ingredients to getting into your Dream Career. Inevitably you are going to encounter challenges, and you will make some mistakes, as I have. The key is how you respond to those challenges that will determine what you do next. W. Mitchell, noted author and speaker, became a quadriplegic in an airplane accident after having suffered very serious burns in a motorcycle accident years before. In his case you could argue that self-pity would be justified. He chose a different route though, and his attitude is articulated clearly in the title of one of his books, *"It's not what happens to you, it's what you do about it."* (1997, Partners Publisher's Group).

Focusing on what's wrong has rarely helped anyone know the

right thing to do. If you want to follow your dreams, begin to adopt some of the behaviours of these people who have done it. Read about their attitudes, thinking patterns, habits and behaviours. Make them contagious, and then catch them.

One main difference between people who are living their dreams, and those who are still dreaming, is the former take action while the latter sit back and accept, or often bemoan, their fate. As you will see from the stories in this book, living your dream is not easy. It takes hard work, discipline, perseverance and a good attitude – among other traits. The people in this book came up against many barriers that would stop a less motivated group. But this group of inspiring individuals would not be denied. Individually they had to find a way around financial obstacles, language barriers, failures and ill health. They dealt with the attitudes and fears of well-intentioned family and friends who tried to dissuade them from their dreams. And they had to overcome their own fears of inferiority and rejection.

Each of these inspiring individuals had to overcome at least one major challenge. To name a few, Daniella Santana had a life-long dream of becoming a police officer. But before she could do that, she had to find a way to overcome her husband's discouragement and her own fears in order to make it happen. Doug Sole was floundering in his musical life quest until he found the courage to face his demons. Mark Gelgor was running out of money and was contemplating returning to his native South Africa before he found a way of making his dream work.

People who are following their dreams often didn't charge headlong into the obstacles they faced. Instead, they looked for a way around them. Rabbi Plotkin looked at how he could fit into the community instead of forcing the community to fit into his way. John McCauley looked inward to discover his unique path, instead of trying to change the opinions of his high school teachers who told him he wouldn't amount to anything.

It may be that you are feeling quite low in your life right now because of a poor work situation, or a personal crisis. If that is so, please do not dismay. All is not lost. Although you may not yet see it, you may very well find your lost treasure within during your difficult time, because you are no longer working on autopilot. It is possible that, for the first time in ages, you may be looking for meaning in your life. Only when you are searching, do you find anything. Remember, the sphinx arose out of the ashes.

This reflects a natural law of homeostasis.[1] As an emergency physician I see my role as putting people back in balance. When they come in with a high temperature I seek ways to lower it. If their blood pressure is too low I look for the causes in order to raise it back to normal. Each system in the body has an optimal state in which it functions. This includes the circulatory system, the respiratory system, the nervous system and so on. Not only that, each system has several mechanisms the body uses to return it to its balanced state. It's like the thermostat in your home. If the temperature is too high the air conditioning is triggered, and conversely, if it gets too low the heating system will come on to warm things up.

This is not to say that air temperature should not change. It has to. That is the nature of our world. Temperatures go up and then go down. Your blood pressure goes up and down all day. Your mood goes up, then down and then up again. Life is always changing. The only true constant in all of life is change. Your body is always changing. The cells are continually being replaced in every organ of your body at different rates. Hair and stomach cells turn over quickly whereas bone cells remodel at a slower pace. By the end of a year every cell in your body will have been replaced with new cells. You are actually a new person each year! Remember this the next time something bad happens to you.

A job loss may not be bad in the long run if it spurs you on to discovering your Dream Path. Things will get better when things go wrong. It's as natural as breathing. If you can, it may even be worthwhile to begin looking for the good in every 'catastrophe' to help yourself bounce back as quickly as possible.

In this book, you will read about some "tragedies," which turned out to be turning points in the lives of my story tellers. Michael McGauley turned his life around after he almost died when a car hit him. In retrospect, the accident may have actually saved his life. Ila Faye Turley had already given up on her dream of becoming an actor. But after witnessing a friend die, she retuned to it in earnest at forty years of age.

---

1. Homeostasis: the state of equilibrium in the body with respect to various functions…e.g., temperature, heart rate, blood pressure, water content, blood sugar, etc. (Stedman's Medical Dictionary)

Those are just a few examples of what people did to make their dreams come true. They pursued them in a very un-dreamlike fashion. It required courage and determination. But everyone told me that if they had to do it all over again they would in an instant. It was definitely worth the trip.

The people in this book are ordinary people whose passions and life purpose spurred them on to do extraordinary things. They had the courage to not only dream, but to do whatever it took to make that dream a reality. Because of space limitations, there was simply not enough room to include the stories of everyone I interviewed. But as a testament to my respect, I would and have used their services, and have happily referred them to my friends. You see, what I found was that these people who loved what they were doing, were also really good at it, and I don't think this was merely a coincidence. If you love what you do, you will have the passion and the interest and the motivation to continually learn and grow and improve. Researching your field will no longer be a laborious task just to get it done. Rather, it will be a labour of love. That is what I discovered when I undertook the task of writing this book. It became my labour of love, and my gift to you.

A Big Myth Debunked

Let me take a moment right now to debunk one of the most common myths about dream careers. There is no such thing as **The Dream Job**. It does not exist. How could it? The world is made up of six billion people – each with a unique set of talents, skills and passions. We all grow up in different families and cultures that emphasize a variety of values. How could one or even a hundred careers satisfy everyone? The research for this book has shown me that the Dream Career for you is the one that fits **YOU** best. Nobody knows you like you do. Don't let anyone tell you what you should be doing. You will know it when you find it because it will resonate within you. You may have to create it but, when you do – find it or create it – it will feel like you are coming home.

Here's the good news – our dreams never die. For many of us they remain in a comatose state as we hypnotically carry on with our life's routines. Too often when I treat people, I notice they have given up on their dreams. They have buried them so far down in their subconscious that they don't even realize their dreams still exist. However, after speaking with hundreds of people about their dreams, I believe our dreams never die until we do. They may be in a coma, but they are still there. According to the *Stedman's Medical Dictionary*, a coma is defined as: *A state of profound unconsciousness from which one cannot be roused. It may be due to the action of an ingested poison or one formed in the body.*

In the case of one's dreams the ingested poison may be swallowing the popular beliefs held by other people about your potential, and your own poison may be internalizing those beliefs and accepting those limitations as fact.

Reversing a physical coma requires a chemical, nutrient or vitamin to replace the toxic compound affecting the brain. Reversing a spiritual coma requires finding that element within that will offset the poison we allowed to affect our dreams. And that element can be found in the desires that still quietly smolder deep in our emotional heart. There have been numerous cases of individuals waking up after months or even years lost in a coma. So too can people wake up after spending years doing something that doesn't fit them. One day, perhaps after a traumatic life event like a physical illness or a marital breakup, they actually take the time to look, listen and feel what has been burning deep within them all along.

As a doctor I have witnessed many people who decide to change their life after they are diagnosed with a major illness. By then they figure they have nothing to lose, so they change their life and decide to pursue their dreams. Sadly, many die before they have a chance to fulfill those dreams.

So the question is, **why wait until you're too sick to do anything?** Why not allow someone else's story to wake you up to what could happen if you don't act now? When we are young we think we are invincible. But after the teen years I think we become aware that anyone can become sick. As responsible adults I'm sure most people realize it could happen to them. I just treated a thirty-one-year-old woman with a bleed in her brain. She was probably born with a weak blood vessel and it ruptured. Stuff like that happens and I witness it all the time. It tears people apart.

The tragedy of September 11, 2001 caused many people to sit

back and take stock of their lives. If life can end so suddenly, they are saying they want to do something worthwhile while they are on this ride called planet Earth. The bad news is that work stress does lead to illness. No question. The good news is that you **can** do something about it. There are steps you can take right now. Remember the flip-side of this situation: People who are satisfied with their careers and love what they do, live longer and are less prone to illness.

I am not telling you this to be a doomsayer. I am telling you this because I want you to wake up from your slumber. We are not immortal. If you dislike what you are doing, start doing something else – today. At least begin. Ask yourself, "What was it I always wanted to do?" Ask yourself what you loved to do as a child. Look into that course you always wanted to take. Turn off the TV and take a half-hour to dream of the possibilities. Write them down. I am not talking about financial riches here. What I am talking about is how you live your life on a day-to-day basis. What I learned from talking to hundreds of people who love their work, is that there is no better reward than being happy with what you are doing.

We are living in a new paradigm. As we walk into the early stages of the Information Age, many of us feel it is a time of great opportunity. There have never before been so many options open to us. With the popularity of the personal computer and the home office, people now have the ability to do what only large corporations could do just a few years ago. When there weren't as many options, the goal of doing what you loved may have seemed completely out of reach. Now people realize they have a choice, and this is causing many people to question their role and their purpose in life. Just go to your favourite bookstore and see what the top selling nonfiction books are. They cover such subjects as spirituality, personal development and environmental consciousness. We are becoming more aware of who we are as individuals, and where we fit in this world. And we are taking more responsibility in doing something about it in our own lives.

There are many benefits of living your dream. Aside from the health benefits mentioned above, many people I spoke with feel energized by a new sense of purpose that gives their life a whole new meaning. They are happier – and that carries over to other areas of their lives. Phil Solomon's story is a prime example of this virtuous cycle. When you get one part of your life back on track, there can be an inner angst to deal with other parts of your life no longer congruent with your new beliefs and actions. Several of the people I interviewed were able to capitalize on the momentum of following their dream, and extricate themselves from a disempowering relationship. Others used it as a time to bring peacefulness back into their life, and sometimes it happened that their dream grew out of that peaceful state.

How to Use This Book

"Don't die with your dreams still in you."

Benjamin Disraeli

This book is organized into chapters according to the myths (read "major obstacles") people have had to overcome to reach their goal. I called them "myth-diagnoses" because the people in the respective chapters were, in fact, misdiagnosed with a false label at some point in their lives. The people featured in this book are "Myth Busters" because they did not allow those myth-diagnoses to stop them from following their dreams.

I now believe that all obstacles anyone might put in front of you, are merely myths, accepted dogmatically by prior generations as truth. As I said previously, this is a new era. The common thinking that used to apply at one time, no longer applies. Some of those old ideas never applied; they were always myths, and were merely used as excuses to rationalize a life not fully lived.

These myths are phrased as statements that you might have heard many times during your life. I've heard them over and over again when dealing with my patients, as the reasons they are unable to follow their dreams. They include comments like:

"I am too old."

"I don't have enough money to do it."

"I have failed already; I might as well just give up."

"I am not _____ enough to do what I love." (You can fill in the blank with any or all of the following terms: smart, healthy, good, tall, educated, etc...)

Most of us have adopted these patterns of thinking from our parents, teachers or other significant people in our childhood. We were young so we didn't question their validity. We believed and lived by these myths as if they were absolute truth. By never challenging the veracity of these statements, we will stop ourselves from pursuing what we really want.

But what if they were wrong? What if what they told you no longer applies? What if it were never true? What if you *could* do what you loved, but never even tried because of some misconceptions you learned in childhood? How would you feel knowing that?

You may wish to start with the chapter that highlights the obstacle you have been facing in your own life. Or you may choose to begin with an industry that interests you. (Each person's career is cross-referenced in the index). Look for the person who works in an area you have always dreamed about or in which you are interested, and begin with their story.

Then move on to other stories to discover the secrets of how these people overcame all the obstacles in their path. These secrets are highlighted in key learning boxes in each chapter. The statements in bold and/or italics are points that *I have chosen* to emphasize as important concepts in living your dream.

Following each story you will find my comments. Here, I have teased out one (of several) key lesson from that story and expanded on it so you will be able to apply it to your life. The next time someone says you can't do what you love because of some mythical reason, just refer them to the most appropriate story.

Following each chapter I have included some questions for you to ponder regarding the major myth featured in that chapter. Take time to contemplate these questions and write out your answers if you've identified with the myth-diagnosis or the people (Myth-Busters) in the chapter.

Very few people take time to reflect upon their lives. Most people spend more time deciding on their next vacation than they do considering their life's purpose. I want to congratulate YOU right now, for taking the time to pause and reflect on your life, and to hopefully be inspired by how others rediscovered their dreams.

Someone may have told you that your ideas were not practical or realistic. If you listened, (and it can be hard not to), you may have allowed them to squash your dream. Have you ever been camping? I used to love camping. When I was a Boy Scout we'd go out into the woods and learn how to live in nature. One of the skills I learned was to build a fire. First I started by clearing out an area to make a fire pit. Then I collected dry leaves and small twigs and placed them neatly around the centre of the pit. I had the big pieces of wood placed along side for later. When I lit my fire, I protected the small flame from the wind. I then fanned the flames carefully until it was strong enough to burn on its own. It then took a few minutes before the fire was big enough for me to add the bigger pieces.

If I had placed the larger logs onto the fire too early, I would have put out the flame. You have to nurture your small flame at first; this applies equally to making fires as it does to making dreams come true. If you let others step on your flame in its early stages they will reduce it to a flicker. (In the metaphysical sense no one can ever put out your fire if you are still breathing.) Later, once it has evolved into a blazing bonfire, a person will get burned if he tries to step on your fire.

Many of your burning desires were doused before they had a chance to grow. They were stepped on by people whose own flame had been crushed, and knew no other way. They may have thought they were helping by saving you pain. Or, they may have feared you would succeed where they could not, leaving them behind to feel like even more of a failure. Therefore, they stepped on your flame and kept you from moving ahead of them. And so it continues as limitations are passed down from one generation to the next. Isn't it time to melt the chains that limit you?

Nurture your flame early on. Care for it, protect it. Don't let the naysayers **anywhere** near it. Only when you have built it up to the point it can withstand the winds of doubters is it time to release it to the world.

Baruch Spinoza, the great 17th century philosopher once said, "Life happens when you are busy planning for tomorrow." Now, I don't think for one minute he meant for people not to plan ahead. I do think he saw how many people spend their present moments in future thoughts, and therefore miss their present moments. However, the other extreme is not very useful either – only focusing on today and ignoring the future, or hoping the future will take care of itself. The answer must be found in the space between these two extremes. It is planning for the future, and focusing on what you are doing in the moment. It is balance.

I often ask people if they plan on living another five years. Do you? If so, then start something today. Here's why: David G. Myers, a social psychologist and author of, *The Pursuit of Happiness* (Harper Paperbacks) said, "Although we often overestimate how much we will accomplish in any given day, we generally underestimate how much we can accomplish in a year." If you don't like what you are doing, then take the time to discover what it is you do want to do. Get a coach. Look at the recurring themes in your life. Take action. You'll be surprised by how much you learn and grow in one year.

Wishing and hoping will only bring you more frustration. You can think about things all day long, but until you actually **do something**, they will remain thoughts. Once you start to break free of the force of inertia and do something, you will start noticing other opportunities you couldn't possibly have seen when you were still just thinking about it. The scenery changes when you actually put the wheels in motion.

Once you are in motion, it's time to draw up a game plan of what your ideal situation might be. At first, put aside a small chunk of time each week to do something towards your dream. That may be only one or two hours, and that's okay. At the beginning you don't want to set really high expectations, and then fall way short. That is a sure fire way of sabotaging yourself.

Be easy on yourself when you start. Set the bar really low at first. You want to build momentum. As a physician I have seen so many people break their New Year's resolutions of getting into shape with an overuse injury, generally around February. They rush into their exercise program so quickly that it doesn't allow their body to adapt to the new routine.

Nothing succeeds like success.

Allow your new passion to develop its own momentum. If you have found something you really love, rest assured you will be motivated to do it. You won't have to push yourself. It won't feel like a chore. Still, resist the urge to surge ahead at top speed before you are ready. Hold the reigns back for the first six months, and slowly increase your allotted time for your dream. Before long you may find yourself doing it for an hour each evening. Omitting one hour of TV a night will easily accomplish that. Most North Americans spend over twenty-two hours a week watching TV!

After a year you will have built up some momentum and gained some knowledge towards sustaining your interest. It won't feel like work. You might now begin wondering why you didn't start it earlier, but that's not the point. You should know that when you follow your dream – you are already in your dream! Let me repeat that – **When you**

follow your dream you are already in your dream.

Your dream is not a destination. It is a path – and just getting on that path can make you feel great and give your life meaning. Did you ever notice when you are playing a sport you truly enjoy, it's the sport itself that brings you pleasure? Myself, I play golf. I am an average player and would like to improve, but that doesn't drive me. I play golf because I enjoy it. I pick up golf magazines. When looking at vacation choices I consider the quality of their golf courses. I look forward to a golf game, weeks in advance. When I wake up on the morning of a game, I'm excited. I don't have to reach a certain level of expertise to enjoy golf, I enjoy it now.

Similarly, just following your dream will start to bring you joy. It often won't feel like work. To be sure there will be struggles; there are struggles for anything worthwhile. But if you go slowly you will continually be drawn back to it because it is what you love.

Remember, these obstacles or myths may be the echo of the doubting voices still chattering away in your own head. They may be the principles you have erroneously adopted as truth. Now is the time to separate fact from fiction. Read the true stories of people who have personally debunked the myth that you cannot live your dreams. Indeed you can, and these people are the proof. They have each followed their dream.

You are not alone in your quest for living your dream. The only difference between the people in this book and you may be that the former group found their Dream Career Path and you haven't yet. Their fires are burning strong and yours maybe simmering embers. Let the people in this book help rekindle your own inner flame. See how they overcame their struggles, and by association, let them show you how you can overcome yours.

They did it. Now it's your turn.

Dr. Samuel Gerstein, M.D.
The Author's Story:

As an emergency physician it is my job to help people in pain. I had been doing that for fifteen years, doing the very best I could for my patients. At times I overlooked my own pain, and ignored the growing void inside of me, hiding behind a façade that everything was going well. However, the longer I ignored it, the larger the void became, and the harder it became to ignore it.

I now understand a universal law: The universe has lessons to teach everyone. If you don't get the lesson the first time it will increase the intensity of the lesson until you have to pay attention. I finally got my lesson when the universe sent a startling coincidence onto my path.

In his bestselling book *The Celestine Prophecy*, author James Redfield speaks about nine insights the human race will discover as it enters the era of spiritual awareness. The first insight is to pay attention to mysterious coincidences. He says once you interpret these sudden, synchronistic events, they will lead you to your destiny. I don't know about the validity of all the insights he suggests, but I have witnessed some startling scenes of synchronicity in my own life, as well as in the lives of the people whose stories I share in this book.

About nine years ago I realized I was growing frustrated at work and wanted something more. I had seen so much despair in people who had given up on themselves, and I knew I could do more for them. This angst carried over to my family life where small things began to irritate me. I knew this because one summer while on vacation I found myself in a heated argument with my wife Michelle, over a seemingly negligible matter. I was on a break for some R&R, and here I was arguing and upset over some small matter. Maybe I didn't really need a break. Maybe what I needed was to scratch that itch that had been nagging at me for some time.

I told Michelle I had felt myself to be very tense lately, and maybe a massage would help relax me. Prior to that I had received maybe two paid massages in my life, so it certainly wasn't a part of my routine. Years before someone had told me about a specific spa downtown. We had tickets to go to a Blue Jays baseball game the same day so, on the spur of the moment, I made a reservation to go to that particular spa right before the game. Michelle took advantage of my plan and made an appointment herself for a manicure, pedicure and facial.

After my massage and while waiting for my wife, I went to the counter to pass the time. I picked up what looked like an interesting book, bought it and promptly headed to the hot tub to begin reading. I couldn't put it down and was almost a prune when I emerged.

The book was called *Passionate Longevity*, by Elaine Dembe, and the concepts in the book enthralled me. In it she talked about the life lessons of elderly people as they looked back over their lives. They spoke about what was truly meaningful for them, and about things they would and wouldn't do if they had the chance to live over again.

We went to the ball game, but I couldn't take my mind off that book and how it related to my life. Was I really doing what I wanted? Would I regret it when I was in my eighties? I couldn't tell you the score of the game, but I finished the book the next day. I was so inspired I wanted to call the author and speak with her. Now there were dozens of books on spirituality, personal development and motivation in the bookstores at the time, most of them by American authors. I could have chosen any one of those best sellers in the spa that day but it was hers I picked up. When I read that the author worked and lived in Toronto not far from me, I was floored.

I contacted Elaine immediately and she happily agreed to speak to me. It happened that I was suffering from some back pain at the time. It turned out that Elaine was also a chiropractor, and one very energetic lady. I met with her several times for my back, and also to talk to her about my frustrations. She suggested I explore two centres in the United States to continue my journey. When I received their brochures, one course stood out above the rest so I signed up for it immediately. It was called *Lifeshaping*, and was a big factor in how I changed my life.

The content and facilitator of the course were excellent. However, it was as much about me being ready to hear the message that was instrumental in changing my life direction. That old Buddhist saying, *when the pupil is ready the teacher appears,* really is true. Over the next two summers I ended up assisting and then co-facilitating the course with its creator, Ingrid Brendenburg, and that was what got me started on the path to what I am doing now.

I decided to start listening to my heart and begin doing what feels good and right to me. It only made sense that if I wanted others to do that, I should be doing it myself. My intention was to not evaluate myself on the results as I have done for so many things in my life, but rather to simply enjoy the process.

In the transition period I began taking extra courses that interested me. I didn't have a specific plan; I just followed where my passions led me. I took a psychology course in NLP – (Neuro-Linguistic Programming) and became a master practitioner. I took an Adult Education Facilitation course, joined a Toastmasters Club and became a local member of CAPS – the Canadian Association of Professional Speakers in Toronto. I also had fun doing some improvisational acting at Second City. Over the next three years I juggled these extracurricular activities while continuing to work in the ER, and spending time with my young family. I simply trusted I was moving in the right direction because I was following my heart.

I began reading more of Dr. Abraham Maslow's and Dr. Carl Roger's theories of self-actualization, and about people reaching their full potential and how they did it. Somewhere in there I began writing material to help people follow *their* dreams.

Shortly thereafter I dug into my savings to create my own company, *Dreams For Real Incorporated*. For the first four years our family cut back on some nonessentials like vacations, and I picked up some extra shifts in the ER to help with the expenses.

After having worked in socialized medicine for so long I knew I had to become skilled in the world of business. I took marketing courses to help me promote my seminars and my professional speaking services. They showed me ways to make my own dream real, and turn it into a viable business. I gave free speeches to several community service organizations like the Rotary Club. I did my first no-fee seminar out of my home. The anxiety I felt *before* the seminar was nothing compared to the exhilaration I experienced after it was done. I would never have known that if I had just sat back and hoped it would happen. *I had to actually take action.*

I did a lot on my own, and I take great pride in going after my goal and achieving it. But I soon realized I would go a lot further, a lot faster if I had help. Besides, it would be more fun having others with whom to share my experiences. I began asking for help.

I started a Mastermind group comprised of like-minded people who had information they wanted to share with others. Whenever I felt frightened or worried I opened up to them. I was no longer hiding behind the façade that everything was going well. Besides, no one had ever believed it anyway. I had just been fooling myself, and was really afraid to admit I had challenges too. I found that just naming them and talking about them in front of my friends was a huge relief. The people in that group have been a tremendous resource for support and assistance.

I soon realized I could not do it all, and began delegating parts of my business I had no interest in. For me this included computer and web-based issues and publishing. I focused on what I loved – writing about living your dreams and helping other people do it.

Despite all of this, I realized something was still missing. This time I was conscious to the message, and paid attention. I had woken up. Through my work I was now delivering to people a lot of important information and techniques, but I was lacking key role models for following one's dreams. As Yogi Berra said, *"You've got to be careful if you don't know where you're going 'cause you might not get there."* From my patients, I had many role models for the mental and physical effects of work stress. But I realized I had very little in the way of what dreams look like in the real world once they've been manifested and realized.

That was it! That was the missing ingredient. I knew I had to go out and find people who were living their dreams and get their stories before I could really show others how to do it. It made so much sense. To the naysayers, they would be living proof that it was possible. To the curious, they would be an enigma. And to the people who were secretly or openly interested in living their own dreams, they would be a roadmap.

And so I began what I didn't realize would become a huge undertaking. I had no idea what I was getting myself into. I interviewed over two hundred people, over a hundred of which were formal meetings. I drove to wherever they worked or lived, at any hour that was convenient to them. My journey took me to many corners of Toronto and its neighbouring cities and towns. Each and every person I met inspired me in some way, and I knew they would inspire others too. It took me two-and-a-half years to complete the interviews, and another year-and-a-half to transcribe them and write this book. I did this work around my family times and while continuing my ER duties at the hospital. I enjoyed every minute of it.

Pouring over the notes I had taken, I teased out the key common themes to how the people who were living their dreams had actually done it. Once that was done, I put it all together in a program, and then used that program to overhaul my seminars. It also became the cornerstone for setting up my own psychotherapy practice, where I help individuals overcome their personal struggles to follow their own true path.

My biggest obstacle was there was no roadmap to follow to do this. Unlike medical training, there was no curriculum to follow and no test with which to measure my competencies. There were weeks when I didn't have any leads for where I would find the next person to interview in their dream career. I was often disappointed and dejected. At those times my wife would step up to the plate and reassure me this was only a temporary lull. My Mastermind group was a tremendous support as well.

What kept me motivated was my belief in what I was doing, and my enthusiasm to help others live their dreams. I have witnessed so much despair in my years at the hospital, and I've been so saddened watching people give up on themselves, not realizing they could live their life by following their own script. I would think of the quizzical looks on the faces of the people I asked about their dreams – people who had never even been asked what they wanted, who had been told what they should be doing. I knew it wasn't right, and they could be so much happier if they were true to themselves. I refused to let my despair win, and I vowed not to give up.

On my good days I remembered the other side of the coin of not having a set path to follow. I reminded myself I could be creative and follow my own instincts. I was not hamstrung by other people's agendas. I was free to do what I thought was best for my clients. The obstacle that I was facing, having no roadmap or set course to follow, was inherently also a benefit.

I can say in all honesty that I now feel more complete in my vocation as a doctor – as a healer. I help people both proactively and reactively. I know that in stress-related diseases there is often a five- to ten-year lag time between emotional distress and the physical manifestation of that stress. I feel that I now have more balance in my life, and I'm more at peace with myself. I know I am doing what I love because no one has to tell me to do it.

I look forward to creating better techniques to help people achieve their Dream Goals. After working in the ER and playing with my young children, I often work in my home office for hours some evenings. It is definitely a labour of love. I also know it is a good fit because I continually talk to my wife about ideas I have for such and such a seminar or book. Sometimes I forget that it's my dream and not hers. Sometimes I go on a tad too much – to the point where *she* is the one needing a break from my dream. I am having so much fun I don't even consider it work.

It took me forty years to hear the true message of what my heart had been whispering to me all along. It was a "coincidence" that woke me up. You can bet that I have been paying close attention ever since.

"Dreams without action are fantasy.
Actions without dreams are empty.
Dreams combined with actions
manifest one's destiny."

Samuel Gerstein

Part 1
Your Inner World

Myth - Diagnosis #1
Low Dream Esteem
"I'm not good enough."

"You gain strength, courage and confidence by every experience in which you really stop to look fear in the face. You are able to say to yourself, I have lived through this horror. I can take the next thing that comes along. You must do the thing you think you cannot do."

Eleanor Roosevelt

Doug Sole

Drum Circle Facilitator, Professional Speaker,
and Retail Music Store Owner

*"I was curled up in a fetal position
and I didn't want to get out of bed."*

When I was four years old I went to see my father play in the symphony orchestra. I clearly remember sitting in the front row of the balcony with my mother and two older sisters. First, the place went dark. Then, as the hall fell silent, the maestro walked onto the stage, raised his arms to bring the orchestra to readiness, and then pointed his baton right at my father who stood behind the kettle-drums. I gasped inside, and as soon as my dad struck the first note of the drum crescendo that begins *O Canada*, I felt a surge of energy inside of me. The moment was electric. Leaping out of my chair and pointing to my father I yelled with excitement, "That's my Dad!" There was laughter, and my sisters and my mum shushed and tried to pull me back down, but I didn't care. Then, the entire audience came to their feet with me and began to sing *O Canada*.

For the rest of the concert, every time I heard my father accentuate the music with the drums I felt a surge of energy that brought me to a peak of excitement. I was mesmerized; it was the emotional focus of the entire evening for me. I really feel the reason I remain so excited today about drumming is because of that magical moment when the energy of the kettle drum first filled the room – and I was there.

With my dad as my inspiration, music became the focus of my entire life. I wish I could say it was that easy, but I had a major hurdle to overcome before I could claim my destiny. I had to face unknown demons head on.

My dad put himself through university playing drums in a band. Although his career was a pharmacist, music was a passionate pastime that permeated his life. He sang in the church choir, played the organ when the organist was sick, played drums in bands, and he played percussion with the local International Symphony Orchestra. Tuesday evenings were symphony practice; performances were Sunday afternoons. I loved Sunday afternoons because I got to listen to him play. From my father I inherited a fervent love of music, which I played and studied throughout my formative years.

I started with piano lessons when I was five. By the time I was in grade nine I had achieved my grade eight piano, which actually gave me a high school credit. Studying the piano gave me an appreciation for the classics, the history of music and how important it was in many cultures.

When I finished high school I was accepted to study music at Humber College. I got a part-time job at Canadian Tire, but I wanted to be around music so much, I quit that job to teach private drumming lessons on the weekends. So it was music, music, music, twelve hours a day. **I totally immersed myself in music.**

After graduating I played full-time for a while in a percussion ensemble. Then I auditioned and was selected to play for an established rock band, *New Hollywood*. I left all of my musical connections behind and toured with this group for three years in Ontario, Quebec, and the Caribbean. As the only classically trained musician in that band I was often asked to help the piano and guitar players write out their parts for any new song we played. It was a fun top-forty group, but it didn't do anything for my soul, no pun intended. I really needed to be more creative. So, after discussing my intentions and the future needs of the band, the bandleader and I both knew it was time for us to part company. Playing in the rock band taught me a lot about the music business, but I also learned that it wasn't for me. There was so much more I could be doing in music.

What to do next? I knew I had to stay close to music, so I got a job selling pianos, and did that for a couple of years. I knew this wasn't my dream, and yet somehow I believed if I stuck with it and stayed close to music, I would find a way to make my dream come true. I had no idea how, I just had faith that it would. Everything I did all seemed to be part of a journey linked together by a common theme of music.

During this period I reconnected with some of my former drumming students. One day I went with some of them to help them buy drums. When I came out of the drum store, I had a job selling drums. My thinking was I would meet other drummers who would then help me with my career. I came out of that experience with ideas for a book on hand drumming. It was the needs of my students that helped me frame the principles of my book, *The Soul of Hand Drumming*. My dream was starting to come together.

One day, one of my students approached me and said, "I take drumming not for the sake of drumming, but because I feel better about myself when I finish a lesson. While I'm drumming, you always get me to think about my life, my direction and my relationships." I have found that drumming helps people focus on the present because, to play well, you have to clear your mind of all other clutter.

I was helping others, but deep down I knew I had to clear my own clutter before I could break through my major barrier – a huge fear of not being good enough.

I had studied music all of my life. I had played in several groups. I taught music and was writing a book on drumming. I had more than enough tools in the box. But my tool box had a major leak. I believed I wasn't worthy of being successful in the music industry, and this belief was holding me back.

While writing my book on hand drumming, I said to myself, "Who am I to write a book about hand drumming? Cripes, I grew up in a small town in Southwestern, Ontario."

That fear was stopping me from going for my dream. It was so frustrating I wanted to scream. No matter what I tried, I couldn't seem to find a way around it!

In the meantime, I rationalized that if I kept the book simple, it would help many people. If people didn't like it, the worst they could do was jump on it or tear it up and that would mean it wasn't for them anyway. That was how I dealt with it on the surface.

But to truly believe that I was worthy I needed to dig deeper. I had to go to the source of my fears. I had buried them so far down I was afraid to face them. To do this, I sought help from two psychologists. I got support from my fiancé, (who I'm very pleased to say is now my wife). I talked about my fears to good friends who really listened. I listened to tapes from Tony Robbins to help me overcome my poor self-image. All of that talking finally led to the breakthrough moment in my drumming career.

I was hired to do a drumming clinic with Anton Fig from *The David Letterman Show*. Yamaha Corporation of America endorsed the clinic, and was the big name used to draw people to the show. I was the 'shmoe' they selected to do the percussion teaching – at least that was how I thought of myself back then. My low self-worth caused me to be very focused on what Anton would think of me, instead of what my job was. I put all of this pressure on myself to make sure I didn't make a mistake in front of Anton.

On the evening before the clinic I was practicing my hardest piece. I was playing it perfectly that night and things were really humming along. Then, just before turning in I decided to do it one more time. That's when it happened. Right in the middle of it, I totally froze. I couldn't think of what came next. I began to sweat, my hands grew clammy and my heart raced. My breathing became shallow. Now in total panic, I said to myself, "I can't do this!" "Who do I think I am? Who am I fooling?"

I had to lie down. I curled up in the fetal position and stayed that way all night. I didn't get any sleep that night. Each time I found myself dozing off I quickly remembered what I would be facing in the morning. And so it was that when the sun agonizingly rose over the horizon, I couldn't get myself out of bed.

It was the worst feeling in my life. My dad called and told me to get out of bed. My best friend, who was teaching trombone at the same clinic, forced me to get out of bed. It took every ounce of energy for me to focus on the lessons of Tony Robbins.

I had to get my butt out of that bed and **step through that wall of fear.** Somehow I had to do it. This was my defining moment. If I didn't do it then I knew I would regret that moment for the rest of my life. What got me out of bed was the realization that this was my chosen career path. I knew I would disappoint myself more than anybody else if I didn't get up. Somehow I finally managed to pull myself up and get dressed. I was petrified.

As my friend drove us down to the show I sat in the front seat shaking like a leaf. I kept saying to myself, "I can't do this. I can't do this." Backstage I paced back and forth. I couldn't sit still. Then they announced my name. I had to decide. Should I go out there or not? It was put-up or shut-up time.

As I took those first few steps on stage I looked up and saw the large audience in front of me. I wanted to stop, but I didn't. I kept putting one foot in front of the other. Everything became so clear. It was as if I had broken through that imaginary wall I had been holding in front of me my whole life. When the wall came down my true self emerged. You couldn't shut me up. There was no stopping me now. I played all of my pieces beautifully. It felt so natural. And why not? After all, I had put in thousands of hours of learning and practice. I was totally focused on what I was playing.

I forgot about impressing Anton Fig while I was on stage. The irony was that right after my performance Anton walked right up to me and said, "I haven't learned that much about percussion since I went to college. Thanks for that refresher course." "Thank you," I replied calmly with a smile. And then I turned and quietly screamed to myself, "Yes! I did it!"

I learned a big lesson that day. I couldn't walk around that wall of fear. I had to walk through it and when I did, I became a free man.

My confidence grew. I started to believe the audience was there because they wanted to hear me. Soon I began leading community drumming circles. After one of those events one of the participants hired me to do corporate events. He said to me, "It's already built right into you. You are doing it naturally and I want to hire you for my next retreat as a speaker because I believe you're an example of someone who lives their passion."

One of those events involved speaking to a hundred and fifty off-shore oil rig drillers. "This is going to be a tough crowd," I thought to myself. After I was introduced as "Doug Sole," a heckler yelled out, "Sole, is this an 'Ah-sole?" And to make matters worse, right before that the CEO had said to me, "By the way, I'm retiring right after this event; this is the last time I'll have to address this rowdy group. Good luck."

As I walked out I was saying to myself, "Holy %#$@! Good thing I've overcome some other challenges in my life. I have the experience to draw from and I know how to react now." It was an affirmation and it helped.

The first thing I said to them was, "Yeah, well, I've heard that one before, and you know what? I'm glad you said 'Ah-sole' because my great-grandfather's first name was Albert. I take great pride in my great-grandfather because he spent his life serving others. His first initial was the letter A so I do come from a long lineage of 'Ah... Soles." Everyone laughed then, and I was able to turn a negative moment into a positive.

Soon after that I opened up my own drumming store with my business partner Paul Bailiel. For the first two years we worked eighty-hour weeks, but I really enjoyed it because I had finally found my true path.

Drumming is a lifestyle, and an extension of people's lives. People's personalities come out in their playing, and the lessons learned in drumming can be transferred back to life lessons. This is why drumming and corporate team building work so well together. I often use it in my team building exercises for corporations, and in the community. This makes me feel like I'm contributing to my community, but I really feel I get back much more than I put in.

Whatever energy you give to the drum it will give it right back. Whatever intention you put into the drum, whether it's positive or negative, it will give it right back. This is what I feel about life. You can't get anything out of life unless you contribute to it. I treat drumming like a metaphor for life. I believe I was put on this planet to serve others. This is just a part of my spiritual beliefs. It is hard for me to think of any of my experiences as failures, because I just think of them as learning experiences. They are a natural progression of what I was meant to go through to get to where I am today. The events of my Dream Career fell into place only because I kept taking the next step, regardless of how big and how frightening that next step seemed.

Dr. Gerstein's Comments

In order to grow you have to stretch yourself.

Doug had a passion for music. You could say it was in his blood. He played, wrote and taught music for most of his life. However, at thirty-two years old he still lacked confidence in his abilities as a musician. He had to step right out into his area of discomfort before he could overcome this block.

You can study and practice and you can read all of the books written by the experts in your chosen field. But until you take it out into the world and test it, you will never achieve what you want.

Don't get me wrong. You have to do the preparation. You have to know what you are doing or talking about in whatever area you choose. But usually that is not where the problem lies. Most of us are abundantly prepared and very knowledgeable about our respective subject matters. In fact, many of the so-called experts with acclaimed celebrity status are not the smartest or the most skilled in their field. They are just the ones who have stepped forward and taken action.

Here is a little secret – very few people are confident when they begin. When you look at the history of people basking in the limelight of fame, you will often find rocky beginnings. The sounds you hear are not the clanging of skeleton bones in the closet; they are the normal chattering of teeth coming from terrified people just starting out.

Just like Doug, begin slowly. Take small bites from the world pie. It's great to have big aspirations but every foundation is weak when it is just being built. **Nothing succeeds like success. The more you do the more you can do.** To put it another way, if you don't take a small risk and put yourself out there, you will not be able to take on the harder challenges you come across later. **Challenges are really**

Dr. Gerstein's Comments

opportunities in disguise. Build on your successes in the arena where it really counts – out in the world. It will be scary at first. Take solace in the fact that you are not alone, and know that fear will put you among the greats in history.

Even Mahatma Gandhi, India's former fearless leader, who fought for his country's freedom with words, started his public speaking career at a snail's pace. In his first address, he had to retake his seat after no words came from his mouth. He simply couldn't speak, and it was an utter disaster. He didn't fare much better his second time either. But look at what he ultimately did with his words.

You have no idea how far you will go by merely imagining what you will do. Start small. Take a risk. It's normal to feel uncomfortable at first. In fact, I would say if you are not feeling uncomfortable you are not stretching yourself far enough. Just as your muscles get stronger when pushed beyond their normal limits, your courage and mental toughness will also be fortified when you push yourself beyond your comfort zone.

"And as we let our own light shine, we unconsciously give other people permission to do the same. As we are liberated from our fear, our presence automatically liberates others."

Marianne Williamson

Charles Marcus

Professional Speaker

"I was playing the victim instead of the victor I wanted to be."

I stutter.

Two simple words that even a five-year-old could say. But it took me about thirty-five years before I could say it to myself and to the world. However, once I did there was no turning back. I had made a decision that I would no longer play the victim role, that I would no longer wallow in self-pity, and that I would no longer allow other people's remarks to crush me. Then over a period of time, I did what I once would not have dreamed possible not in a million years, I became a professional speaker.

Growing up in England, stuttering was a problem I carried with me everywhere I went. I was ridiculed in school. I avoided answering questions I knew the answers to, because of my fear of ridicule from the other kids and because I lacked the courage to try and speak up for myself. I became withdrawn. People mistook my stuttering and consequent withdrawal as signs of lower intelligence, not as a disability as it is recognized to be today. It took an enormous toll on my confidence and self-esteem.

Adults were often no different. Growing up, even they did not realize my struggles with routine daily activities that they took for granted. Things like making a simple phone call or getting change in a bank were nightmares for me. Going out to a restaurant and ordering a meal was a nerve-wracking experience. If I was taking a girl out to dinner I would start thinking about how I would order three days in advance in an attempt to avoid the inevitable humiliation. I tried very hard to hide my problem, generally unsuccessfully.

I had taken speech therapy for years and while my speech improved slightly, it hardly made a dent in the stresses I felt. People would laugh and hurl insults at me if I held them up in line like at the grocery store or purchasing tickets for a train or an event. I endured verbal abuse like, "You should be ashamed of yourself." "You are a freak." "Get on with it. What's your problem?" I don't hold it against them, they had no idea of how hurtful or inappropriate their words were, but I certainly felt different than everybody else. I was so ashamed of myself. The more I attempted to control my stuttering, the worse it got. I grew up carrying my shame with me wherever I went.

As a career, I chose hairdressing, or should I say, it chose me, a career where listening and artistic talent was valued more than talking. To begin with, I was fortunate enough to have been given an opportunity with the world famous Vidal Sassoon Company where I learned so much about business and life. I then went on to own and operate my own hair salons in Manchester, England for a number of years. While my stuttering still affected me, there was some improvement for a time. However, in my mid-thirties my speech started degenerating again. It came to a point where I began to avoid answering the phone. I coughed when I spoke, to cover up my hesitation or inability to speak. I chose my words very carefully so as not to embarrass myself. Life was hard enough, but this behaviour was exhausting me. I was bitter and angry, and my self-esteem was at an all time low.

I was suffering from pain, shame, rejection and humiliation, and now I became seriously depressed. I wallowed in self-pity, and took all that pain out on the people who loved me. I didn't like myself much. **I was the victim instead of the victor I wanted to be.** I felt sorry for myself instead of taking responsibility for what I knew I had to do. I thought of drowning my sorrows in alcohol. I even contemplated suicide.

One day something inside me caused me to finally look in the mirror and convince myself that I had to do something about my speech. This meant accepting responsibility and doing something about my stuttering that was mentally, emotionally and physically destroying me.

Interestingly, around that time, call it fate if you would like, while channel surfing on the television, I saw a documentary program about a course in Scotland for people who stutter, put on by Andrew Bell. What I witnessed on that documentary was astounding. People with stutters even more severe than mine, being able to speak relatively fluently. I wrote a letter to the BBC requesting the address and phone number for Mr. Bell. Because of its popularity, the next course I could register for was a long twelve months away.

I immediately signed up, but because of my fear of facing my speech demons, I cancelled and rebooked twice before finally finding the nerve to go through with it. I was waiting for someone else to save me, to come along with that quick fix or magic bullet to make all my problems go away. The truth is there is no easy way. People had reached out to me before, but I knew that I alone had to take the first step. Finally I took that step, and I attended the course *eighteen months* after I first saw the program.

I remember lining up at the train station, in my home city of Manchester, England, on the way to the course. I kept rehearsing what I would say at the ticket office, "A one way ticket to Edinburgh, Scotland please." Over and over again I rehearsed but, despite all that work, when I got up to the ticket wicket, I just froze. I couldn't get anything out of my mouth. I felt the pressure from the people behind me in line. And then they started. "Get on with it you freak," "Get on with it," came the taunts. My gut was in my throat. I couldn't speak. I turned red with embarrassment. I stammered out a broken apology for my stuttering, quickly wrote out my destination on a piece of paper and handed it to the ticket agent.

When I got out of line I breathed a sigh of relief. I gathered myself and turned around to face my tormentors, the people still in line. I said to myself, **"Never again will I be humiliated like that."** I carried that thought with me for the whole seven-hour trip to Scotland. That was a DEFINING MOMENT for me. I still have that train ticket in my office. It is worn and tattered now, yet it is very significant to me.

When I got to the course the hardest thing I ever had to do was to stand up and admit to everyone else: "I NEED HELP." I had to first accept I had a problem before I could start fixing it. Mr. Bell conducted a very strict course, and I needed that guidance and focus. I discovered that stutterers are people who generally want to please everybody, probably because of low self-esteem or inability to articulate otherwise. I learned I had to become a little selfish and I found out that was okay. Mr. Bell told us we had to convince ourselves that we had a new way of speaking. He taught us to be confident, to face our demons and to believe in ourselves. He inspired me greatly. **One of the first affirmations we learned on the course was, "I am the most important person in my life." I learned that if I didn't like and respect myself first, how could I expect other people to like and respect me?** If other people were uncomfortable with my new voice, that was tough. Recognizing this did a lot to raise my self-esteem, and knowing that Mr. Bell believed in each and every one of us on his course, and that we could personally contact him at any time, kept me going over the weeks to come.

Those were tough weeks, but it was also a transformational period for me. I learned a lot about myself in those sometimes dark moments. But I never, for a moment this time, felt like quitting or blaming other people. There was no going back this time; no failing. Very slowly, I began to improve. I left the course with a new way of speaking; strange, slow and very protracted, however if I concentrated, it was virtually stutter free. That was amazing to me and a real confidence booster.

The hard work really began when I left the safe confines of Andrew Bell's course. As I headed back to the real world, I knew I was going to be challenged. I would have to actually use the techniques I had just learned and draw on all my strength and determination to stick with it. Over the next few years I took two steps forward and one step back, but I stuck to Mr. Bell's plan religiously. I was very motivated and disciplined, I had made my decision to work on it, and I was going to make it happen. **There was no going back. I was no longer going to be the victim, but rather the victor I wanted to be.**

To support my efforts, I joined a local drama club. I began reading motivational and goal-setting books instead of just the soccer scores at the back of the newspaper. I was now so focused on improving my speech that other people's looks and abrasive comments didn't affect me as much. I finally had a direction. I knew where I was going and I was not going to let anyone stop me from walking in my path. I also surrounded myself with very positive people who supported what I was doing and I stayed away from negative people at all costs – the "dream stealers" as I call them now. This was a very important decision on my part.

Another pivotal point during that time was being prepared to talk about the elephant standing in the middle of the room (a.k.a. my speech). For years my speech was a topic that was avoided by both my family and friends. Everyone knew it was there, but they and I had strangely chosen to never talk about it. That changed after my time with Andrew Bell. I started talking to my friends and family about my stuttering and disability, and the steps I was taking to work on it. Admitting that I had a disability, and telling them I was working on a method to control my stuttering, was probably one of the hardest things I had ever had to do. I told them to expect my speech to sound slower and more mechanical, and I asked for their understanding and support. I had spent a good part of my life trying to hide the problem, and now I was asking for help and support. The impact on my longer term success and sense of self-esteem was noticeable.

In 1990, with my speech generally under control, I came to Canada. To challenge myself, I took a sales job in the hair products industry with a large corporation called Nexus. Part of my job was to educate hair stylists about our products. In sales I experienced incredible success, growing my territory by over 346% and managing my speech challenges every day. Within a few years I was promoted to Ontario district manager with new responsibilities including training new sales reps. By working in sales **I started to become the person I knew I always could be.**

Meanwhile, I had found a new skill, giving presentations. This started with the educational seminars to the salon employees and training of the sales representatives. I soon realized I was good at it. I joined an international speaking group called Toastmasters. It was an excellent training ground and challenged me even further.

Soon I was speaking quite frequently. Here I was a stutterer giving speeches. It seemed ridiculous, *but I was doing it.* Stuttering groups began to ask me to come and share my story with them, and the media picked up the story of how a stutterer was giving speeches.

My impact in these presentations caused me to become intrigued by the speaking industry, and the skills and techniques of professional speakers. In 1996 I recognized the need to challenge my speech further. I began to focus on those professional speakers as a way to encourage me to continue learning and growing or else I'd risk slipping back into a comfort zone and stagnating. In this vein, I went to a couple of meetings held by The Canadian Association of Professional Speakers (CAPS) and shortly thereafter I joined. Throwing myself into that organization, I volunteered on a program committee and began attending speaking conferences. I was now rubbing shoulders with famous speakers.

In 2001 I sat down with my wife to discuss my dreams and my future. At the time we had one child, my wife had a full time job, and we had some savings, but I also knew that to become successful as a speaker I had to commit to it a hundred per cent. She was very supportive and believed in me. Together we decided that I should give speaking my full focus, at least for a time, and pursue my dream. With that, I gave notice to my employer, leaving a fifty- to sixty-hour a week executive position, not to mention a very good salary.

Professional speaking is a business. Many people approach it like a hobby, but it is a serious business. As with everything I take on, I was not interested in becoming an average speaker. When I do something I want to rise to the very top of whatever profession I am in. That is just the way I am.

In the beginning, I had no clients and few leads but I believed in myself. I also had support from my wife and some wonderful people from the speaking community who believed in me. Those first couple of years were tough, very tough. I struggled financially, but my public speaking skills were slowly improving. I went for coaching and attended training seminars, but most of all I sought out every opportunity to speak.

Now, six years later, I have made a successful career for myself as a speaker and a best-selling author. I will always have a speech challenge because there is no cure for stuttering, however, that probably makes me appear more real and genuine to my audiences.

People tell me they find encouragement, inspiration and hope from my story and the message that I deliver in my presentations. This gives me a tremendous sense of satisfaction and a sense of giving something of myself to others. **I am humbled by the privilege of being able to speak to people,** but I also frequently have the privilege of listening to others share their personal struggles with me. As a professional speaker, I have also, ironically, become a better listener. One of the problems I had when I was wallowing in self-pity was that I could only see my own pain. I was only focused on me and my problems. Today, I have a broader view of the world and deeper empathy for others. This shift in me has also helped my business. As Zig Ziglar says, "People don't care how much you know until they know how much you care."

I've learned to control my speech instead of having my speech control me. My speech used to control my life – where I went and what I did. Now it no longer stops me from doing anything. I used to portray myself as a victim, and that made me feel awful. For years I sold myself short because I never believed I could do what I wanted to do. Now I am the victor but I don't feel arrogant. Having come so far makes me appreciate everything I have in life. Every day is a blessing for me. Every time I step off the stage I have to pinch myself to remind myself I am not dreaming. I know when we have the courage to dream and the commitment to succeed, a whole new world of opportunity opens up for us.

Dr. Gerstein's Comments

"Asking for help was the hardest thing for me to do."

Charles was a very good hairdresser. He pushed himself and paid the price to succeed in the Vidal Sassoon industry. That was not easy. He took courses and received a lot of help and training. He got support. He learned from the best. He did what was necessary to succeed at work. But at that time he just didn't have the strength to pay the price with his speech impediment.

He took pride in being an independent person. But was he? Is anyone truly independent? There is no such thing as a self-made man or woman. It's a fallacy. Show me a successful person at the top of his or her industry and I'll show you someone who got a lot of help. It might not have been formal help but they had assistance. They asked questions, they received advice, they paid for expert support.

To become a successful hairdresser, Charles received a tremendous amount of teaching, support and assistance. But for thirty-five years he had blinders on when it came to being successful with his own speech challenge.

Things turned around for him when he started to openly ask for help. It was probably the hardest thing for him to do. To ask for help means you actually need help. You are admitting you actually have a problem. It took him thirty-five years to admit he had a problem. Once he did, he asked for help, and the world opened up for him.

The truth is people generally want to help you. The biggest fear people have is if they ask for help, they will be denied. That is not what I have found personally, or professionally. Think of how you feel when someone turns to you and says, "I need your help." How did that make you feel right now when you read that sentence? Here is another secret: We live in an inter-dependent

Dr. Gerstein's Comments

world. We want to be needed. It feels good for the giver to help. When you ask for help, you are actually doing someone a favour by allowing them an outlet to express that need of giving. In this way, the giver benefits.

The receiver benefits in three ways. He/she receives the help and in turn will be eager to give to others. Others who receive that help will pass the favour forward to even more people. And so the "virtuous cycle" continues.

Where have you needed help but have avoided asking for it? Who can you ask now?

Do it. You'll be doing both of you a favour.

"What You Think of Me Is None of My Business"

Terry Cole-Whittaker

Penny Simmons

President and Founder of
Penny Loafers Shoe Shine Company Inc.

I used to think I wasn't particularly smart. My biggest challenge has been a constant struggle in overcoming this misconception. As a result, I allowed my lack of confidence in my abilities to hold me back. I just didn't believe in myself. I made several mistakes; including dropping the ball on what became a million dollar invention. But I never gave up. I used the inspiration of other people to keep me in the game until I won.

I did not have much of a formal education, and as a child I was teased a lot by my two older siblings for not being very smart. One of them even called me stupid and no one ever corrected him.

My dad was a successful business man. He was always tough on me, and preferred to tell me what to do instead of asking me what I wanted to do. He often sent mixed messages such as, "Do what you want," while at the same time saying, "Learn how to type, just get by and conform." It was the classic push-me-pull-me tug of war. As I internalized this belief, I lost all confidence in who I really was. When

I was in my late twenties, some of my friends sat me down and pointed out that I was always apologizing. I had not realized I was doing that, and that day was the beginning of a long road to recovery in my area of self-confidence. I am still on that road but I feel much better about myself now that I understand it was all perception and not truth.

When I was seventeen I came home one day and announced I wanted to buy a Taco Bell franchise. My brother was dumbfounded, and said the idea was crazy. "Who would want a franchise?" he asked. So, I never did it.

I naively followed my conditioning and started working as a secretary at a major brokerage firm. That honoured one of the messages I received as a kid – "just get by." The other message – "do what you want" – didn't click in until much later. Eventually, I convinced the firm to give me a shot at selling stocks, but I simply didn't have the passion for it. I tried catering for a while, grew bored with that, and then did some marketing in my father's business. I had no idea – no vision for where I was going.

I was eager to do something I loved. Around 1990 I saw the popularity of a line of toys called the *Cabbage Patch Dolls.* You couldn't wash them, and I felt the children's market needed a line of toys that could be washed. I was jazzed; I had never been this excited about an idea for work.

I began brainstorming and sourcing appropriate materials. Beanbags were popular in my childhood, and the idea could be recycled in the form of a doll. I thought beanbag toys would be perfect. I found a source of cheap recycled PVC pellets, and envisioned using the ends of fabric bolts as the cover. I would be environmentally conscious as well as entrepreneurial.

A friend of mine made some prototypes, and another friend who was a children's author was keen on writing little books for the characters. We began to brainstorm lists of animals and possible names for them. For research I watched Saturday morning cartoons and hung out in toy stores. I had connections with a toy company, and a manufacturer lined up. I trademarked the name The *Has-Beans* for comic books, movies, toys, cartoons and merchandise. Our working name was *The Beanies.*

Then it happened. My fiancée abruptly broke off our engagement, I had a falling out with a close friend (the designer whom

I'd enlisted for *The Beanies*), and I underwent a business setback. Those three significant personal losses knocked me off course, and clouded my judgment. **I lost sight of my goal,** and concluded it was all just a dumb idea. *I never followed through.*

Years later I saw a front page headline, and froze. It announced the phenomenal success of a new line of toys called *Beanie Babies*. I was devastated. There was even a picture of a rabbit – almost identical to one of my prototypes. When you register a trademark you must sell at least one unit within a year for it to remain protected. I had taken my eye off the ball, and let the ball drop. My trademark had expired, and someone else grabbed it.

I had blown off what might have been a million dollar idea all because my confidence wavered. I was upset for weeks. After moping around for a while I finally realized, "If I could do it once I can do it again. Dwelling on my mistakes won't help me now."

I picked myself up and moved on. "How?" you may ask. I used the inspiration of people like Thomas Edison. He had about 1,000 "failures" before he invented the incandescent light filament. I played the tunes of Tina Turner, who resembles the Phoenix rising from the ashes as she reinvents her career every decade. I thought of people like Katherine Hepburn who was unceremoniously dropped by her studio when her early movies struggled at the box office. She didn't sulk. She bought her movie rights from the studio, hired Cary Grant to play opposite her, and then starred in her own movies. The rest is history. Moving on, I turned my focus to the next opportunity.

I looked at ideas that had come to market. I wrote down what had worked for me and what had failed. It was important that I know who my cheerleading section was, so I listed the people in my life that might assist me with my goals. With no idea what I wanted, I turned to a career counselor for help. After weeks of searching and introspection I discovered I wanted and needed to go into business for myself. BUT DOING WHAT? I was determined to find something by keeping my eyes, ears and heart open.

While doing international sales and marketing for a family business I met a young woman with an invention whom I had mentored with such things as the ins and outs of government agency requirements. Her invention soon won an award from Canada's scientific research community. That's when she called me with her dilemma. She wanted to accept the award in person in Vancouver, but was already committed to a trade show in the U.S. that same week. She asked if I would I go and represent her at the trade show. I was free, and agreed to go for only the cost of my expenses.

While there, I discovered two items that intrigued me – miniature menus and a shoe shine business. *The Mini Menus*™ appeared years later in Canadian hotels and restaurants as business advertising. But at the time, none of my contacts in the tourism industry had heard of it, so I dismissed it. (Looking back, I can see I dismissed things too quickly as a result of not believing in my abilities.)

I didn't have a chance to see the shoe shine business, but the fellow in the next booth raved about it. He told me there were two girls giving shoe shines with their bare hands, and it was phenomenal. I wasn't overly impressed, but he persisted. "There's a business for you" he said. "What were you smoking in the men's room?" I asked jokingly. "Do you have any idea what I've done? I've been a stockbroker, a caterer, and I'm now working in international marketing. I am not going to shine shoes." Or so I believed at the time….**never say never.**

Eight months later I went on a trip to unwind. I shopped, walked and exercised to Jane Fonda tapes as I tried to clear my head and get focused. I reviewed my strengths and weaknesses. Then, while driving down a country road with a girlfriend, it hit me like a ton of bricks!

That shoe shine business had everything I was looking for. I could own my own business, the environment was right, and I could be an entrepreneur and still interact with people. My customers would fit the profile I had identified with the career counselor. I guess I really did listen to that man who told me about this business; it just took a while to realize it. Fortunately, for some unknown reason, I remembered the name of the company even though I had discarded the business card almost immediately.

The next day I was so wound up thinking about my future that I got up with the birds. To track down the number of the company from the trade show, I called directory assistance. I was so excited I told the operator about my plans. He was delightful, but despite an intense search he couldn't find it. But just as I was hanging up, I heard him yell, "Wait a minute. I found it!" He gave me the number, and with many thanks and his best wishes, I hung up.

As it was early on a Saturday morning, I sat there waiting for the appropriate time to phone the manager of the business. When I finally dialed the number at 8:30 a.m., I heard a very sleepy voice on the other end. Somehow I had forgotten about the two hour time difference, and had wakened her at 6:30 a.m.!

"I love your business," I said, "and I'm wondering what I can pay you to teach me to do what you do." She was very gracious, and set up a conference call with the owner, who then mentored me in starting my own shoeshine business.

I wonder if I would have lost faith in myself again had the operator not found the number that day. I'm not sure. I almost didn't do this because of my age, which at that time was thirty-nine. I knew the other girls doing this were in their twenties, and all of a sudden this older gal was going to hit the scene. My old conditioning was nipping at my heels again. This time I refused to listen.

I registered the business in September 1994. I shelled out thousands of dollars in consulting fees and in building my first chair. It wasn't easy in the beginning. For the first nine months I applied to and was rejected by what felt like every landlord in the city.

To get my name out there I volunteered to shine shoes for free at a Harry Rosen location prior to Father's Day. I had nowhere else to go, and it was important that I get out to where the people were. I never told anyone I wasn't being paid. I never asked for gratuities but accepted them if they were offered. For three months I brought home about $20 a day.

During this time I had to find ways to make ends meet. I cut down on my expenses in as many creative ways that I could. I received about $1,000 a month from my family business, and still had some employment benefits for a few months. I took secretarial work and even did some catering, often with dubious results. One lady refused to pay me for an evening when I just about ruined the whole dinner. I knew my heart was no longer in it. I lived that way for a year to get my business off the ground.

I opened my first location at a downtown building in 1995. That first year I had few clients. As I watched thousands of people walk by without stopping, but instead snickering and whispering, I smiled and told myself I could always chop it up and use the wood for kindling. It took a lot of grit to get through those early days.

By the end of 1996 I had opened my second shoe shine shop at the TD Centre. Then, life once again threw me some setbacks. My brother had been diagnosed with brain cancer. He was having frequent seizures, and had to be restrained in a hospital bed. Down the road in another hospital, my mother was suffering from the effects of dementia. I found myself shuffling between the two, keeping vigil over them. I slept on a little cot alternating between the two rooms at different hospitals. I was mentally and physically exhausted, and I wanted to curl up in a corner and make this bad dream go away. But I had a business and responsibilities, and I wasn't going to drop the ball this time. *Instead, I held on tight.*

I knew I was in the right career because my personal stress dissipated after working on my first customer of each day. I felt invigorated and rejuvenated. I enjoyed the physical activity of the shoeshine and the relationships I was creating with my customers. I swear if I had been in an office job or in a business I disliked, I don't know how I would have gotten by.

When my mother and my brother both died only a few months apart in 1998, the vice chairman of one of the financial institutions expressed his condolences and brought me a lovely plant. His genuine interest was shared by many of my customers and that helped me at what was certainly one of the lowest times in my life.

There were setbacks. I lost my first location to a barbershop, who liked my ideas so much that they took my chair designs, and then I lost another one in Casino Niagara. The latter had wooed me with promises of a bustling business. They spoke about the success of the shoeshine at the casino in Windsor, so I spent thousands on new chairs and set-up fees. The result was only a few customers a day. Casino Niagara was drawing the bingo bus crowd, and that differed markedly from the customer demographics at Casino Windsor. I was commuting back and forth in support of my people who were working for me for free, hoping it would turn around.

It all ended when I was told they had changed their minds about my services, and would I please come and pick up my chairs from storage.

I was absolutely furious. I had fulfilled their requirements, and they didn't honour their commitment. There was no way I was going quietly. They had taken six months of my life at the time my brother was told he had only eight months left to live. I was a dog with a bone and I wasn't about to let go. I told them this was not acceptable, and I wanted a settlement. I went to the president of the Ontario Casino Corporation, and eventually received a full settlement.

Today I have many people working for me in different locations in the downtown core of Toronto. We have more than 30,000 clients a year, yet I am always asking myself, "What can I do next for my business?" I thought of running a weekly anonymous poll on social, economical and political issues. My clients could be the white-collar voice on many subjects. It might even attract media attention and thus, more exposure for my company.

My fears and self-doubt prevented me from acting on this great idea for years. I hemmed and hawed, and procrastinated. Finally, I just did it. I put together three questions and conducted a pilot test at one of my sites. One of my customers in the pilot test knew a writer who worked at the *National Post* newspaper. He told him about my idea, who in turn relayed it to his editor. The editor liked it so much that it became a weekly national feature in May 2003.

I still hear the voices of inadequacy whispering in my ear now and then. They are the same voices I heard when I allowed my Beanie Baby idea and others, slip though my fingers. **The difference is now I take action in spite of my fears.** I realize those feelings are just that – feelings. It doesn't mean they are true. The irony is that one of the best ways to diminish those feelings is by taking action in the face of them. It is just like Susan Jeffers says in the title of her book, *"Feel the Fear and Do it Anyway"* (Ballantine Books, 1988).

Dr. Gerstein's Comments

The biggest obstacle - ourselves.

As Walt Kelly's comic strip character Pogo, once said, "I have faced the enemy and it is us."

Outside of a calamity, whenever we don't do what we want to, we only have to look in the mirror to see the reason. Rarely however, do we see our own reflection looking back, but rather, we see a litany of people including our parents, former teachers, mates, former and current bosses and friends and family, just to name a few. It's as if we have created a cloud in front of our faces that blurs our own responsibility for our situation.

Well it's time to bring clarity to the image. It's true that we have been affected by a myriad of influencers that may have steered us in the wrong direction, and may not even have had our best interests at heart. But at some point we have to realize we have the right to choose the direction in which we want to go. We have no obligation to keep replaying the same old disempowering scenarios we have been conditioned to. *If we are not happy with our lives, we can change, and the first step to any change always begins with awareness.* We must become aware of our sole responsibility for our lives. We must somehow come to realize that blaming and pointing fingers at anyone or anything "out there" is not only inaccurate, it will never help us get what we really want. It is in fact, a total waste of time, and only keeps that mirror cloudy.

It is important to really understand that if we are not doing what we say we want, there is no one responsible but ourselves. That might seem harsh, but reality is seldom easy to face. It is always easier to rationalize our failures on the backs of others. Looking back through the cold lens of time, the bottom line is that all of those rationalizations are just stories. And while some stories have more validity than others, they are still just stories.

Dr. Gerstein's Comments

To gain some clarity, look back on the results in your life. *Your* results are the effects of your actions. An action is the effect of your thoughts and feelings, and those all exist within you. We can muddy the waters by blurring the recall of certain thoughts and feelings we may have had in our past. But it's a lot harder to be confused about the actions we took and the results we got. Start there and be honest with yourself.

Penny is a very creative and dynamic person, but for many years she didn't believe she was good enough. She carried around the erroneous belief that she wasn't smart enough because she lacked formal education. Well-meaning but inaccurate family members propagated, then re-enforced this misconception. It didn't matter that they were wrong; it only mattered that she believed them and internalized their values about her intelligence.

World history is filled with rich, famous, smart and successful people who had little formal education. Just to name a few, Albert Einstein was kicked out of school. Bill Gates left before finishing university. Donald Trump had little formal education.

I am by no means condoning quitting school. Formal education brings an invaluable contribution to one's thinking process, and can provide numerous advantages in your life's work. Statistics have shown that people with university degrees get better jobs and earn more than those who don't. What I am saying is that education does not start or end there.

Penny said she dropped her "Beanies" creation because of all of the turmoil in her life. But it was likely based more on how she felt about herself, than on her life situation. This became evident when she suffered through even more intense emotional pain caring for her dying mother and brother while getting her shoe shine company off the ground. With years of maturity and

Dr. Gerstein's Comments

insightful awareness, this time she did not fold up and walk away. She was learning how smart she really was, and beginning to believe in herself.

It is generally a lifelong struggle. It is not easy to cast off years of childhood conditioning, but Penny's story shows it can be done. She also shows it is not necessary to cure all your internal doubts before you take action and start. In fact, by taking action in the face of her fears she was able to speed up her process of inner healing. Success breeds success and nothing builds confidence like success. You can't think about success – you have to actually go out and make it happen. Bravo to Penny for doing that.

When you look in the mirror, who do you see? Who is responsible for your situation? Until you can see only yourself, you are operating under the illusion that someone else is responsible for your results. At first it may hurt to realize you are the creator of your situation. Here's the good news. By reclaiming your sole responsibility for your life, you will also be reclaiming your own personal power.

If you take away nothing else from this book remember this one thing: Never again allow anyone to steal your dreams. That includes you – yourself. Many of our beliefs about ourselves are wrong. You have no idea how high you can soar if you are still allowing someone else's negative conditioning to weigh you down. Cast off the chains and look in the mirror. Who do you see now?

"No one can make you feel inferior without your consent"

Eleanor Roosevelt

Susan Regenstreif

Music Specialist and Teacher

"But when you are FAT, you always think you're FAT.
So I thought I was FAT."

As a little girl I loved to sing songs from musicals, and dance around in my basement. I participated in musicals and plays at school, camp and synagogue. I always just seemed to have a natural interest in music. So you think I smoothly and easily flowed into a career in music? Not! I had some big issues to overcome first.

Music wasn't my only love. I also thought about becoming a veterinarian because I had a soft spot in my heart for animals. As a child I would bring stray animals home and care for them. There was only one problem – I couldn't stand the sight of blood! While I was at McGill University in Montreal I worked at The Jewish General Hospital as a nurse's aid. When I saw critically ill people I would become dizzy and nauseous. That plan would obviously not work.

I studied music in high school. From there I went into a CEGEP (*Collège d'enseignement général et professionel* or in English, *general and professional education college)* academic diploma program, which had a music program in Montreal. At McGill I majored in piano and voice. I sang opera and did so well I received several bursary scholarships to attend performing arts schools in Banff, Aspen, and Toronto. I still had to audition, but eventually I was able to take advantage of all three opportunities. While I was in Banff, I performed at Lake Louise and at The Calgary Stampede. The following summer I received another scholarship, which paid my way to study in Aspen, Colorado.

However, despite all this talent, I had a problem. As I child I had been overweight, and back then obesity was a stigma of inferiority. I was constantly ridiculed about it. In time I internalized these criticisms to mean I wasn't good enough. It made me not only self-conscious about my appearance, but I began to doubt myself in other areas of my life, like my musical talent.

Now, as an adult, I was unable to shake my Achilles heel. I was doing what I loved, yet I was burdened with feelings of not being good enough.

This issue had a serious effect on my musical career. My opera directors in Banff often told me I had a pretty face; I would look great *if only I could lose the weight.* They told me I looked like a potato sack in my dresses.

Auditioning was tough. I remember once getting dressed for an audition, and choosing something I thought I looked good in – a one-piece jump suit. *But when you are FAT, you always think you're FAT. So I thought I was FAT.* When I walked on stage my mind was preoccupied with my looks, and I was too nervous. I was not comfortable with my body, and all I could think about was how FAT I was. I didn't do well, and I knew it. The negative self-image I developed in childhood was continuing to haunt me as an adult, and my self-doubt sabotaged my performance.

Needless to say I didn't get the part, and I was devastated. I began thinking maybe opera wasn't for me after all. Maybe I should just stop. I was constantly being judged, and the level I had to reach to be accepted was just too high for my low self-image.

Ultimately I found opera to be too adjudicating. There were always critics, panels, teachers and evaluations. The burden of rules stifled my creativity, and I felt I couldn't express myself freely.

The final push that resulted in my exit from opera was my

realization of what I was becoming. I was a performer, and I had always thought that was my dream. I thought I wanted to be a star. However, I found myself becoming totally self-absorbed, and selfish. Everything I did during that time all began to relate to how it would affect my opera performances. Will this activity make me too tired? Will that experience affect my voice? It began affecting my relationships. I could see what I was becoming, and I didn't like it.

I have a special bond with children – maybe because I'm a kid at heart. So I left performing and went back to McGill and studied music therapy for children.

When I graduated, I started teaching piano to individuals. The good thing was there were no start-up costs. I was building my teaching skills, and my students benefited from my diverse musical background. My husband supported my entrepreneurial endeavor, and I got very positive feedback. But I soon realized this was not my passion. It was just a way to bring in some income. I really needed something more creative.

I wanted to develop a program that would boost children's confidence and allow them to express themselves freely. I started by researching children's music, and then I began creating my own material. I knew from personal experience that talent was not enough. Self-confidence was just as important, if not more important, than being good at something. If I could get children to feel comfortable in their bodies I reasoned, they would feel better about themselves.

Rhythm became the foundation of my program. I knew I wanted to do it in a group setting, because I really enjoy working with groups. There is a blend of entertaining and educating that takes place that I have a real affinity for. I find that learning is much more successful when the process is enjoyable.

When my own children got older, the after-school piano lessons began to conflict with their needs. I needed to work during the day, so I began approaching local schools and offering to teach my program. All of the musical scholarships I received at McGill gave me the confidence I needed in my new undertaking, and I was positive it was going to work. **I didn't even have a back up plan in case I failed. Failure was not an option, and it didn't even enter my mind.**

At the same time, I'm a perfectionist and never completely satisfied with my work. Artists can always make their product better, and that need creates self-doubt in my mind. I used that self-doubt to drive me to study more, and continuously improve my program. **It's a paradox. On one hand I was positive I was going to succeed; on the other I feared not being good enough. The combination kept me motivated.**

Once I began to market myself, the news spread by word-of-mouth and local schools began calling me to work for them. Camps became interested in my program. At one camp I used music as therapy to help autistic children. The counselors and parents noticed that music had a definite calming effect on the kids. It became a method of communication able to cross the barriers of normal language, and I found it so gratifying to be able help children that way.

Over the years, while creatively developing my children's musical program, I have found that I have developed too. An example occurred not long ago.

I had just finished a successful session of music for young children, when the parents who had hired me told me it was not what they wanted. Their vision had included more props and musical instruments. I experienced them as very critical in the way they communicated their message to me. I was hurt, and I felt angry and upset with them for telling me how to run my class. My opinion was they were naïve and ignorant of what I was doing musically for their children. I eventually realized they didn't have the musical background to understand all the subtle benefits of my program. All they could see was a lack of props and instruments. But that was their reality.

What did I do? I regrouped. Even though I was then a size eight, criticisms about my work sometimes still brought up old self-image wounds. But I didn't allow these criticisms to shut me down and cause me to retreat inside and hide. Instead, I looked at the situation from my client's perspective and incorporated their suggestions into my program. It would still work. I understood I could be flexible, adapt to a new situation, and still maintain my integrity in sticking with my principles. I learned a difference of opinion isn't necessarily a personal rejection. That was so liberating.

It was also freeing to accept that I can't please everyone. As I matured, I began to accept my imperfections and myself. Trying to change who I am to please others is more of a reflection of my own self-esteem, than it is about the people doing the criticizing.

I can now laugh at most criticisms. Some people remark that I bounce around a lot while teaching children's groups. There was a time when that remark might have devastated me, but now I find it amusing. Giving others permission to disagree with me and not fall apart, is an indication of how much I've grown in my confidence.

A key to enjoying my work has been in my gradual acceptance of my total self with all my imperfections. By releasing the entrepreneurial spirit within me, I also released my need to be perfect. Even if I had overcome my self-doubt earlier I believe I still would have felt too stifled in opera. I'm a very creative person who likes to play like a child and move around a lot, and that's why I'm so comfortable around children. When I took the focus off of myself and put it onto the children, I began to relax. My energy level rose, and the children had more fun. This career fits me perfectly, which is in direct contrast to the one-piece jump suit I wore for that opera audition.

Dr. Gerstein's Comments

Overcoming yourself as an obstacle

Often the biggest obstacle to doing what you love will be you. So many things we name as obstacles are really just challenges we can walk around. Why are some people able to move around them while others get stuck? It all links back to our beliefs about ourselves and the world around us. If you see yourself as a competent, confident person, you will take action to make that vision a reality. If you see the world as an encouraging, helpful place, you will seek help and get it.

If you think you don't deserve to be successful or happy, you will find a way to fulfill that prophecy. If you think the world is a scary place and people are out to get you, you will find a way to make yourself right. Frank Lloyd Wright, the great American architect said, *"The thing always happens that you really believe in; and the belief in a thing makes it happen."* By making our outer lives like the inner ways we see the world, we remain congruent. It makes sense and we go on with our lives thinking all is as it should be. It doesn't matter if we are suffering. If our outer world matches our inner world we think that is all we can do.

But what if your inner image is wrong? What if what you were taught to believe about yourself or the world was not true? Wouldn't this change your view of what's possible? Wouldn't it make you doubt some of your limitations, which heretofore you have unquestionably accepted?

Susan was made to believe she was inferior because she was overweight. The truth of that statement is immaterial. What matters is Susan believed it and internalized it, and that became her reality. No amount of proof could change her mind. Look at the evidence she could have used to counter that claim: She had excelled in music throughout her school years. She had won awards in music. She received scholarships from three different

Dr. Gerstein's Comments

performing arts schools, and was further taught by some of the best in the business. Yet when she auditioned, she could only think of how fat she was.

She may have left opera to keep her outer world – people criticizing her in auditions in a closely judged art form – and her inner world of self-doubt, consistent. Changing her self-image earlier may have changed her career direction. Conversely, she might have left because opera was too constraining for her creative, energetic self. That's not the point. The point is how powerful your self-image is.

What things about yourself have you allowed to stop you from doing what you want? What life-long beliefs that you hold about yourself or about the world may be wrong? If you want to look at one of the biggest obstacles in your life, start by examining yourself and your belief systems.

Myth-Diagnosis #1
Low Dream Esteem

✦

How You Can Bust This Myth

Now that you have had a chance to see the flaws in the belief systems of people who at one point didn't believe they were "good enough," this may be an ideal time to think of areas in your life where you don't feel as worthy as others. First, you must be aware that this notion may not even be true. If you do not feel worthy enough to do what you love, you might just be repeating someone else's opinion. It might have been something you heard as a child and took it as truth. From where did you get that idea? Who said it to you? Remember that how someone treated you and the names they called you were more about them than you. They were more likely projecting their own sense of unworthiness onto you and you were too young to reject their offer.

Even if part of what you feel about yourself is based in truth, it may have been about something for which you had little passion. Bear in mind that you don't have to excel in areas that you have little passion for or that you don't feel are important to you. Too many people become caught in what they are not good at and spend far too little time focusing on where they have talent. No one can be great at all things. Bill Gates might be a really bad golfer and Tiger Woods might not be good at software programming but notice that those "deficiencies" didn't stop these two talents from excelling in their own strengths.

You need only find your own tiny niche to begin building your esteem. You can always delegate other parts you deem necessary for your Dream Career to other people who do enjoy that area.

Myth – Diagnosis #2
Confusion Illusion

"I don't even know what
I want or who I am."

"A child-like adult is not one whose development is arrested;
On the contrary. He is an adult who has given himself a chance of
continuing to develop long after most people have muffled themselves
into a cocoon of middle age habit and convention."

Aldus Huxley

Laura Koot

News Presentation Editor

"I wanted to understand every single section of
the newspaper before I masqueraded as someone
who could lead this group."

Although I never saw it, my Dream Career was in front of my nose the whole time. My father encouraged me to go into a secure field. I was young and naïve, and didn't know any better. Thankfully I was a quick learner and discovered what I should have known all along.

I was born in Dorchester, New Brunswick, and when I was small we moved around a bit. When I was twelve we took a six-week camping trip through thirty states, setting up our tent in a different camp ground every night. We didn't know when or if we would find a camping spot each time, but that was part of the thrill. Experiences like that nurtured my childhood curiosity and spirit of adventure.

As a child I was an avid reader, and always enjoyed both reading and writing. In grade three I did classroom reports for the school newspaper, in time becoming editor of that newspaper. I was also to become editor of my high school newspaper.

I enjoyed it so much I volunteered to be a reporter for the town newspaper. I went on interviews with their reporters, and stayed late at night because I was curious about the industry. We taped up the stories – literally. The lines on the paper were actually tape where we pasted up the story. I was involved in the composing and production end of putting a newspaper to press.

After high school I went to the University of Western Ontario. For the first two days of school I was thinking of going into speech therapy because my dad had seen lots of current job postings in that field. I listened to him because he was my father, and it seemed the sensible thing to do. I thought I was supposed to enter a respectable career after I had gotten my play period out of my system. We were kids then, and I was just doing what many of my peers did when they reached university age. It never dawned on us that we could actually do what we really loved as a career.

By the third day of school it occurred to me I could work at the student university newspaper, *The Gazette*. When I volunteered as a reporter, I was immediately surrounded by enthusiastic people. We had interesting conversations and I began learning new things every day. There was no teacher advisor. All the information at *The Gazette* had been passed along from previous generations of students. I wrote a story the first day, and returned the next day to write another one. I was being creative *and* having fun! I began to think this could be my career, but I still wasn't sure.

In my first year at Western I took English and discovered I had already read just about everything on the reading list. I wasn't getting anything out of it, so in my second year I switched to politics. They spent the first two weeks explaining what 'liberal' was, and I was bored out of my mind. Most of the people in my class did not know a lot about world affairs or politics. My classroom education was a big disappointment. I had worked my tail off earning enough money to get to university doing part-time work in grocery stores, libraries and museums. When I finally got there, it was an enormous letdown.

Meanwhile, the student newspaper was completely stimulating. It was there, outside of class, where I was getting my true education. I was able to interview whomever I wanted including former prime ministers and authors. I got something published in every section. I did sports stories, feature art stories and took photographs. Once I even drew something for the graphic department that made the paper. I found I was a better editor than reporter, but before I masqueraded as someone who could lead this group, I wanted to understand every single section of the newspaper.

An editor is like a conductor. She has to know how to play instruments from each section of her orchestra. After volunteering my whole first year of university, I became the news editor in second year and received a small honorarium. To supplement my income I worked in a donut shop in the winter, and in the summer I conducted bus tours.

In third year I simultaneously quit university and became one of three supervising editors for the university newspaper. I was now making real money – $20,000 per year, versus the weekly fifty dollars from working at the donut shop. We had a $600,000 operating income, and it was our responsibility to get the paper out four times a week. We had to recruit volunteer staff and hire editors. We had deadlines, controversial editorials, and crossword puzzles. If the crosswords weren't clear we would get hundreds of complaints. It was real. Most of all, we learned to work in harmony, and the entire experience was worth more to me than any journalism school.

I enjoyed this unconventional route of education. I liked the practical aspects of learning as an apprentice because it had immediate applications. It was not just theory. Every day I worked at the newspaper I witnessed the reality of my future career.

In one particular project, I put together a special homecoming section for Western's ninetieth anniversary reunion. I called many successful alumni and asked them to do a piece for the section. That student newspaper had a lot of thriving alumni, and I considered that one of those contacts might pay off for me one day. Little did I know how right I was.

I knew it was time to move on from the university position when the challenge was no longer there. I was now ready to intern at a city newspaper. I began looking around, but both *The Globe and Mail* and the *Toronto Star* turned me down. *The New Brunswick Telegraph Journal* in Saint John accepted me, but I didn't really want to return there. I had spent my life trying to get away from my home and grow. But the offer was a good one and I couldn't turn it down. I reasoned it was a good provincial paper and it was a four-month opportunity. It wasn't as if I was locked in for life.

They hired me as a reporter and copy editor, but I didn't do a single story for them. It was rare to find a young person who was interested in editing. Most young people are eager to report. I on the other hand, liked the editing part of it.

Just as I did at the university paper, I volunteered to work in as many different areas of the paper as possible in order to gain understanding of each section. I was doing what I loved and wanted to soak it all in. I worked in sports, business, art and provincial news. I even learned how to fix the computers. That was important because at a small newspaper like that computer crashes weren't uncommon. We could avoid missing deadline if I could get it going again.

Three months into it the editor hired me as the Canada/World Editor. That meant I was in charge of finding Canadian and world stories, laying them out on the computer and finding the art to go with them. My salary rose accordingly with my higher position.

When they hired a new editor-in-chief, he came around to meet the staff. When he asked me what my goals were, I said, "I'd like to do the front page." In a newspaper the front page is the most important page. Then he said, "The front-page editor is off on Friday, would you like to do it then?" I was shocked, but managed to say, "Absolutely," the words fairly leaping out of my mouth.

Front page editing meant shuffling late breaking stories and getting it all done in time. I am proud to say we made deadline, which we almost never did at that newspaper. That was the beginning of my front-page duties and the end of the other person's. Making deadline saves newspapers a lot of money and when given the opportunity, I proved I was up to the task.

I was still only twenty-one. Everyone else on the desk was older, and they were all male. I stuck out like an art story in the sports section. I was young and had a lot to learn, but fortunately I knew it, and wasn't too proud to ask for help when I needed it. When I did, the others were very gracious with their assistance.

My forward thinking in university was about to pay off. I had kept in touch with the preeminent contacts I made while doing the Ninetieth Anniversary special section at Western. Whenever one of them came to New Brunswick to cover a special event such as a

Premier's conference, I met them for lunch. One day I got a call from one of those contacts, Paul Wells. He told me about a new newspaper that Conrad Black was starting up in Toronto. It was to become the *National Post*. He said they were hiring copy editors and would I be interested? He himself had just been hired as a columnist. I knew this was the break I had been waiting for.

When I came to Toronto for the interview there were a few people typing away in an empty office space; my interviewer sat in another room. I admit to being a bit apprehensive. I didn't know if this new paper was going to get off the ground. On one hand I had a great job in New Brunswick that I loved. I loved the people and I loved the place. But my long-term plan was to work in different newspapers across Canada, and this was Toronto. Even so, my peers in New Brunswick didn't believe there was going to be a new newspaper. I guess Toronto's inside news didn't reach all the way to the east coast. Well, I had my interview, and they offered me a job. To say I was excited would be an understatement.

I was told if I didn't work out they would send me packing. No one knew me in Toronto, and I had no security. I was the youngest person on staff, and it was anything but safe. I decided to take a risk, and embrace the unknown. My fear became my motivator.

There were many benefits to being in Toronto, including more social opportunities. In Saint John, if I didn't like the movie playing at the one theatre, I had a choice between the two bars downtown. Yes, Toronto was looking brighter all the time.

When I finally arrived in Toronto, all my fears melted away. Other people on staff were quite welcoming and helpful. We were excited to get the new paper off the ground. Many people in the journalism industry thought we were going to fail, and even now they are calling for our demise. But that didn't stop us; in fact it may have even motivated us even more to succeed. Our first edition came out on October 27, 1998.

I love what I do. **I am doing the same thing now that I did in grade three** although I didn't realize until much later that it could become my career.

Dr. Gerstein's Comments

Opportunities – Who you know is often more important than what you know.

In any career I have found that networking is key. Who you know is often more important than what you know. That phrase often brings with it negative connotations. However, let us look at it in a positive way. It is the relationships that grow out of those networking opportunities that often propel people to the next step on their dream path.

Laura began developing important contacts in university and maintained those contacts through lunches and telephone conversations while back in New Brunswick. This ultimately paid off when one of those contacts recommended her for a position at a new start-up newspaper in Toronto.

There is no such thing as a self-made man or woman. We all need people to help us develop and nurture our passions and talents. Begin developing relationships with people in your field of interest. Who knows when and where those relationships will pay off for you?

"Pain is temporary. It may last a minute, or an hour, or a day, or a year, but eventually it will subside and something else will take its place. If I quit, however, it lasts forever."

Lance Armstrong

Ricky Ramos

Sportball™ Coach

*"When I look at a challenge I look at all
the ways I can make it work.
I do not look at how it can fail."*

I've always been playful. The trouble was none of my family would play with me. My dad was distant. My mom was warm but not the type to horse around a lot, and I didn't get along with my sister until I was fifteen. So as a child I had to play by myself. As an adult I found a way to keep playing.

I grew up in Mexico City, and as a child I was hyperactive. My mind worked so quickly that my tongue had trouble keeping up. My parents once took me to a specialist, and he told them to give me plenty of outlets to burn all the energy I had. They put me in football, karate and other activities.

I was a kid with a lot of needs, yet my dad was very distant. I wanted a lot of attention, but he pushed me away because he needed his space. I think his poor marriage to my mom was a factor in his aloofness. He was a strict disciplinarian, and made me organize my toys as young as five years old. All my trucks had to be put away together, and the other toys sorted in kind. My room had to be clean and my hair couldn't be messy. Later I discovered that his father was even more of a disciplinarian to him than he was with me.

But my dad was also very protective of me. He didn't want me to take a lot of chances because he wanted to save me from hurt or disappointment. That may have been true from his perspective, but as a child I only saw him as continuously putting obstacles in my path.

I stopped telling him about my dreams because whenever I did he would poke holes in my ideas. He only ever saw what could go wrong, not what could be great, and that just brought me down. For the longest time I wanted to be a pilot. I loved the air – and it was extreme too.[2] My dad didn't want me to do it, so he said, "Ricky, to be a pilot you have to be tall and have perfect teeth." I believed him, and as I met neither criterion I gave up on that idea.

When I was twelve, my parents' marital problems forced me to go and live with my aunt for a year. I needed some reprieve from all the chaos and turmoil. As a result I ended up missing a year of middle school, and then I wasn't allowed to enter high school.

My aunt had a friend who was the president of a university, and she asked him if I could take a computer course. She told him I had nothing else to do, and this might help point me in the right direction. Surprisingly he agreed. The irony is, I couldn't go to high school but at twelve I was going to university. I was still hyperactive, but because I didn't have anyone my own age to distract me, I concentrated on my work, and it paid off.

By the time I was fourteen I had a university degree in computer programming. I was doing so well my parents urged me to go to high school, which I did, with plans of taking advanced computer courses after I graduated. When I graduated I decided to take a few years off to decide what my next step should be.

It was time to experiment. My dad got me a job working on computers at his place of work, Roché, the large Swiss pharmaceutical company. I lasted a total of four hours. My energy was too high, and I

[2] In sports, extreme refers to: a. Very dangerous or difficult: extreme rafting. b. Participating or tending to participate in a very dangerous or difficult sport: an extreme skier.

knew I wouldn't have the patience for this type of work. I did well in computer programming in school because I was forced to focus – I didn't have another option. But now was the time explore my options.

I started by taking a position at a Sheraton Resort in Puerto Vallarta, where I was put in charge of the kids club. I enjoyed working with the children in different sports activities. Over the next few years I worked at several resorts.

I took an interest in scuba diving, and soon became a dive master. It was very good money and I quite enjoyed living at the beach. I did that for a number of years and was on my way to becoming a director of activities at the resort. I was having a good time – maybe a little too good. I've never met a director who was happily married and faithful. You were always around scantily clad women who came from all over the world and were looking for fun. The temptations were just too great, and I couldn't see myself settling down and raising a family in that atmosphere. It's hard for me to separate business from family. It's all one package for me and I have to be comfortable with the whole package.

I followed my girlfriend to Canada, where we got married. I worked at a sporting goods store. The marriage didn't work out (she was cheating on me). I went back to Mexico and got a position at another resort in the children's program. I soon discovered that it was effectively just a baby-sitting program. Parents would drop off their children and then leave for seven hours. Sometimes I wound up with children ranging in age from two to seven years old. I found it very frustrating coming up with activities to appease such a diverse group. I liked the kids, but didn't enjoy the position I was put in. I returned to scuba diving.

The terrorist activity of September 11, 2001 forced me to quit scuba teaching and look in a new direction. People stopped flying, and many hotels in Mexico closed. I began nurturing the idea of going to Canada.

Before I moved to Canada I took a chance and asked my dad what he thought. I did it because I had distanced myself from him, and I knew he was feeling rejected. I told him I no longer wanted to live in Mexico City because of the high crime rate and the pollution problem. I surely didn't want to raise a family here. He shocked me by asking me, "What does your heart tell you to do now?"

I told him I wanted to go to Canada because I had been there before and loved it, despite the heartbreak of my divorce. Over the years at the resorts, people from Canada had promised me positions should I ever move to Canada. I was sure I could get a job. He said, "Then go ahead. I trust you because whatever you do, you do it well. You don't do drugs. You are a responsible person."

I was taken aback. Was this my dad? Why was he being so understanding? When I reflected on his career history I got a deeper appreciation of his situation. When his best friend at work betrayed him, my dad refused to squeal on him. He took responsibility for what his so-called friend did, and my dad was the one who lost his job. He could have been president of that company one day. He had worked his way up to directing the import-export branch of Roché. All that happened about ten years ago, and after that he was never the same. He valued his career so much that when he lost it he just gave up saying, "My life here is done." He became depressed. He was diabetic but didn't take care of himself, and it was almost like he was trying to die. In 2005 at the age of fifty-eight, he did die.

My dad once asked me, "Why don't you come to me for advice any more?" I could tell he was hurt. I told him, "I no longer do because you have always knocked my dreams." Looking wounded he said to me, "You don't love me as much as you love your mother, you never did."

"That's not true," I replied, "I love you both equally. I would give my life for either of you. Don't you know that? If I had to live my life over I would want the same parents because I am who I am because of you."

I felt his pain, and when I did, I finally understood. I now knew he had always loved me deeply. He had knocked my dreams because he was trying to protect me. Because he had always been afraid of going for his own dreams, he projected his fears onto me. Sadly, by blocking my dreams he thought he could save me from the hurt he had experienced in his life. However, it just doesn't work that way. I love you dad.

I believe if you want to do something with all your heart, then nothing can stop you. I used this belief to move me forward in my plan to come and live in Canada. My parents supported me, but my friends told me my computer diplomas and diving credentials wouldn't count in Canada. They warned me that as a Mexican I would be relegated to menial jobs. But I didn't let their negative thinking stop me. The more negative their comments were, the stronger I became. **It was as if their**

negative energy was feeding my positive energy. Even if their words turned out to be true I had plans of getting my dive instructor certification at the diving school at Tobermory, Ontario. Then I would move to Vancouver. Or, I could get a job in a restaurant and take a college course in industrial diving.

When I look at a challenge I look at all the ways I can make it work. I do not look at how it can fail. Perhaps that is why I always manage to make it work. Once I have committed my heart to an idea, I will do it. Nothing can stop me. There are no real obstacles. I had years of negative conditioning by my dad, but I learned to overcome all of my dad's cautious warnings and do what I wanted. I believe there is a solution to every problem, and if you have a big problem, there is a big solution out there somewhere.

When I came to Canada I had $1,000 in my pocket. That's it. Over my years working at the resort I'd had the privilege of meeting many gracious visitors. Many had told me to call them if I ever came to Canada; *I kept all of their phone numbers.*

When I arrived here, I did just that and when I called one Portuguese man, he immediately gave me a job at his restaurant. Another man, one of my former scuba clients, bought some furniture and rented me a room in his house in the Beaches for only $300 a month. He lived on his boat during the summer and left the house to me. I consider myself fortunate to have had good people in my life. I believe that people were so hospitable to me because of the energy I put into my scuba program at the resorts in Mexico. I was enthusiastic even when I didn't feel like it, and that enthusiasm came back to me ten-fold when I moved here.

After settling down I called one of my friends, Mark, with whom I had worked at an all-inclusive resort in Puerto Vallarta. He was the entertainment director for a few years and I was a scuba instructor. Our paths crossed for a couple of months and I kept in contact with him. When I called he invited me down to the Beaches to see him at work. He was now working for a company called Sportball™, a company that teaches young children the skills of sports through play.

Immediately I liked the concept. A job where I could earn money *and* play – that was what I was looking for. That was my childhood dream. But I was hesitant because of my previous experience as a program director for children at the resort in Mexico. "I don't want to end up baby sitting kids," I told him.

"This is different," Mark insisted, "this is truly coaching. We are there to teach skill sets in a fun energetic atmosphere. The children are grouped according to age, and we make the program age-appropriate."

He convinced me and he was right. I noticed the difference immediately, and it felt right for me from the get-go. I felt I was doing something useful for them. Every child had their own unique personality and I enjoyed relating to them. Every child was a mirror for me. They brought me back to my own childhood, and from that perspective I could better understand their behaviours. As a bonus I got a deeper understanding of why I did certain things as a child.

I believe everything that happens in life has a purpose. I believe I was meant to get this job. I went with it and have loved it ever since. I know I can always take my dive instructor test if I need it in the future.

I have two passions – coaching children and teaching scuba diving. Oddly enough I see them as very similar. As a scuba diver I get to take people to a different world – it's peaceful and beautiful. Similarly, working with children is like working in a different world – a world of innocence and simplicity. All of my stress disappears as soon as I begin working with the children or submerge under water in a scuba class.

I have a business plan for an aqua sports centre. I am now doing what I love. Imagine when I combine both things I love. Where there's a will there's a way, and so far I have accomplished everything I set out to do. If I ever gave up on something I would always think to myself, "What if I had tried that and it worked out?" It would be hard to live with myself if I didn't try every possible solution to my big challenges in life. I go for everything.

Dr. Gerstein's Comments

Adopt the 'Never give up' attitude

Ricky's relationship with his dad was estranged but I felt a strong, deeper connection there. His dad came down hard on Ricky's dreams, not in malice, but from fear for his son's well being. It was more his issue than Ricky's. Yet it drove a wedge between them, and Ricky learned to manage on his own. He believed in himself even when others doubted him. There is no bigger opposition than your father throwing bricks at your dream balloons.

It is telling how Ricky's father met his own fate in his career. His dream was pulled out from under his feet. He had worked his way up to an executive position, with aspirations of eventually running the company. But he was fired when he clung to a noble but misplaced loyalty to a friend who had defrauded the company. His father wouldn't give up his friend's name, and therefore he was terminated. He never recovered. He became depressed and gave up on life. Here was a man who had always been cautious being thrown into a chaotic circumstance filled with uncertainty. He lacked creativity, and the ability to consider other possibilities. He didn't have either the resilience or the willpower to bounce back.

When you play it safe you don't develop creativity, and you don't build any resilience muscle, which you will ultimately need when things fall apart. Very few things in life go as smoothly as planned. Start to prepare now for when things will go wrong. Protect yourself with a PMA – Positive Mental Attitude.

If you have a dream, write out all of the ways you can make it work. On another piece of paper, jot down all the ways it might fail, and then beside each statement, come up with at least three creative ways to overcome each obstacle. That is what Ricky did, and that is what gave him the confidence to immigrate to a foreign country alone with no job and only $1,000 in his pocket.

"Money Can't Buy Me Love"

John Lennon and Paul McCartney

Elaine Morton

Owner and Operator of an Aesthetic Salon

*"I was living what some call
a dream life, a life of opulence.
Yet after three years I felt like I was caught in a web.
I couldn't breathe. I had to get out."*

While doing interior design work twenty years ago I had a premonition. It involved me working in a tiny salon in a remote small town. It was located in a little house with a white picket fence and a squeaky gate. Eventually my vision came to fruition – save for the fence.

Who says premonitions can't come true?

After high school I did not continue with my formal education. I found work as a legal secretary working for a couple of firms in downtown Toronto.

Soon after that, I married a man many years my senior, and spent the next fifteen years raising children. When my children were still in school, my husband retired. He was now very wealthy, so we moved to California to play. We traveled, went horseback riding, played bridge and joined clubs. Our lifestyle included many opulent activities. For example, while my children were at private school we would sometimes take a private plane to Las Vegas for the day. In the beginning playing was fun. But after a while, although this may sound strange, it became horrible. I was living everyone's fantasy life, but I realized that all of that privilege did not make me happy.

After three years of playing I felt totally empty. I was lonely, I was depressed, and I was angry because I feared there would be nothing left for me. After experiencing all that money could buy, what else was there for me to look forward to? I was afraid there was nothing purposeful for me to do. Part of the reason for my depression was I didn't feel like I had accomplished anything myself. I had married into all this money; I hadn't earned it. I wanted to make a difference, however, I was freeloading off someone else.

I wanted my life to have meaning, and my husband understood where I was coming from. He was very supportive of my needs, and encouraged me to do what I wanted. One day at a black-tie yacht party I found myself in conversation with Barbara, one of the only people at the party without a pretentious air about her. She turned out to be a professor at the faculty of architecture at UCLA. She taught interior design, and that interested me. During our conversation I felt myself awakening for the first time in years. I was intrigued, and I signed up for a few classes. I earned a degree in interior design and architecture.

I moved back to Toronto and started my own interior design company. I designed interiors for nursing homes. I also did a lot of work for Tridel, a condominium developer, and for various high-end residential properties. I enjoyed the technical parts of the work, which included space planning, lighting and colours, more than the details of fabric and furnishings – my partner took care of that. When my contract with Tridel ended, my business dried up.

I didn't give up. I was now a member of the Association of Registered Designers of Ontario, and they had a referral list. Everyone on the list got a turn when work came up. When it was my turn, the job was to design the Ministry of the Attorney General's offices.

Embracing the challenge, I designed judge's chambers and courthouses. It was boring, horrid, mundane work. I was overqualified, and I had no interest. I no longer felt like going to work and sought out ways to waste time. I felt like I was caught in a web. I couldn't breathe. In time they replaced me with an external consultant.

All was not lost. While I was working at the ministry, I assisted Diane Litchen, representative of Posters International, in getting an exclusive contract with the ministry. This would later prove to be quite beneficial.

I tried more interior design work for other firms. It didn't work out because no one could pay me what I was worth. Then one day in 1991 a flyer came in the mail that stuck out from all the others. It was advertising a course in manicures and pedicures. I didn't need the money, but I was intrigued by the idea. *It just felt right.*

The woman I had helped, Diane Litchen, recommended I speak with her own esthetician, Vicky Sutherland, who owned a wonderful Forest Hill salon. "Vicky is looking for a manicurist," she told me. Indignant, I responded: "I have a degree in interior design and architecture. I'm not going to do manicures for a living." Innocently she countered, "Why not?" Taken aback, I realized I didn't have an answer.

I contacted Vicky, applied, and got the job. **I was excited and somehow nervous. I had led a life of extreme privilege, and now I was actually nervous about applying for a job as a manicurist. I think it was because I was now on my path. It felt like an adventure, and I was earning my own way.**

On the personal financial front I became careless with my investments and lost a lot of money. I joined a group that was basically an investment course for women. There I met a lady who owned a very large business in body hair removal, and she offered to make me a partner. I was interested, but I wanted to know the details before I put up any money for a partnership. When I asked her what specifically they do, she refused to tell me! She said first I had to give her the money, and only then – once I had become her partner – would she tell me the trade secrets.

When I went back and explained to Vicky what had transpired, she said, "Tell that lady to %&*$ #% #! Then she said, "I didn't realize you were looking to open up your own business. I didn't know you had the capital to do that." Vicky then mentioned that her sister often got her hair done at the Nottawasaga Inn in the small town of Alliston, Ontario. She knew the owners of the inn were looking for someone to open their own independent salon. I thanked her for the referral and thought to myself, "Alliston? All the way out there?" Nonetheless I kept my mind open.

I considered the suggestion. Could I do it? Did I have the courage to leave the security of a job and start a business in another town? I'd have to give up my Saturdays to work. The more I thought about it the more nervous I became. At the same time, the more excited I grew.

When I talked to the leasing manager at the inn, I learned they were looking for someone to sign a five-year lease. The only thing I had ever signed was a marriage license! Five years. What a commitment. It felt like I would be signing my life away.

So I drove out to meet with the owners. I put the convertible top down, and played my country music loud. I was continuing my adventure, and I was excited. With my hair blowing in the breeze I sang along with Dolly Parton. It felt like a whole new beginning. Even if I struggled at the salon, that would be part of my journey. The second I pulled into the Inn's parking lot to meet with the owners, I just knew it was right. We had a great meeting, and I signed the lease without even checking if this small farm town of 7,000 strong would come in for facials and manicures. Not too smart but I had to go with my feelings – *I felt it in my gut.*

Everyone but my husband was down on the whole idea. My lawyer warned me of locking in long term. My accountant said that I didn't know the market. My mother thought I was being impractical. My children thought I was crazy. And my friends exclaimed, "Alliston! Where is Alliston? Why would you want to go there?"

They all had a point. But I had to go with this feeling in my gut that told me it was the right thing to do. I realized this was my twenty-year-old premonition coming to fruition. Okay, it didn't have the white picket fence, but it was a salon located in a small town. I was willing to accept full responsibility for my actions, and face the consequences. I was ready to take the leap.

I was determined to make it on my own, and not ride on my husband's coat tails. I put $50,000 of my own money into the salon furnishings, the lease, hiring employees and advertising. Then in 1996 my husband died, and I was not the beneficiary of any of his money. His will instructed that it all go to trusts and other functions.

Due to hard work, my business turned a profit in the first year of operation. In the ensuing years I lost my focus, and threw money away on products and advertising. I reigned in that habit, and learned to direct my marketing costs to specific niche markets. It's been quite a ride.

Many people wait until they retire to have fun. I did it backwards. I had my fun early on, and grew bored with it. It wasn't all it is cracked up to be. I was living off of someone else's money. Granted it was my husband whom I loved deeply, but I still yearned for my own purpose.

Finding my purpose was like going on an adventure. It had everything you would expect in an adventure – premonitions, heroes, villains, interesting twists and unpredictable turns. At the end of it I found my Dream Career just as I had envisioned it early on in my journey.

Dr. Gerstein's Comments

The Big Lie: If only I were wealthy I'd be happy.

Elaine's story illustrates how it takes more than money to make people happy. A study of lottery winners revealed that while their level of happiness rose at the time of their win, within eight weeks that level returned to what it was prior to their big windfall.

People need a purpose to give meaning to their lives. Humans are social animals. We need each other. We are not merely hedonistic beings. Wealth may seem like a fantasy life until you live it. Elaine had the rare opportunity of living it. It was a fun ride but after three years she wanted to get off. She felt empty, lonely and depressed. At the age of forty-three she had the courage to not bemoan her situation, but to actually go and do something about it.

Don't be fooled by false advertising. Once you are clothed, have a roof over your head and have enough to eat, anything more will not make you happier. Find a way to contribute to your community. Who would you like to help? Figure out what gives your life meaning, and then go out and do it. It is in the 'doing' where you will find true happiness.

"I have never let my schooling interfere with my education."

Mark Twain

Jeff Wilson
Children's Camp Owner

"Everything I learned in life came from camp."

I never did well in school. I was one of those kids that couldn't see how dissecting a frog would help me find my life direction. I knew I never wanted to be a scientist or a doctor. Add to that, I just couldn't sit still. Today I would likely be labeled with ADD, (attention deficit disorder). To compensate for my lack of school prowess I became the class clown, and laughed things off a lot.

Inside I always knew I'd be able to do whatever I wanted. I was the middle child and I wasn't going to follow the playbook. Luckily for me my parents gave me room to pursue my dreams, and never pushed me into a specific profession. They respected and supported me throughout my life. I think that allowed me to explore what I wanted in an open manner, and gave me time to realize what my dream was.

It was obvious I wasn't going to find my passion through the school system, so I never attended university. But I did have one serious passion – I loved summer camp. Who knew my real education would start and end there?

Camp was an incredible experience for me. I went every year, and all of the friends I have kept in my life I originally met at camp. I have always felt that camp was the most important thing in my childhood. **Everything I learned in life of value, I learned at camp.** I learned how to live in nature, pitch a tent, build a fire, paddle a canoe and respect the animals. I became a more responsible person at camp. As campers, we each had responsibilities that included making your bed, cleaning the cabin and cleaning up after meals. Camp is where I developed my passion for tennis and baseball. Water sports didn't intrigue me so much, but my best friend at camp loved to water ski, and I learned to respect that. I learned how to get along with my peers – even people I didn't like. When twelve guys are thrown together for the summer and have to live under one roof, you're forced to do that. Camp is where I encountered many of life's little lessons, like fending for myself or how to organize a ball game. All of this took place in a safe environment, with people who really cared about you.

I was recently at a White Pine Camp reunion where we honoured one of our long-time directors. It was just incredible! Over three hundred former counselors and campers dropped everything to be there, and it was as if time had stood still. We hugged and retold our favourite camp stories. We laughed and relived our experiences with old friends who were still the same. All in all, it was a magical evening.

I was introduced to photography at camp. I liked it so much I thought it might be a good career for me. As a result I enrolled in a photography course after high school at Sheridan College. But my heart wasn't in it. I really didn't know what I wanted to do next. I was twenty-one, and many of my friends were now following professional paths, but the idea just didn't interest me at all.

Around this time I got a call from Joe Kronick, the director of Camp White Pine. I was elated when I learned his call was to offer me the position of Program Director, and I jumped at the opportunity. Joe became my mentor and taught me a lot about running a camp. I took it all in enthusiastically. No job was too small for me, and I realized *this* was the school I had always longed for. When I finally found the education that interested me, you can be sure I paid attention.

I worked for Joe Kronick year 'round until 1990 when his son decided to take over the family-run business. The writing was on the wall for me, and I knew it was time to move on. Interestingly enough,

I was ready. Joe had given me the foundation upon which I would build my dream.

I began looking around for other camp opportunities. Someone put me in touch with the owners of Camp Tamakwa. They were looking to pursue other interests, and brought me in as a partner to run their camp. As camp director for eight years, I learned all facets of running a camp including recruiting the children, hiring the staff, developing the menus and marketing the business.

After a while I became restless. By now I had my own vision of the kind of camp I wanted to run. It would combine the fun and sports activities of a Camp White Pine, with the canoe tripping, outdoor activities and traditional spirit of a Camp Tamakwa. I could see things were not going to change at Camp Tamakwa, so I began looking around with the idea of buying my own camp. My vision was not to take over a well-established camp, but rather to find one that needed some work. It would be cheaper to buy one in that shape, and I wanted to build my own legacy and put my own mark on a camp.

I had heard the owners of Camp Manitou were looking to sell, and I was considering making a pitch for it, alone, or with a partner. Coincidentally just at that time, I ran into Mark, an *old camp friend*. We met for lunch, and he told me he wasn't happy with what he was doing, but he'd *love* to do what I was doing.

I went home and pondered the idea. I had a solid camp programming background and street smarts, and he had business acumen and legal smarts. The more I thought about it, the more I was confident we would make a great team. It seemed to be falling into my lap at just the right time. After meeting several more times, we decided to do it. We were actually going to buy our own camp, and I was over the moon excited!

They say that partnership is a hard ship to sail. Before Mark came along I'd had several offers from people wanting to partner with me in buying a camp. But Mark was the only person I felt I could work with. Besides his integrity and honesty, he had all the skill sets I didn't have. We complemented each other perfectly, and it has turned out to be a great partnership.

Many people don't see camp as a business, but it certainly *is* a business in every sense of the word. We had to make a good real estate deal, and money was a challenge. I couldn't do it alone. Mark and I both received financial backing from our families. We both put up our own personal savings, and in addition to all that, we took out a bank loan. I put my dream on the line. I guess I was never truly afraid of failing. In the back of my head I always felt that if it all fell apart and I lost everything, we could always move into my parent's house. By now I had a wife and one child. My wife is a psychologist and she amended her schedule to help me follow my dream. I have always had great support from all my family.

This was what I was meant to do, I now had the opportunity to do it, and somehow I was going to make it work. You might say that I was confidently naïve about the whole thing. There are many things I was not confident about. However, when it came to camp and what we each had to bring to the table, I knew my niche. Historically, the camp we were buying drew two-hundred and fifty campers each summer. I knew we could easily accommodate four hundred children. We had room to grow.

When I finally found the camp of my dreams, the process was anything but easy. The owner wasn't completely ready to divest himself of the camp he had built. First, the land the camp was on had to be subdivided so they could keep their well-established inn. Then we had to jump through many government regulation hoops. When real estate such as a camp changes hands, it's an ideal time for the government to bring things up to code. And this it did. We were faced with many upgrades around environmental issues, waste management, drinking water, fire regulations and even the height of all of our perimeter fencing. The entire process took a full year of hard work. A less enthusiastic person would have surely given up long before the challenging year was over. But we persevered, and in the end, the camp was ours. I finally had my dream.

I think camp is a terrific opportunity for children to develop a variety of life skills. For many it is the first time they are away from their parents for a substantial amount of time. They learn how to interact with their peers, develop interests in activities they may never encounter in the city, and grow in confidence. I remember one seven-year-old girl who, on the first day of camp, refused to get on the bus, and clung to her mother very tightly. Eventually one counselor had to just take her and put her on the bus, and then tried to comfort her while she wailed all the way up to camp. She cried the first few days and had a severe case of homesickness. I was actually quite concerned about her.

But the counselors kept nurturing and encouraging her, and introducing her to new activities. Even her bunkmates supported her. By the fourth day those tears had turned to laughter as she slowly grew comfortable with the environment. She began to participate and soon she was enjoying herself.

The next summer, in anticipation of a similar drama on opening day, we had our new camp mascot, a moose, all ready to comfort her. She surprised us all by excitedly getting on the bus by herself. Her confidence had taken a giant leap forward, and camp had a lot to do with that. She even helped another child who was showing signs of homesickness.

Those kinds of stories are not unique, and each one warms my heart. It really is what camp is all about. We give children the time and space to grow and mature outdoors, in a fun and nurturing environment. To be able to offer that opportunity to children is worth everything to me. That is what touched me thirty years ago when I was a camper, and it is what inspired me to make it my dream career. I can't imagine doing anything else.

Dr. Gerstein's Comments

Learning is more than what you did in school

If you were to look at Jeff Wilson during his high school days, most people would never have accused him of being interested in learning. But when I asked Jeff if he had any regrets in his work life here is what he said:

"I learned so much from Joe Kronick, the first owner to hire me as camp director. I learned every day from him. In my mind I believed I could learn from anybody. I learned that as a kid. A wise man can learn from anybody and every situation. I took in lessons from every activity I did, both the ones I liked and the ones I didn't. It all sunk in somewhere for me."

I went back to our interview and counted the number of times he used the word learn or some related word in his brief answer. He used it no fewer than seven times – without prompting. As opposed to popular belief, learning does not start or end in formal schooling. Don't get me wrong, I have great respect for formal education. It gives us a foundation to build on. It helped me build my thinking processes, which included memorizing, analyzing, hypothesizing and innovating. But by no means does it end there.

School worked well for me because it fit my passions. I love to think of new ways of doing things, and I've always enjoyed figuring out puzzles, whether they were math puzzles in high school or human puzzles like re-discovering people's lost passions.

But it does not work for everyone. Jeff said he never did well in school, and admits that today he might be regarded as having attention deficit disorder. His parents allowed him to discover his niche, and supported him as he pursued interests outside of mainstream education. When Jeff finally found something he

Dr. Gerstein's Comments

loved he excelled in it. He did extremely well in the school he created for himself. Actually, he had two burning passions – music and camp. He knows more about those "subjects" than most people I know. Jeff was actually an excellent learner once he found something he wanted to learn. In his own words he absorbed everything in those two fields.

If you are not excelling in your field perhaps it is because you are not very passionate about it. What things excite you? What makes you want to learn? School and learning have received bad raps. Most people picture education as a classroom, with students sitting in ordered rows, and teachers imparting words of wisdom upon them. In fact, that's only one of many ways we learn. We learn all the time, using all of our senses. To name a few, we learn behavioural skills from our parents, social skills in the schoolyards and motor skills when we play sports.

In his book, *Frames of Mind* (1983), renowned Harvard professor Howard Gardner has debunked the IQ testing many baby boomers endured as children. Before him it was theorized that people were born with a blank slate, and only had to be educated in the right way at the correct time in their development to become well educated. In his research, Gardner theorized that we have multiple interdependent intelligences. These include logical-mathematical intelligence, linguistic intelligence, musical intelligence, bodily-kinesthetic intelligence, spatial intelligence, interpersonal and intrapersonal intelligence, and naturalist intelligence.

Formal education has always emphasized only two intelligences – logical-mathematics and linguistic. If your particular mix didn't mesh with those two you were out of luck, and often given less than glowing labels in school.

It seems one of the key reasons for Jeff's success in his career is

Dr. Gerstein's Comments

that he made maximal use of his above average interpersonal intelligence. I got more than a glimpse at that when I asked him his reason for his success. He answered:

"Respect for every person is the key to my success. That includes the maintenance person who cleans the septic tanks, the banker who loans us money, the young camper who is homesick and the counselor who is trying his best but is not yet getting it. Each of those people deserves my full attention. If you want respect, you must first give it."

Howard Gardner has said that our individual genetics and culture both have an influence on the type of intelligence(s) for which we have a predilection. What is your particular mix? Where are your strengths? When you find where your strengths and passions are, you too will find a new interest in learning because it will be the kind of learning you enjoy. And the likelihood is it will bear very little resemblance to the way you learned in school.

*"The great enemy of the truth is very often not the lie -
deliberate, contrived and dishonest - but the myth -
persistent, persuasive and unrealistic."*

President John F. Kennedy

Mark Diamond
Camp Owner

*"For years I worked in "respectable" careers.
I was doing what I thought was expected of me.
How could I have been so wrong all that time?"*

As a kid I wanted to be a teacher, work with charities or run a camp. But growing up in an affluent family I felt an unspoken expectation to be a lawyer, doctor or successful businessman. My father was a successful businessman, and all my brothers went to law school. I felt I had something to prove, so I went to law school too because I didn't know what else to do, and figured at least I would learn something. I felt a pressure to do something "respectful" with my life because I always felt my friends and family only considered a stereotypical corporate business or professional career had merit. I carried that stress for years. If I had only known then what I know now.

My strength has always been dealing with people. I communicate well with others, and people have always sought me out to help them solve problems. I was often called upon to mediate arguments between friends or family members.

As I was growing up, attending kids' camp meant a lot to me. I made all of my good friendships at camp. My self-esteem was developed at camp. At school, I was quite insecure. I worked hard but was quite shy. But when I went to camp that all turned around. At camp I was well liked, I was popular and had friends. People saw me in a different light. They saw more of my facets because I lived with the other kids 24/7. They appreciated my sense of humour and how much I enjoyed helping others. I even became a leader when given a chance. Camp allowed my self-confidence to blossom, and the real Mark to emerge. I might have gotten there on my own, but camp was the catalyst that accelerated my personal growth. It was also to be a key piece of my career puzzle.

Being born with a silver spoon in my mouth meant I did not struggle financially but I was raised with the values of hard work and discipline to get the most out of life. I'm glad I went to law school if for no other reason than to prove I was going to do something with my life. Had I gone into camping right away I would have worried about how my family would view me. I felt they would have thought that camping was not a real job. It was important to me that others see me as a success in my own right. Intellectually I know it is misguided to depend on others' opinions about you, but at that time I was not very high up on Abraham Maslow's self-actualization scale.

After only one year of law practice I found myself to be extremely stressed. I was doing civil litigation, the only law I really liked, but on a stress scale of one to ten, where one is no stress and ten is imminent explosion, I was already at a ten. I found preparing for court to be exhausting and emotionally draining because I didn't like what I was doing. I was doing it because I thought this was what success looked like. I wasn't doing it for me and that kind of strain really took its toll.

Because I knew law wasn't for me, I began to subconsciously sabotage my career by turning away many potential clients. I also knew if I continued to act that way I would not be long with the firm. After another year of more of the same, enough was enough. I walked out the door never to look back. Just walking out felt like a weight being lifted off my shoulders, and I immediately began to breathe more easily.

Now I was unemployed. It didn't feel right being without work, and I didn't want people thinking I was goofing off. I was getting bored and wanted to get back to it. My father was a real estate developer and that influenced me a great deal. Looking back I realize I was still being guided by my false impressions of my family's expectations of me. I got together with two other people and started building industrial and office condos and townhouses. It was fun and my stress level came down to an eight – still high, but now more tolerable. I didn't love it, but I did enjoy working with the trades and seeing the finished physical product after all of our work. I also loved the nonprofit housing we built. I have a strong sense of social responsibility and it gave me pleasure to be able to help people through my work.

For the next nine years I did that. However, when the real estate recession hit in 1991, business slowed to a crawl and my partner wanted to close the business. I found I was ready for something new too.

At that time the Internet was just in its infancy. I was approached by a headhunter told me about a high-tech group doing websites for big businesses. They needed someone who knew business and finance. **Again I responded instead of initiating my own next career move.** It sounded respectable, so again I leaped without fully thinking it through.

It didn't take long before once again I was very stressed, mostly because the industry was completely foreign to me. Firstly, we grew from a company of six to twenty people while continuing to lose money in the process. I didn't know that was the norm for internet-based businesses. I had learned to look for a 20% profit year after year to define a successful company.

Secondly, I had difficulty relating to the people in this business. I liked to talk with people, yet all day long I was surrounded by techies who kept their heads buried behind their computer screens. That was their safety zone. But it wasn't mine.

Lastly I was continually frustrated by the amount of information I had to absorb. Information technology was growing exponentially and it was impossible to stay abreast of the latest developments. I worked very long hours just trying to keep up.

It was overwhelming. I became run down, I got pneumonia and then my asthma worsened. I found myself snapping at my children. Then I would get upset at myself for losing it, and that made me feel even worse. I wasn't happy. Luckily for me our internet company was bought out, and I walked away with a tiny profit. At that point just getting out with my original investment would have sufficed, so the profit was a bonus.

Afterward I felt totally drained. **I decided to not just react this time and jump at the next opportunity that came along.** I decided I was going to give myself a full year to contemplate my next move.

I went to career counselors to identify my strengths and see where my heart was. Several aptitude tests confirmed what I had dreamed of as a child. They showed I was best suited to work with people, specifically children. Careers in mediation and teaching also came up. During the ensuing months of self discovery my emotions were on a roller coaster. I'd fluctuate between euphoria when I thought I had finally found my true fit and then depression when I realized it wasn't going to work. Not being busy was a stressor all in itself, even though I knew this time was necessary.

During this period of introspection I began to think again of what camp had done for my development. I felt a growing urge to give back to other children what I had received in my youth. I realized that if I became involved in a children's camp, I could do that. For the first time in ages I could feel myself getting excited about work.

When I asked the career counselors about that possibility, they agreed it fit very well with my profile. I was a generalist and liked a position with a variety of roles. I liked running a business in a non-stressful way. To me, that meant understanding the whole process and being in control. I also loved kids and the outdoors. It was a great match they said.

I am convinced I came up with it myself because I immersed myself in the question for the first time in my life. All I had ever needed was some time off to think. I had finally given myself permission, and time to rediscover myself. That created a situation that allowed me to put the puzzle together.

I made another important distinction during this time when I realized **that who I worked with was probably more important than**

what I did. I am an emotional person and take things very personally. Relationships are everything. I realized I would be better off working with someone I liked, doing something I didn't love, than working with someone I didn't like in a career I loved. I had to work with someone I respected and enjoyed.

During this break I went out with different friends to keep my spirits up. One of those people was Jeff Wilson, a childhood friend from a summer camp we had both attended. He had been in camping his whole life. One evening about four months into my year long sabbatical, I was out with Jeff and we were chatting. **After a few drinks I blurted out, "Wouldn't it be neat if we ran a camp together?"** He looked at me in bewilderment as if to say, "What are you talking about? You wear a suit every day. You're not a camp guy." I explained that I was doing a lot of soul searching and felt it would be a great thing to do.

Jeff is a very calm, level-headed, intelligent guy. He responded with a casual, "That's neat." I was a bit put off. I was expecting him to jump at the idea. But that's me. I tend to be impulsive. That's the trait that had gotten me into trouble when I jumped into real estate and the techie world without a lot of thought.

About a week later I got a call from Jeff. "Hey Mark, were you serious about what you asked me that day?" he asked. "Do you really want to run a camp?" I answered with a resounding, "Yes!!" I guess he waited to see if I was still as enthusiastic after the alcohol had left my body.

Over the next few weeks we met several times to develop the idea. It turned out we shared the same ideals and goals. Our strengths complimented each other. I needed his expertise about camp, and he needed my legal and financial knowledge and experience in running a business. My background in real estate development would help in buying the property and setting up the cabins. But I made it clear I didn't want to be relegated to the administrative part of it. "I love kids and I love interacting with people," I told him. "I want to be totally involved." He agreed.

Coincidentally Jeff was at a point in his life where he had just told his camp he wanted to leave and start his own camp. I believe the whole thing was meant to be.

Now I had to decide if I could work with a friend. I didn't want to lose his friendship over a job, but as it turned out, it has only gotten stronger. I think a lot of that stems from our mutual respect for each other.

One's own demons and the external reality of life are sometimes not even remotely close. Now I had to tell my father about my decision of becoming a children's camp owner. I was pretty sure my father, the successful businessman, would be more than a little disappointed. I was nervous but for the first time in my career life I grew up and made the decision rather than asking him for advice. Incredibly, he said, "Mark – Fantastic!" I was blown away. Shaking my head I remarked, "I guess I should have done this a long time ago." My dad replied, "Yeah, you should have. What's your problem?"

How could I have been so wrong for all those years? The surprises kept coming. Far from being judgmental, all three of my older brothers helped me map the strategy of my dream. With my family's support I was able to quickly overcome the fear of not being good enough once I had the guts to say, "This is what I'm doing."

Once Jeff and I decided we wanted to own a camp, our next job was to decide which one to buy. When we finally agreed on a camp the negotiations took a few months. Then we had a lot of government regulation hoops to jump through. It was a stressful year for me but as opposed to my other careers, this was a healthy stress. I was doing what I wanted and I viewed it as an exciting challenge. I kept thinking of how upset I would be if the deal fell through, as opposed to disliking the work. Deep down I realized I was truly happy.

Now my biggest concern was how I was going to relate to the staff. Here I was, a former corporate lawyer, now in a camp setting. I'll never forget that first meeting with the staff in our first summer of operation. I told them my story, and encouraged them not to give up on their dreams. Here were a group of eighteen year olds paying attention to what this old fart had to say. After the meeting I turned to my wife with the biggest smile and proclaimed, **"This is my career. I have found my calling."**

Finding my Dream Career has positively affected my other relationships. I no longer get upset at stupid little things in my family, because I am basically happy. I can let them go now. I treat my family better now, and I show more appreciation for my wife. Relationships take work, and I now have more energy to do the work. I always wanted to do it, but when I was in corporate law I constantly felt drained and had little left over for other things.

I have truly enjoyed the past six years as a camp owner. By no means does that mean I am free of stress. As I am a person who doesn't handle stress terribly well, it's ironic that I ended up in a career with lots of potential stress. Think of it. I am responsible for hundreds of children each summer. Their safety is in my hands, and sometimes I get anxious about that. In the first couple of years I had a tougher time handling those thoughts. But I wouldn't trade this job for any other. **I have found that any big stressor can be mitigated if you are in the right fit. Conversely, any small stress can be magnified if you dislike what you are doing. It's all about perspective.**

I feel like an uncle to many of the children whose personal growth I have witnessed over several camp seasons. I have gotten to know many of these kids well, and some have even become part of our staff. Knowing I have positively affected their lives is a fantastic feeling, and my ultimate goal; it is something I am very proud of. I can't imagine a better career for me. Pardon the pun but now I am truly a happy camper.

✦

Dr. Gerstein's Comments

What false beliefs are you living by?

Fears are often bigger than real obstacles. Mark had no idea his family would support his dream. His first step was to announce his decision to buy a camp. He was not asking for permission. That move took courage considering he felt immense internal pressure to live up to a mythical family expectation. But, he firmly announced his goal and went for it.

What false fears are you harboring? What false beliefs are you living under? How would you feel if you discovered that the imaginary obstacle you are afraid of is a mirage? Many fear pursuing their dreams because they fear ridicule and rejection. What I have found is that people who dislike what they are doing are looking for inspiration. Some will not like it if you follow your dream. Others will support you and be inspired by you. They will thrive on your ambition.

What if you had a dream buried deep inside and stopped looking a long time ago because you thought it was gone? What if you could earn an income from your buried dream? What if it isn't too late to go for your dream? The people in this book followed their dreams. If they did it, so can you because they are really not very different from you. I have done my best to show the personal side of the people here who are living their dreams. They have real fears. Many feel inferior in some aspect of their lives. Many were confused. Many struggled financially and some still do. Many had to find courage to face obstacles in their path and find a way around them.

They are not better than you. As individuals they have learned how to do it, and you can too. It is not easy. It takes courage and hard work but your dreams are definitely real. Prove it to yourself. Take on those false beliefs you are carrying around. Test them and see if they are real. You will find that many of your perceived obstacles are paper tigers.

Myth-Diagnosis #2
Confusion Illusion

◆

How *You* Can Bust This Myth

If you are confused by your future you can see from these stories that you are not alone. The accounts you have read in this chapter typify the clients I treat in my own private practice. It is less about what is wrong with the client and more about people not yet finding the optimal "fit" for them.

There are many ways to search for the best "fit." I use them all in my *Your Unique Life Path Discovery System®*, which I created for my clients. There is not enough space in this book to delve into all of the methods available. To discover more about your own unique life path, check out the *Discover Your Life Direction©* course at **www.dreamsforreal.com**. As a start, notice how the people in this chapter used clues from their childhood to discover their true Life Path.

Think back to your own childhood. What did you love to do? What couldn't you wait to get up for? What activities made time pass so quickly you could hardly believe it? What did you collect? What was your favorite place to play?

Don't worry about making your answers relate to a career. That is too logical and logic is not the way the people I interviewed found their passions.

Myth – Diagnosis #3 Chronologically Challenged

"I'm too old. I'm too young."

*"And in the end, it's not the years in your life that count.
It's the life in your years."*

Abraham Lincoln

Ila Faye Turley

Actor

*"I was not being myself and the worst part was
that I felt stuck. Then something happened that
instantly shook me out of my comatose state."*

At college in Calgary I studied broadcasting and journalism. At that time the "arts" scene was fun and exciting but it was also rampant with drugs and alcohol. Afraid of being drawn into that life, I left it. I might have stuck with it if my parents had supported me in acting, but their expectations for their daughter included a "respectable" career. Acting just didn't fit into their definition of respectable. It would be many years before I was able to return to my first career choice, and even then people told me it was wrong, but for a completely different reason.

If I wasn't going to be an actor, my second choice was to become an athletic trainer. As a student I worked with the Calgary Stampeders professional football team. I became involved in many sporting events hosted by the university such as synchronized swimming, the Olympic

Trials and The University Games. Working with these motivated athletes was really a thrill. But in the 1970s, there was no program for the athletic training field in Canada. I could have gone to the U.S., but that would have cost a lot of money. So I tossed out that dream as well. Strike two.

Undaunted, I decided to get a registered nursing degree. My plan was to bring credibility of medical knowledge when I applied for careers working with athletes. And then life's realities got in the way. At the time that was the excuse I used.

By my mid-twenties I was married and had two children. My husband was away a lot working the oil fields in the Northwest Territories, and we divorced soon after the birth of our second child. I had to start thinking practically and nursing pays a lot more than being an athletic trainer. I now had two children to raise on my own, and I needed the money. I took a job in general nursing, and then moved to a position at a trauma centre in 1988. I remained there for thirteen years, and my aspirations for working with athletes slowly faded into the background.

The pay was good but the cost was high. I was tired all the time. Ironically, helping other sick people in this setting was making me sick. I often didn't want to get out of bed to go to work. My sick time went up as my happiness went down. I found myself yelling at my kids with very little provocation. It wasn't that I didn't enjoy helping patients, I did. I liked helping people in need and seeing the quick successful results that often occur in a trauma centre. But I found the rules very stifling, and it was not acceptable to display your feelings in the culture of the hospital setting. I was not being true to myself, and the worst part was I felt totally stuck.

Then something happened that instantly shook me out of my comatose state. The husband of a nurse in my department was brought in by ambulance one day, having suffered a seizure. A negative brain CT scan was reassuring, and he was sent home. However, over the next few months his personality began to change. He became more and more irritable, and was fired from his job. Then he had a second seizure. This time, a more penetrating magnetic resonance imaging (MRI) scan was ordered because no cause had yet been found for his changed behaviour. The result was shocking. The MRI revealed a deep brain tumor inaccessible to surgery. Three weeks later, he was dead.

That was a wake-up call for me. It was 1996 and I was now forty-one. In an instant I realized if that could happen to him, a seemingly healthy man in midlife, it could happen to me. I knew inside I must not put off my dream any longer.

I had always been so creative. I loved to act, and had been involved in plays and writing stories since I was five years old. Imagine, I thought. I gave all that up because of what other people were doing, (drugs) or not doing, (my parents who didn't support me). My only regret is not listening to myself back then, and instead allowing other people to influence me. But no more! For the first time in my life I realized just how precious our time is here on this earth. I didn't care how old I was. I was going for my dream.

I immediately signed up for an acting course. I was excited to begin, but right from the very first class I discovered it was not going to be easy. The teacher asked us, "Who here expects to be working in this industry?" Like everyone else, I naturally put up my hand. Then she continued; "Every female over twenty-five, put your hand down. Every male keep your hand up. As for the rest of the females, only ten percent of you will find work."

Well, I thought to myself, I'm here to stay. I'm giving it my best shot. She can't discourage me that easily.

She harassed me in every class. If this was an attempt to see if I had the mental fortitude to stick it out. It was a very crude way of doing it and I grew to hate her. But I went back for another class with her because her acting school was the only one accredited in Calgary. I wanted to learn from the best, and I was damned if I was going to allow her to stop me.

I began to audition around town and within a year had completed three big roles in community theatre. Word of my abilities began to slowly seep out, and then semi-professional theatres started calling me for auditions.

It was now 2001, and I was ready for the next step. If I really wanted to make it as an actor I had to be where the action was, and that was Toronto. My two children were now eighteen and twenty, and out of the house. There was nothing holding me back, and I was pretty excited.

Before I made my move I found a Toronto hospital that agreed to hire me part-time. That would provide me with an income while I went out and pursued my dream. I would not be desperate, and I could still take acting courses and continue my learning.

Through these courses I met Kevin McCormack, an inspirational teacher and an artistic director who started his own theatre company. He accepted me into his conservatory company, and I have worked steadily in semi-professional theater and independent films ever since.

I have given myself ten years to succeed or fail in this industry. That is about how long it took me to feel really comfortable in nursing. There is no such thing as an overnight success. I will not pressure myself out of the industry. I will give myself ample time to learn and grow in the field I love. I will do it. I am doing it. Life is too short not to go for it.

Dr. Gerstein's Comments

Real Dreamers are more practical than so called realistic people

It irks me when people tell me they have to face reality, and have no time for their dreams. They have serious responsibilities, mortgages to pay and a family to look after. I tell them that going for your dreams is not the same as fantasizing about your life. The latter is for fairy tales while the former requires hard work, as can be seen by the stories in this book. Hans Selye, the *'Father of Stress'* and the physician who first described the effects of stress on our health, once said, ***"The practical and realistic people in the world are not so practical and realistic in the long run of life, as the dreamers who pursue their dreams."***

As you can see, the quiet whispers of Ila Faye's original passion were persistent, and she finally listened to her own voice. Think of the all of the experiences she may have enjoyed had she been less "practical" and followed her heart. She can't pull back the time, but you can learn from her lesson.

*"I'm not interested in age. People who tell me their age are silly.
You're as old as you feel."*

Elizabeth Arden

Shavey Tishler
Director of Day Care

"If I didn't do this a part of me would die."

It was the sign of the times. I was married and living in suburbia. I sat in the backyard with my girlfriends and we talked about everything. Married life was bliss. Why would I ever work?

But times change and I changed along with them. Actually, deep down I always knew what I wanted to do. I just had to wait until the right time to express it. The irony is that it might have cost me my marriage.

I was the youngest of six siblings. When I was ten, I baby-sat our nephew and loved it. I continued to baby-sit for the neighbourhood children, and created this fantasy of family life. I always felt that being married and having children was my dream. Maybe one day I'd be a social worker and work with children, but that was a distant second to marriage.

I was married at eighteen. I was thrilled, and by the time I was nineteen I had two children. Married life to me was real Donna Reed.

Nobody had any money. We lived in the subdivision, sat outside on our patios, drank tea and played scrabble. We talked about cleaning products, looked through catalogues, and imagined what we would buy if we had more money.

One of our girlfriends went out to work, and we laughed at her. Why would she go to work? My husband was in sales and his income fluctuated wildly. We'd be doing very well, then suddenly we'd be in debt, but I never felt any pressure to go to work.

When their children began school, many of my girlfriends started going to work. I wasn't one to sit around, so when my youngest reached that age I did the same. I got odd jobs enumerating for the government, telemarketing, and working in a doctor's office.

One of my close girlfriends was a social worker with the Jewish Community and Child Services. Some of the children they cared for were developmentally challenged, and they were searching for a summer program to fill the gap for them. My friend asked if I would be interested in running a camp at my farm if they provided the proper support staff. I was interested, and after a series of meetings it began shaping up perfectly.

When we opened up we had about a dozen children. They didn't provide us with enough staff, and the kids ran wild. It turned out they had sent us the most behaviourally challenged children. The situation was uncontrollable and we had to close after only one month. The camp failed miserably. However, for me the experience was not a total loss. It rekindled within me the flame to work with children. But first I had to overcome a personal struggle with my own mental health.

Working at the camp with these behaviourally challenged kids brought a lot of my own unresolved issues to the surface. The result was I had a nervous breakdown. I saw several different doctors who prescribed tranquilizers, but they just made me sleepy. Other meds I tried made me hyper. So I went off all medications and just struggled with my emotional imbalance for two more years. I have since found stability with the newer generation of antidepressants, which have far fewer side effects.

When I was forty, I decided to take a childcare course at George Brown College. There I met a woman named Margo, and we hit it off. In the middle of the course we both realized that we couldn't do childcare. We agreed it was too strenuous for people our age to work with emotionally disturbed children. However, I still liked kids and still really wanted to work with them. We both decided not to complete the program. Instead we became business partners and opened up a day care centre.

On the outside, my husband Bryan supported my new venture. But deep down I knew that starting the day care centre was the beginning of the end of our marriage. Bryan wanted to live at the farm. But to make the day care work, I had to live in the city. He was looking forward to retiring at fifty, and here I was starting a new career at forty. He hated his work, and I loved mine. We were like two trains heading for a collision, and one was going to have to give way.

Margo asked me what I would do if Bryan gave me an ultimatum – stay with him or open the day care. She knew I had inherited a nice sum of money, and I didn't need this new venture to live. I think she was sure I wouldn't stay, but she was wrong. I was in the midst of an internal struggle: If I open the day care I might lose my marriage; if I don't open it, part of me will die. At some level I knew that if I followed my heart I would risk my marriage, but I did it anyway, and my marriage did end.

Children are everything to me. They are the world. From the time a baby is born until it is two years old they learn so much – how to love, how to ask for what they want, how to be angry. And it's all pure. If I could help children even a little during those precious years, I wanted to be a part of it.

Now that I knew what I wanted, I would not be denied. I would accept no excuses from myself. When Margo and I went to the bank to borrow money for our centre, they turned us down – because we were women. But, they told us, they would give us the money if our husbands co-signed on the loan. We wanted to do this on our own, so off we trotted to other banks and just came up against more rejections. We would have to do it without a loan.

We knew the area we wanted to locate in, and went to the Ministry of Community and Social Services to get a license. They said there were no children in that area, but we knew the rules. If we fulfilled all the criteria set out by the Ministry, they had to grant us a license. Part of the criteria required us to hire an accredited early childhood educator (ECE). We found one, but did not particularly like her. Our philosophy was learning through play, and everything she wanted to bring in was the opposite. She really acted like a police warden, but we needed her to open, so we endured her for a while.

Then the church we selected as our location didn't want to rent to us. Some of the elderly church members did not believe in day care centres. They felt that mothers should stay home and raise their own children. However, the young minister was sympathetic to our cause, and agreed to rent us some space.

The government had told us we required at least $20,000 for toys, equipment and marketing. We only had $2,000. Undaunted, we were determined to get it started. Margo began shopping garage sales, and her house quickly filled with toys, bicycles, scooters and whatever else one could imagine a day care might use. Eventually she had enough things to open the centre. The church already used the room as a nursery, so it came with tables and chairs and a fully equipped kitchen, and we saved some money there.

We needed a logo, so one of our artistic friends drew one on a serviette at dinner one night – it's still our logo. With that we created a flyer announcing the opening of our day care centre, and put them up around the park, and sent them out in the mail. Women returning to work would call the ministry and ask for day care centres in their area. A couple of children with whom I worked at another day care came with me. We were licensed for twenty-four children, and when we opened we already had thirteen.

During the first year, we applied for a government subsidy. They laughed at us, saying the income demographics of families in that area were too high. In our second year when we filled our day care to capacity, they came to us offering a subsidy. We turned them down because there were too many strings attached to their subsidy payments. As well, subsidized children are more of a transient clientele, and we were in it for the long haul.

We started the whole thing flying by the seat of our pants. Margo and I didn't have a joint venture agreement. We did everything on a handshake, agreeing to split all the expenses and revenues fifty-fifty. Meeting Margo at that course was only the first of several coincidences. We later discovered we had been in the same class in kindergarten, as well as grades one and two. Our oldest children are only one day apart in age, and they also attended school together. We lived around the corner from each other, and never even knew it!

On the other hand, we were as opposite as two people could be. It worked in our favour because we complimented each other. If the children were hungry, I would say, let's feed them. She would say no, they have to wait until snack time. I came from a very permissive background, and that's how we raised our kids. Margo was more the disciplinarian.

On top of starting the centre, during that first year Margo and I decided to go for our ECE certificates, partly so we could remove the sergeant we had reluctantly hired. It took me four-and-a-half years to complete a two year program going to school two evenings a week. I enjoyed it and realized how smart I was, even though I was one of the oldest in the class. I'm proud to say I graduated with honours.

Overall we have been quite successful. We've both gone from working full time to working four half-days a week – twenty-one years later. Not bad for a couple of old broads.

Dr. Gerstein's Comments

What is your heart saying to you?
And are you listening to it?

No matter how old you are, or how you were raised, you have an internal flame that still burns inside if you are still breathing. Shavy was brought up in a family-centred environment. All she ever wanted, she thought, was to be a wife and mother. It was a fantasy because she rarely talked about the struggles of married life when she was young.

If you had come to her when she was nineteen and said, "I have a crystal ball and can see your future. In about twenty years you will become an entrepreneur and you will say, 'I will never retire from work.' What do you think of that?" she would probably have asked what planet you were from. She would have definitely thought you were talking about someone else.

The theme running through Shavy's life is children, and her love for them. Remember, her own mental health issues were precipitated by the developmentally challenged children at her failed summer camp. Despite this she enrolled in a childcare course within two years of the onset of her depression. Realizing she couldn't cope with the needs of these children and her own mental health, she sought another way to work with children.

Faced with the subconscious awareness that sticking to her dream would probably mean the end of her marriage, she chose her dream. In her words, if she didn't open up the day care centre, some part of her would die. Thank goodness she listened to her heart.

What is your heart saying to you? And are you listening to it?

"The young do not know enough to be prudent, and therefore they attempt the impossible – and achieve it, generation after generation."

Pearl S. Buck

Jeffrey Prosserman
Filmmaker

*"I was hanging onto the rope with the water far below.
If I cut the cord I would gain my independence but
may also lose my security. What should I do?"*

I always had a passion for the arts. Beginning in early childhood my drawings drew rave reviews from family and friends. When I was fifteen I decided I would make a film. If Hollywood could do it with large casts and multimillion-dollar budgets, I had the courage to believe I could make one of equal quality, albeit on a smaller scale. I was excited and began planning for it every day after school and on weekends.

Then the powers that be threw the biggest monkey wrench into my dream – my parents separated and my world fell apart.

As I child I spent a lot of time drawing while most of my friends played sports. I began with crayons and my father fed my passion by bringing home more artistic materials. He always supported my dreams, and I think this led me down a somewhat different path than my friends. It was a path full of creativity.

When I was about fourteen, I was sitting around watching a movie with a friend. It was some comedy, one of those movies that seemed like it didn't take much effort to make. We looked at each other and thought if they got millions of dollars for making something like this, what is stopping us from doing just as well or better? So, we created our company, and called it Twisted Cow Productions. Then we set out to prove we could do it too.

Our naïveté worked to our benefit. When we started, we didn't know that we couldn't do it, so we just did it.

Both my father and grandfather encouraged me to follow my dreams. They didn't see my young age as a barrier. My grandfather had started in the clothing business when he was only ten years old. He was a confident man, and his story had always inspired me. He began in retail and built up enough capital to buy a retail store. Then he got into manufacturing.

The emphasis in our family was to do your best in whatever you were doing. But even though doing well in school was important, following my passion was more important. In school I never pushed myself because I had no passion for what was being taught. My father encouraged me to follow my passion rather than merely fitting into the mold of what the school system taught. It turned out my passion was film making. In many ways the school system pushes you to not follow your dreams, because it's really a conformist environment. They don't want a million leaders; they want a million people to work under them.

I was excited about the film we were going to make. Then my parents separated. Things had been going along so smoothly, why did this have to happen now? I was sixteen and caught in the middle.

I began having to move back and forth from my mom's place to my dad's. My dad was encouraging me to make my own choices and make my film, while my mother wanted me to remain in the old routine. My dad represented uncharted and exciting waters; my mom represented safety and comfort.

It felt like I had fallen off a bridge and was hanging on to a thin rope over water, not knowing what to do. I was being forced to choose between the two most important areas of my life, my work and my family. If I cut the rope I didn't know who would catch me. I didn't know if I had the courage to take the plunge. If I didn't cut the rope, I was afraid of being stuck in a family struggle, relegated to follow my mother's wishes and having to ignore my own. It was one of the hardest decisions I have yet had to make in my young life. I had to decide whether I was going to strive or survive.

I cut the rope, and let go. It was a metaphorical cutting of the adolescent umbilical cord, and my leap into independence. Remaining a passenger in life was just not me – I wanted to make my mark whatever that would be. This was a defining moment for me, and one I will never forget.

I fell, and the fall into the deep dark depths of the water below was long and scary. The water was so murky I couldn't see anything for a while, and I sank almost to the bottom. Eventually, I got my bearings and began to rise. When I resurfaced I saw the light on the other side of the bridge, and quickly regained my vision of the future. I knew in my heart that I was the one who would have to be there for me from now on. I learned that I had to catch myself.

From that day on my relationship with both my parents changed. I still loved them, but I had grown up fast and knew I could never return to being their baby.

It has been very emotionally empowering to see the way my father has influenced my life and career so far. When we registered the name of our production company, he guided me through the legalities. He knew how serious I was. I benefited from his years in business, and he gave me a few thousand dollars to kick start my dream. After that, the ball was in my court. It was my baby.

We wrote a script and built the production around a few people. We looked for people who were exceedingly passionate and who were excited about becoming involved in our film. Nobody was getting paid. I gave the same speech to everyone who wanted to work with us. "I'm not telling you to be here," I would say. "I don't want you here unless you want to be here, and I want the real you to come through no matter what we're doing. If you are excited to do that then we can work together. If not, then I'll see you around school."

I wanted people who were going to bring their own passion and drive to the set every day. I have found the more I surround myself with passionate people, the more success I have.

Once we committed to doing the film, every spare moment was

spent on it. We would begin Friday after school, go to one or two in the morning, and start up again at eight or nine on Saturday morning. When I say all weekend I mean every single hour, the whole weekend.

My enthusiasm was contagious. If nothing else, I was creating an emotional buzz. I feel it doesn't matter what you are selling – it could be pencils or a million-dollar movie. If you can get everyone on board, then you have a good chance of being successful. It's all about creating energy and catching the passion.

Everyone bought into our vision, and that just made it what it was. It was a positive and exciting project to be part of, and we had a lot of fun with it. We shot scenes in different parts of the city, went to different high schools and to several downtown locations. We were sixteen-year-old high school kids, and had thirty-year-olds working for us. It was incredible. They had their own reasons for acting in our film, but the important thing was the passion each one brought with them. There was always something going on – delays, technical problems and personnel issues. Yet I was constantly surprised by the dedication of every individual. I never had a serious problem with anybody – from the student extras we hired at different schools, to the forty-year-old guy who helped us with the camera equipment.

It was inevitable though, that a bunch of green kids would make some mistakes along the way. There is one I will never forget for as long as I live.

We were on location at somebody's house and a female character in the film was threatening someone else with a gun. About twenty minutes into it, the dog in the house began to bark. Annoyed, we had to stop filming and find what he was barking at. We looked outside but saw no one, so my uncle took the dog for a walk. After we resumed filming, my uncle quietly brought the dog back into the house, and then went out again. About ten minutes later the dog started barking again, and once again we had to stop filming. To our amazement, this time when we looked outside we saw my uncle on his hands and knees, his head in the snow, and two policemen pointing shotguns at the back of his head!

People in the house began to panic. "What do we do?" they yelled. I didn't have a clue but felt I should take the lead because after all, it was my production. So I ran outside in the middle of a cold February day in my t-shirt and bare feet. I immediately heard the command, "Freeze!" and stopped dead in my tracks. I found myself surrounded by police in full SWAT uniform, all aiming their weapons at me.

With my head spinning, I tried to figure this madness out quickly while maintaining my composure. Things were happening so fast, it was surreal. I felt as if I had just stepped into the middle of someone else's movie. It was life imitating art.

Before I could get out the words, "It's all a misunderstanding," I was ordered to walk slowly to the edge of the driveway. Amazingly, this scene was repeated three more times as three of the actors followed me out into the cold. We were handcuffed and put into the back of police cruisers. Meanwhile everyone else in the house was freaking out.

Eventually the cops broke into the house and quickly realized the gun scene being played out was part of a movie. They removed the handcuffs, brought us all back into the house, and lined us up. Then, the captain came in.

He stared at us for what seemed like an eternity with a look of total disgust. He opened his mouth to speak, and while pointing at each one of us in turn he said, "You are all stupid. Stupid. Stupid. Stupid." He only stopped after he had pointed to all twenty people on the set. Then he pointed at my uncle, the only one over the age of twenty, and said, "And you sir. You are the stupidest one of them all." Half-wittedly I began to giggle, still not yet fully comprehending what had just happened.

It turned out that a neighbour had overheard the girl in the scene threatening to kill someone, and called the police. Later we discovered the street had been completely barricaded with eighteen police cruisers, and all the residents had been evacuated. Police helicopters were circling above, and snipers were positioned in the house across the street.

They were seething mad and wanted to lay criminal charges, but couldn't. They told us if we were going to film a violent scene, we had to let the local police station know ahead of time. This was a lesson I'll never forget. We were all shaken up, but the director in me still had the *chutzpah* to ask one of the police officers if I could get a picture with him – for nostalgic purposes.

Yes, we were making sacrifices. We could all have been doing something else on those weekends, like going out with friends to a movie. But we were with friends and we were making that movie, and that turned out to be as much or even more entertaining than anything else we could have been doing.

The film was called *Crazy Things Happen*. In retrospect, the film was not magnificent, but the sheer experience for everyone involved was incredible. Together, a bunch of teenagers wrote a script, rehearsed, choreographed, directed, shot and produced this film. Essentially we went through every step the Hollywood production companies go through, except on a tiny scale. Our budget was a couple of thousand dollars compared with the multimillion-dollar budgets of the well-known Hollywood studios. It was an invaluable experience for me.

My friend and I continued to make films. We recruited people from the community and built our brand image. I can't say I was tiring of it, but I was definitely ready for the next level, and more exposure in the film industry. It's one thing to do it on a student level as an independent, but another thing altogether to begin earning an income in this business. My friend was not interested in taking the next step, but I went on to the film studies program at Ryerson University in Toronto.

To make it in the film industry I knew I had to learn a lot more about it, so I became involved in corporate advertising. Here, I am learning skills that will help me when I launch my film career. These include CD Rom and DVD promotional video inserts, web design, HTML code, Flash animations and interactive presentations.

One day I want to get back to my passion – making independent films. In the meantime I am learning all about the business and really enjoying myself. I can't see myself doing anything else. I know it will work because I love what I do. I am never satisfied with my work and I keep pushing myself to improve.

It took just under a year to complete my first amateur film and I felt as if I was reborn upon completion of the project. Ironically, in my second birth, I had cut the cord before I was born. I haven't looked back since.

Dr. Gerstein's Comments

Are you still holding on to your metaphorical umbilical cord?

Are you still doing what your parents expected you to do? Are you doing what others want you to do? Have you allowed family members, authority figures, the culture or society you live in, or anyone else to influence your choice of your life direction? If the answer was "yes" to any of the questions above you owe it to yourself to rethink what you are doing.

Your life direction has nothing to do with anyone else. This is your life and your dream. No one else could possibly know it as intimately as you do. Even if they are genuinely concerned about your welfare, *only you* know in the innermost part of your heart whether you are doing what you love.

When a baby is born we are able to cut the umbilical cord because the heart and lungs have matured to the point where the baby can now breathe, and utilize oxygen on its own. Similarly, you may be afraid to cut your own safe metaphorical cord until you have allowed your dream to mature and become strong. Nurture it with baby steps.

What small step can you do today to begin to strengthen your dream? It could be signing up for a writing course one evening a week, or working on a project with your hands on the weekend. It might involve gathering information for your dream, and for one year dedicating one morning or evening every week to that task.

Don't share these activities with anyone except those who will support you fully. Don't let the critics and cynics of the world anywhere near your Dream, until it too has matured and grown to the point where it can breathe on its own. Family or friends may have told you your ideas were not practical or realistic. They

Dr. Gerstein's Comments

may mean well but what they are doing is projecting their own fears and limitations onto you. I call them Dream Killers and you don't have to allow them to stop you.

After a while you will be amazed by how much you have grown in your area of passion. It won't be long before you too can start breathing on your own.

"You will either step forward into growth, or step back into safety."

Abraham Maslow

Janice Lindsay
Interior Colour Designer

*"Popping people's corks about colour and getting them rolling
and excited is just the best feeling for me. I am allowing
their passion to come out of the bottle."*

I believe if you ask a question the answer will eventually come to you. It's as if the question points your subconscious in the right direction. Things start to happen almost without you. Then I created a list of goals – things I wanted in my career, and did whatever I had to do to make it happen.

I grew up in Stratford, Ontario, the home of Shakespearean theatre. My dad was a surgeon and my mom, who was trained as a social worker, was a full time mom. I was always surrounded by the arts. I grew up with opera and other classical music on in our house. As a child I would draw, paint and sew. I thought of becoming an artist when I got older, but I didn't like the loneliness of the craft.

I studied art and art history at the University of Toronto. One summer I landed a job in the prop shop of Stratford Shakespearean

Theatre. I loved the work. I was creating, being artistic and working in a room with about fifteen other energetic artistic people with whom I could collaborate. It was a beautiful blend of collaborative and independent efforts. The music would be on while we worked our respective crafts. It was a very creative and happy time for me.

After I graduated I intended to study theatre, but then The Stratford Festival called and asked me to come and dye for them. When I told them I didn't know how, they said I was great with colour and they'd teach me the rest, so I accepted.

Other people saw my talent long before I saw it. Working with colour came so naturally for me I didn't realize it was an expertise I could market. In theatre, colour sets the mood of the scene, and the colour of the costumes reveals the character. Colour was a language I was always speaking in theatre.

Fortunately (or unfortunately) I was promoted to design assistant and then to theatre designer, where my responsibilities included managing people and budgets. People just assumed because I had designed for a theatre like the Stratford Festival that I was good at it. I did this for ten years even though I knew in the back of my mind I was getting away from my passion for art. Yet it educated me in other areas of theatre. It taught me how to manage people, budgets and time, and that put me in good stead when it came time to look for my Dream Career.

With two children and a mortgage to pay, I needed more money. Theatre is always a labour of love. I needed a career where I could earn more than the nanny who was caring for my children so I parlayed the theatre experience into becoming a stylist for photographers. My role was to set up shots for them. This entailed everything from the finding and setting up the props, to selecting the clothes and, sometimes, to choosing people off the street who fit the look the photographer needed. The work was not as satisfying as theatre design, but my income went up about four hundred percent.

I still had dreams of focusing on colour as a career, and began seriously thinking of ways to earn a good income doing what I really loved. My time management skills came in handy as I scheduled my career development around my work as a photographer's stylist.

I developed my game plan. Often I was booked for three to seven days in a row as a stylist. Then I would have some time off. I used that time off to plan my next move. I set goals and an agenda each week, but that didn't mean I had to strictly adhere to it. Some weeks played out to their own rhythm, and I learned to go with the flow. However, I can't imagine how chaotic my schedule would have been if I'd made no plans at all.

Step one in my plan on becoming an interior colour designer was to find a magazine to actually pay me to do the needed research on starting this new career. I would write about what I learned, and my phone number would be included at the end of this column.

I was doing freelance work as a stylist for *Canadian House and Home Magazine.* One day I approached them saying I thought the magazine could use some more colour commentary – figuratively and literally. Next thing I knew they hired me as a colour columnist. Step one was now in place! Some people say I was the first in Toronto to bring colour consulting as a career to people's attention; that I invented the career.

Traditionally architects have handled colour in their buildings, and often badly because they are trained in shape and form more than in colour. Interior designers have also handled colour consulting, but they have tended to be quite conservative. If they are going to charge a lot of money for their services, they don't want to shock their clients. In our society we have this notion that neutral colours are more elegant, and bolder colours are tacky and cheap. I don't see colour that way. I see it as an expression of people's emotional state. I first ask people how they want their room to feel, and then I translate that into colour. Colour does not have to be colourful.

When I landed the column, I was elated. I was actually getting paid for doing what I love! My phone number at the end launched my new career as a colour consultant. I started getting calls from people asking me to do colour consultations for their homes, and all while I was still doing my work for photographers. I did this for the next two years, and it was just incredible.

I found that once I had set my goal and focused on it, things began to fall into place. As my new business took off, calls from the photographers began to diminish as they perceived my waning interest. Again it was as if, by laying in some ground work, goals and questions to be answered, things started happening without my making them happen. Within five months I had made the transition to colour consultant. That was a scary time because my income dropped, but it was manageable. It took me only two years to surpass my former income as a stylist, and it has been climbing ever since.

As I gained experience in this field I was better able to tune into my client's perspective and needs. It wasn't about me. I shifted away from telling people what to do, to enabling them to tell me what they want and building colour ideas from there – like a translator.

I enjoy giving people value. Those who are most critical or skeptical may have the greatest need, and I am more patient with them. The toughest clients are those who have very few things in their home – no art, no books, no colour. They have allowed others to block their true selves. Letting people know how smart they really are is the most satisfying part of this job. People intuitively know so much about themselves and their own needs.

I see my role as popping people's corks and allowing their passion to come out of the bottle. It's a thrill to watch people get excited about colour and to watch colour excite them. It's almost like therapy. At the end of some of my best consultations, people wonder why they needed me. It felt as if they had the ideas inside themselves all along; I just brought it to the surface. Sometimes I have to do a bit of hand holding and encourage them to try it by saying, "What is the worst thing that could happen if you dislike the colour? Just get out the roller and paint it over. Colour is important but it isn't so serious. We are not discussing open heart surgery." That puts them at ease.

I have no regrets about starting this career so late. Everything I did before has prepared me for how I approach my current career. I wouldn't be who I am, and doing it the way I am, if I had started sooner. It was an evolution. Everything is built on what came before.

I began my interior colour design career at the age of forty-five. This has allowed me to be bolder, and try things that might be a little outside the box. I no longer worry about being perfect, knowing everything as I did when I was younger. It is actually quite freeing.

For instance, I am quite comfortable saying, "I don't know" – when I don't. I might have tried to look smarter at a younger age. I am more relaxed now, and that helps my clients relax. During one consultation I was just getting acquainted with the lady and her tastes, when the husband came home and asked suspiciously what colour I thought the room should be. "I haven't got a clue yet," I replied. "I need to know you and your wife's likes and dislikes first. What colour were you thinking of?" He seemed to relax after that.

I bring a humanity that comes with maturity. I know about kids, I know about pets, I know about life. Half of the job is communicating with my clients and getting them to relax and open up. It's not just about being an artist. At fifty-one I am still excited about my career, and I'm always learning.

An example of a good learning experience came when the owner of an apartment building hired me to do a colour consultation for painting his below ground floor. He wanted to market to a new kind of tenant and wanted to spruce things up a bit. I put some bold colours on one side of the hallway and left the other side neutral. I thought it was a big improvement over the previous pale grey and washed out whites, and the owner thought it looked pretty good too.

The reaction from the tenants, however, was nothing short of ballistic. They were angry and thought the colours were outrageous and hideous. I felt bad because I enjoy lifting people's spirits with my colour choices, and their spirits were anything but uplifted. I felt like a failure. I tend to take my successes for granted, and focus on what goes wrong. I learned a valuable lesson: People don't like big changes. You can't get people who are accustomed to eating Pablum, to start eating spicy Mexican food. You have to start small – perhaps getting them to first put a little pepper on their meal before introducing the more robust tastes. That learning experience has become a cornerstone of my work.

I stated that I wanted to be an artist as a child. In some ways I am now. When I am helping someone add colour to their home it's almost as if their entire house becomes a painting, and each part has to relate to the other parts of the home.

I do a monthly column for *The Globe & Mail* called "Rooms that Work." That got me a TV spot on *CityLine*, which turned into a regular monthly appearance. I am also writing a book on colour. My enthusiasm for my work grows with each passing year.

I used to think if I was really good at what I was doing, people would just flood to me. I have since realized I have to continuously create new ways to sell myself, and it all has to come from within. But it's a lot easier when that "within" is filled with love for what I am doing.

$\diamond$

Dr. Gerstein's Comments

Look at the advantages of maturity

Janice has a calmness about her, and she made me feel comfortable during our interview. It was a pleasure speaking with her, and I got to see first hand how she puts people at ease. I felt like I could just be myself because she was so comfortable in her own skin. That acceptance and patience often only comes with the wisdom of maturity.

When we are young we have a lot of what the Chinese refer to as *yang* energy. We want to go out and do something, or tell people how to do things. That energy is abundant and can be overwhelming at times. Janice's work requires much *yin* energy. She has to be receptive to what her clients are really telling her. She has to tune into her clients and really listen to their needs so she can translate these into their corresponding colours. This active listening often takes years to develop and people of mature age have an advantage in this arena, although they can't necessarily lay claim to it just because they have a few years behind them.

Look at the advantages of your age. If you are young, middle aged (which grows every year) or older, there are unique benefits in each category. Each category will attract different types of markets. Don't count yourself out if you are mature, you have a lot more to offer than you think. Janice may not have been as good in her Dream Career had she taken it up in her twenties. Her life experiences gave her an advantage that her clients now appreciate.

Scott McDiarmid

Home Renovator

"My wife was very supportive of my
career transition. Without her behind me it
would have been tough to succeed."

I have always enjoyed working with my hands. Throughout my school years you could find me tinkering with electronics, building AM radios and making electronic meters. In woodworking class I would build tables, stands and chessboards. In metal shop I made a mini-bike and a go-cart.

It took me twenty years to realize that my childhood passions were where my dreams could be found. It was there all along. I was simply not aware of it.

As a teen I worked part-time in a stereo store while going to school to become an electrician. Then in 1977, my last year of high school, there was a seven-month electrician's strike, which resulted in a one-year waiting period for apprenticeship. That's when I decided to work full-time at the stereo store.

Switching directions, I enrolled at York University in a business program. After graduation I moved to the wholesale end of electronics sales and became the sales representative for different manufacturers. I started my own home electronics business as a 'Rep-ing' agency. From my home office I traveled to stereo stores and asked them to carry the products I represented. I worked on straight commission and sold car audios and home stereo equipment for all the big manufacturers. I didn't have children yet so I still had the freedom to travel. Being self-employed taught me how to budget, run a home office and manage my time. These skills would become useful later when I finally realized what I truly wanted to do with my life.

Over time, I grew tired of being on the road and weary of the profession. Needing a change I took on the role of director for a computer reseller, and managed the Canadian retail division. I was responsible for staff hiring, purchasing and promotions. I was earning over $100,000, and I enjoyed the selling aspect of my job, but missed working with my hands. I partially satisfied that need outside of work. I finished our basement and did odd fix-it jobs around the house and for my friends.

Over a period of fifteen years, I slowly lost enthusiasm, and became more and more dissatisfied with work. I would get excited when a new product was released, but after a few months it was the same old grind. I stayed because I didn't know what else to do. Five years ago I decided to approach headhunters and career counselors for advice. The headhunters wanted to keep me in the same role, but the career counselor was more helpful.

When I was thinking forward to what I wanted to do with myself, I looked back to my early years. When I was younger, because I enjoyed working with my hands so much, I also loved to cook. My mother would go up to the cottage each summer and I stayed in the city and experimented with new recipes. I considered cooking as a career that would satisfy my need to work with my hands, but my family was now a priority for me, and the hours were not for me. A good friend who owned a restaurant talked me out of this choice for that very reason.

Carpentry was my next option. Cooking and carpentry don't seem related at first, but both careers actually require envisioning a final product. I am a visual person and have the ability to see completed projects in the planning stages. Both fields involved working with my hands, and finishing the work in a timely manner. For carpentry, that would be a completed renovation; for cooking it would be a five-course meal.

After remaining undecided for a few years, I became seriously depressed. I lacked energy and drive and slept in a lot. I was no longer receiving recognition at work because I was underperforming. It was awful. When I reached this stage I knew I had to get out.

Because I proactively arranged for a severance package, I took a much needed year off. We had four children, from four to eight years old. I spent a lot of time with them and with my wife, while I tried to figure out what to do. I had never been able to do this before. For the first time I was in a position to do exactly what I wanted. I no longer felt like I had to work for financial reasons or in the areas in which I was experienced. Out of much soul searching and many discussions with my wife, I decided to pursue my first passion – the home renovation business. I would finally be working with my hands again.

I researched the market ahead of time. I spoke with contractors and went to several home shows to see what the demands were. I discovered that most the new homes being built in my neighbourhood didn't have finished basements. I read about the current trend where extended families live under one roof. People were fixing up their houses rather than moving into new or bigger ones. I knew that renovations would be a booming business for at least the next seven years.

I cashed in my stock options and purchased professional-quality tools. I had a six-month cushion to get my company rolling. If I became desperate, I could draw on my RRSP savings. I didn't want to get a bank loan because the interest could have hurt me and result in my downfall.

I was willing to change our lifestyle and so was my family. We downsized our home and I drove my car a few years longer than what I was accustomed. My wife and I agreed on a five-year trial period. If in five years, I hadn't grown my business to where it could meet our needs, I would go back to my old business. We were all committed to the five years.

I still had some reservations about my ability to do it. With the encouragement from my wife and mother, and with all of the research

I had done on my potential target market, I gained confidence in my ability to be financially successful. Having my family behind me was a big boost in my career transition. Without their support it would have been very tough.

I was never afraid to seek out successful people to answer any question I had. I also surrounded myself with positive people because I am a person who sees the glass half-full. I want to be, and choose to be, around like-minded people. I never knew when I might need someone's help, so I joined a networking group to have access to professionals with different areas of expertise.

I was excited to begin, and was able to build my business on referrals. My clients seemed very satisfied with my work. If there was a problem I attended to it immediately. One time a client called to tell me there was a leak in the basement bathroom I had built. I sought advice from an excellent plumber in my networking circle, and repaired the problem quickly. The client appreciated my direct attention to the matter.

It was certainly a struggle at the beginning. I only drew out $4,000 and $9,000 from the business in salary for the first two years, respectively. Then, after two years, things began really clicking.

One of my clients wanted to turn part of her house into a rental unit, and she was on a tight budget. I installed a kitchen upstairs, which was a challenging job because there was no plumbing in that bedroom. But I finished the work on time and even suggested where she could save money, and where she could spend it afterwards when her rental income started.

She saw that I was wanted to help her save money. To my surprise, when I gave her the invoice she rounded it up. It is so gratifying knowing I had a satisfied customer, because this is also the best source for more referrals too.

I am making a lot less money today than I was when I worked as the director for the computer company. In spite of that, I have never been more satisfied at work. And I know I will earn a lot more as I grow my business. Switching to this career is one of the most rewarding things I've ever done.

Dr. Gerstein's Comments

Spend some time now to reap the greater benefits of your long-term vision.

Many people are scared of running their own business because it lacks the guarantee of steady pay. The prospect of going out and having to constantly drum up business can be extremely intimidating. This is what prevents many hobbyists from turning their pastime into a career.

Granted, some people want to keep their hobby a hobby. They don't want to make it a business. They enjoy the leisure of doing what they want when they want and at their own pace. They don't want to work for other people. If that is the case I wouldn't recommend turning it into a career. It will sabotage both the career and the hobby.

However, if you are motivated to please others with your talent or would enjoy selling your labour of love, do not allow the fear of marketing yourself to stop you from pursuing your dreams. Marketing is a skill that can be learned. There are hundreds of books and websites that offer tips on marketing. There are probably dozens of marketing experts in your area who can teach you how to get your small business off the ground.

If you have the will and the desire to do what you love as a career you can find the way to make it work.

There is a short-term mindset in society. As a whole we don't put away enough savings for retirement early enough. We don't look at what our eating and exercise habits of today will do for our health in ten or twenty years. And we don't think what our careers will look like in ten or twenty years. Many of us do it backwards – we look at the money we need to support our lifestyles today and then look for any job that supports that need. This is how many people find themselves in a job they dislike for

Dr. Gerstein's Comments

the rest of their working lives. Don't sell yourself short for a measly three to five years of earnings. This is the time it may take to get your new career moving well.

You have to adjust your sights towards a more long-term approach – but the payoffs are tremendous. You can still look at your lifestyle and the income required to maintain it. Then stop and take some time to discover what you love to do. It's a lot easier to take the time here than waiting until you have invested years to an area you dislike. You may need a coach or counselor to assist you. Don't skimp on this investment. It could be one of the most important endeavors of your life. Once you know the area you'd love to get into, look a few years down the road for a way to produce the income from that field that matches your lifestyle requirements.

If you love carpentry and you only require an hourly wage of thirty five dollars then working for someone else will suffice. If you want to earn upwards of eighty dollars to ninety dollars hourly you may wish to look into starting your own business. Other choices include consulting, doing higher end work, writing a newspaper column on carpentry or hosting radio and/or television shows doling out advice about carpentry projects.

Give yourself three to five years to get your business going. Be patient at the beginning. The average work life is forty years. (Even that is being extended as more and more people are choosing to work well past the old paradigm of retirement at sixty-five years old. That is because people at sixty-five are a lot healthier now than they were when that arbitrary retirement age was first chosen. In addition, the idea of living your Dream Career was not even considered a possibility to most people back then) What is three to five years out of forty? You may have to endure a few years of alternate lifestyle choices. However if that

Dr. Gerstein's Comments

enables you to enjoy thirty-five years of a happy prosperous career isn't the trade-off worth it?

Even if you only have twenty years left in your working life, you will probably be able to accelerate the growth phase because of the transferable skills you developed. Many of you will have some equity built up in your home or other investments. You can draw on these funds as bridge financing to support your dream. Is it worth spending a few years developing your passion if it allows you to enjoy seventeen years doing what you love? Only you can answer that question.

Myth-Diagnosis #3
Chronologically Challenged

✦

How *You* Can Bust This Myth

When have you allowed your age to stop you from pursuing a goal? Have you ever pulled yourself out of the running, or better yet, not even entered because you thought you were either too young or too old?

Start reviewing your own beliefs:

What do you think older people can't do?

What do you think younger people can't do?

Then go ahead and look for examples that break your own theoretical rules. If you were wrong about those, perhaps you were mistaken about your own limits.

Some examples of young people accomplishing great things include Marquita Andrews, who broke sales records selling girl scout cookies; Steve Jobs, who at the age of 20 with Steve Wozniak, started Apple computers in his parents' garage; and Craig Kielburger, who after reading about the murder of a Pakistani boy who was speaking out against child labour, started Free The Children at age 12, now the largest network of children helping children through education in the world.

Some examples of people starting their Dream only after they were older include Ronald Reagan, who became president of the United States at age 70, Rodney Dangerfield, who after working as a salesman for many years, really didn't start his acting/comedy career until he was 42 and Grandma Moses, who began painting after she turned 70 leaving behind a career in embroidery because of arthritis. There were many other late bloomers: Colonel Sanders began his Kentucky Fried Chicken (now KFC) franchise of restaurants in his sixties. Laura Ingalls Wilder, author of Little House on the Prairie, became a columnist in her forties but did not write her first novel until her sixties.

It's time to stop accepting the old limiting rules that others have handed down to you. Challenge them and start making new rules that work for you.

Myth - Diagnosis #4
Diploma Deficiency Disorder

"I don't have the education.
I'm not smart enough."

*"I think there is something, more important than believing: Action!
The world is full of dreamers, there aren't enough who will move
ahead and begin to take concrete steps to actualize their vision."*

W. Clement Stone

Elaine Overholt
Vocal Coach and Singer

*"I knew my talent was music. Bigger than my dream of music
was my dream of affecting people in a positive way."*

There was never any question what my talent was as I was
growing up. I had so many affirmations in my life that validated my
musical talent. When I sang my first solo in church at the age of three,
I forgot the words and everyone laughed – probably because I was so
darned cute. I've often said I've spent the rest of my life trying to get it
right.

I grew up in Woodstock, Ontario, in a middle class family. From an
early age I had a good ear and a passion for music, and I am so thankful
to my parents for supporting it. Somehow they always found the money
for my piano lessons because they knew how much I loved it.

I started playing piano when I was four, and practiced from two
to four hours every day after school. I didn't like it much because I was
a very social child, and sitting in front of a piano is a solo endeavor. But
as time passed I got better, and when I was around eight I suddenly

began to hear the beauty of the music. It all came together for me then; it was exhilarating and I became very motivated. I realized then I had to do the work to get the rewards. It's like I tell my students, "Singing is like being an Olympic vocal athlete. You've got to put in the time."

From age eleven to thirteen I won all the senior piano Rose Bowls in my town, and I was always the piano player for the school choir. At fourteen I began teaching piano. In high school I formed a musical group and we toured on weekends. Some would say I was a bit of a child prodigy; I certainly knew I had a talent for music. I found easy success with anything I put my fingers or my voice to. My passion found *me* at an early age.

All this might lead you to believe I was one of the lucky ones. The truth is I never felt I was good enough, and was constantly striving to prove my value to the world. It's ironic – I never felt fully confident in my musical abilities, notwithstanding all the external awards and accolades I received. I just hoped that feeling would disappear with age.

After high school I took a year off and toured the country with a gospel group. I spent the summer in Banff at the School of Fine Arts. While there, I got a lead from a Barbadian man that resulted in me doing a piano tour of Barbados. When I returned, I enrolled at the University of Western Ontario as a piano performance major, but graduated with an Honours Bachelor's of Music in voice performance. Somewhere during my time at university I realized my passion was more in my voice than my fingers.

I wanted to be a star, but starting out I had to pay the bills. In 1975 I got a job as a production assistant at a Toronto recording studio, and did that for a year. To supplement my income, I taught. Then I became a full-time session singer doing jingles for large corporations like McDonald's, Coca Cola and beer companies. Whenever an American commercial was brought across the border it had to be redone using Canadian talent. That money was great while the gigs lasted but it never occurred to me to stash it away or that making money would not always be this easy.

I spent the 1980s doing jingles, performing in clubs, doing R & B and Gospel concerts, and coaching pop and theatre singers. Performing in nightclubs six evenings a week helped me build vocal cords of iron. Then NAFTA was signed, and my little goldmine of jingles dried up.

Perhaps this sudden lack of money necessitated the emergence of my truly creative artistic side. This included singing backup for artists like Ray Charles, Tina Turner, Anne Murray and Chubby Checker. I performed internationally and sang for dignitaries like the former Prime Minister of Canada, the Right Honourable Pierre Elliot Trudeau. And I started to write songs.

Despite all my successes, my biggest challenge has been overcoming my feelings of inferiority. I suffered terribly from it, almost to the point of backing away from doing a certain project. I feared that my musical expressions and/or my public instructional methods would be mocked by those in the know. As a child, my older brother had really teased me for not being smart enough and it had gone in deep. I was afraid of being called stupid. I knew I was talented in music. I just never felt adequate intellectually.

This has been a lifelong battle that improves every day. But music was what I knew I was supposed to be doing, so I just went ahead and did it. It was a God given gift that I wasn't about to squander. **There is something within me that keeps stepping over my fears into action.**

Feeling inferior has made me sensitive. Once I was given a bad review in the *Toronto Sun* and I felt like a kid who had been slapped in the face. I cried a lot and got depressed for a couple of days. But then I asked myself, **"What can I learn from this?"** I've somehow always been able to do that. I've learned to pick myself up, dust myself off and keep going. I told myself it was just one person's opinion – one person didn't like me. On the other hand, I had to admit he was right about some things, such as my choice of material. That prompted me to take action to change what I could change, and then I moved on.

Creating beautiful music is addictive, and those special moments are few and far between. Each one is an emotional high, and once I had experienced it, I wanted to experience it again. It's like creating a baby. It comes from within and it's a magical moment when it happens.

My first album was released in 1978, and it got some radio airplay. I was flown first class across Canada to do TV shows like *The Tommy Hunter Show* and the *Bobby Vinton Show*, and I starred along with *The Fifth Dimension* in Edmonton. It was all glamorous and fun and I was living the high life. I was on my way to the top – or so I thought.

When I returned home, reality quickly set in. My manager had booked me to play in a little Toronto restaurant. Only four people showed up, and I was upset. I thought I was above that. I thought I was going somewhere, and it was below me to sing for only four people. Didn't my manager see my newfound lofty status in the music world?

When my manager came backstage he swiftly brought me back to earth. He said, "Elaine, you think you're such hot stuff, but you don't know what performing is all about. Performing is putting out the same effort for two people as you would for two thousand." And he was right.

It was a good lesson for me, and a wake up call. I had to decide – was I in it for the glitz and glamour or was it truly my passion? I realized then that I really love what I do. The fleeting brush with fame and glamour had briefly carried me away. I was young and impressionable and it was a great ride.

My marriage ended in 1992, and when I became a single parent I stopped performing in the evenings in order to be with my daughter. The divorce was tough on me financially and emotionally. I received no spousal support, and I had to give half of my retirement savings from my jingles to my ex-husband. I've gone through many lean years. In the entertainment business you are only as good as your last DVD or CD. The fear around money is always present, and it can affect your health if you dwell on it. Still, I was determined to stay in the music business and be a good mother.

I took on a variety of jobs along the way – some of which weren't ideal, but I was a single mother and I needed the money. I've never compromised my ideals. I always came back to music. But even **bigger than my dream of music was my dream of being able to affect people in a positive way.** During my career I'd heard so many stories of people who were told when they were young they couldn't sing, and had given up on their dream. I wanted to make a difference, and I knew that I could. I decided I would help other vocalists, and my religious Evangelical background played a role in my new passion for coaching. If this was to become my focus, I wanted to give it my full attention and make it special.

I started by treating this new part of my career as an art form, the way I approach most projects. I have a need to look for the absolutely most ultimate approach to whatever I do, and that search can be both exhausting and exhilarating. Even as a teenager I approached my job at a Harvey Woods underwear factory that way; I didn't care for it, but I wanted to give it my best. It's my creative side that continually wants to leap out from within.

Almost every week I get a call from someone whose voice is shaking with anxiety. They tell me they've always wanted to do this, but they were so nervous about calling me. Then they tell me a story that sounds something like this: "When I was six my father told me to stop singing. He said I sounded awful. I listened and stopped singing, and I am here because I think he was wrong. Can you help me?" When I hear that I just melt. That person could be the worst singer in the world, and I'll still take them on. I really want to honour that person's desire to explore herself.

Because of the negative message I received when I was young, I can really empathize with my students. I am able to help them act on their dream in spite of their feelings. That's what I did in my own life, so I *know* that when you do, the feelings of inferiority diminish. People ask me, "Can anybody sing?" I say, "Yes, and everybody should sing!" Singing is a very deep form of expression, even if you just sing for yourself.

I love helping uncover the voices of people who have a passion for singing, and for those who just want to be able to express themselves better. I have heard, lived and breathed music from the depths of my soul through my own performances, and to me there is nothing more exciting than helping someone unlock their hidden voice. That voice is not just about the *outer voice*, it's also about their *inner voice*. I have found the physical voice is often an obstacle for many people. So many people want to break out into song at a party, but they stop themselves. I want to free their voice and give it sound.

I've had many highs in my career – from singing backup for some great artists, to performing in front of thousands of people, to being a vocal coach to the likes of Renée Zellweger, Catherine Zeta-Jones and Richard Gere for the movie, *Chicago*. In spite of all these accomplishments, I still have to deal with that small voice inside, reminding me of my failings. **What I have learned is to turn down the volume of that voice, and simply carry on in the direction of my**

dream. With time, the voice gets quieter, but it never completely disappears.

Now I have realized another longtime dream – a DVD that features my singing techniques. The music industry is not usually kind to women as they get older, and in addition, the recording industry is in the worst shape ever because of pirating of DVDs. Despite all that, at fifty-one years young I am having my best year ever.

Dr. Gerstein's Comments

What false story do you currently believe about yourself?

I've learned that it's almost impossible to talk someone out of their false beliefs. All of the evidence was there for Elaine to see that she was not stupid; in fact, one could call her brilliant when you look at all the careers she has created for herself using her enormous musical talents. But alas, all that evidence would fall on deaf ears if you tried to sell Elaine on that theory.

We leave our childhood with a set of values and beliefs – and issues – that have been formed, and greatly influenced by our parents, caregivers and teachers. The best they could do was to pass along to us what they were taught by *their* influencers. And so on it goes back generations and generations – it has all been handed down.

Here is my question to you: What if a common theme that has been handed down to you is just wrong? Many families pass down values like they pass down their genes and their family photographs. They believe they are fact and must be accepted.

Here are just some of the beliefs that many people have adopted as fact:

- If you are uneducated you cannot be successful.
- Poor people can't change their financial situation.
- Work has to be hard. If you enjoy it, it is not real work.
- Stop dreaming – this is the real world.
- Get a job with a good company and you'll be set for life.
- Small businesses can't compete with the big companies.

These statements – which represent beliefs – have all been proven false by the people interviewed for this book. If you've carried

Dr. Gerstein's Comments

one or more of these beliefs around with you for your whole life, you can now free yourself. They are not truths – they are myths. It's important to remember they were not passed down with malice. The people who professed these beliefs thought they were true. And some were more true generations ago but today they just no longer apply. You now have a choice. You no longer have to carry the weight of these limitations like a chain around your neck. Once you know the truth, you *can* break free of them and adopt new beliefs. And by adopting a new belief, you can change your life.

People have come to Elaine believing that they had a bad voice, and could never sing. Elaine helps them see that their voice is merely undeveloped, and if they have a passion for music they can learn – she can teach them. Her success with these people speaks volumes to what can happen when you change your beliefs.

Elaine is gradually starting to believe in herself. What you need to notice is that she did not allow those self-doubts to stop her from pursuing her dream. If anything, it made her more determined than ever.

*"It is not that I am smarter than anyone else.
It's just that I stay with my problems longer."*

Albert Einstein

Kim Mitchell
Co-operative Education Instructor

*"In December of 1998 I had had enough. I made a decision.
I quit my job – perhaps not the smartest thing to do. I told myself
I would find something I liked in the New Year."*

I always wanted to be a teacher. Perhaps it was because of the teachers I had in school, particularly my grade eight advancement program teacher. It was a small class, and each person had the benefit of extra individual attention. I was a shy child, and rarely raised my hand to participate. Having to do a book report in front of the class would send chills down my spine. But in that year my confidence grew. My teacher gave me personal attention, and encouraged me to be creative. He challenged me, and then he supported me, and the combination instilled in me a new confidence. It was as if I had been in a dark tunnel for a long time, and when the school year ended it was like a light went on inside me as I came out the other end.

I did eventually become a teacher but not in the way I had envisioned. I had a lot of growing to do. I believe it was fate that I was rejected from teacher's college twice before finding my Dream Career.

In 1979 I graduated with a BA in Sociology and Psychology. But

I put my aspirations for becoming a teacher on hold for two reasons. First, a small part of me didn't think I could do it and second, I figured I had a lot of time to do it later on.

I liked social work, but my aunt, a social worker and an official guardian, who had been responsible for getting many children out of abusive homes, dissuaded me citing the high stress and burnout rate in the field.

Another option that intrigued me was working with people in human resources. My first job was at an employment agency, and my role was to match the applicant with an employer. It was a commission position, and I found it quite stressful. I had to make many cold calls and that just wasn't me.

One day a job came across my desk that appealed to me, so I applied for it and was hired to work in the personnel department at the head office of a retail ladies wear chain. I conducted personnel interviews, assisted with payroll and administered the company's benefit plan. I was fairly content, but after six years the company closed down and I was out looking for work again.

After my second maternity leave I didn't want a full-time job because by now I had young children and I thought it was important they have their mother around. Simultaneously, the teaching bug started to gnaw at me again, and I knew I could no longer ignore it. It just kept growing inside me like a caterpillar anxious to move on to the next natural stage and become a butterfly. I had to listen to that voice. You know the one – that still small voice inside that just won't go away no matter how often you shout it down. It is persistent and it speaks the truth. When I finally started listening, my Dream Career began to take shape.

My oldest daughter was in junior kindergarten at the time. I volunteered in the JK and in the grade five class. I found I was more suited to the grade five age group. I quite enjoyed their intellectual reasoning and decided to set out and reclaim the teaching position I had let slip through my hands *twelve years earlier*.

I applied to the Faculty of Education at the University of Toronto and was rejected. Strike one. The principal of my daughter's school suggested that I would have a better chance of getting in if I got my

Honours BA.

I decided to do it. But now I needed a job that would give me enough flexibility to be with my children and still allow me time to study. I found a part-time position in data entry, and even though I wasn't happy with the work, it met the requirements. I took on the challenge, went back to school, and received my Honours BA in Sociology at the age of thirty-three.

With that in hand I reapplied. I had stiff competition – there were 10,000 applicants and only 1200 acceptances. Those who got in had a Masters degree, a specialty, or spoke another language. I was rejected again. Strike two.

I was disappointed but remained undaunted. Because I still had to pay the bills, I returned to data entry for three more years. This was tough. It was not what I wanted, but this time I knew it. I often found myself not wanting to go to work. It was very robotic-like, and mentally exhausting, not because of the demands it placed on me, but rather the lack of demands. I was unchallenged, stifled, and bored.

Then I saw a school offering a program called *Teaching English as a Second Language* (TESL). It did not require an Ontario Teaching Certificate (OTC) to teach adults, and I became excited. I completed the intensive training by attending classes after work two evenings a week for three months, and graduated with an A. Then I set out to find a job.

When I started submitting applications, I was told I had no practical experience. Catch 22: I couldn't get in because I had no experience and I couldn't get experience because I was not a teacher! I was advised to volunteer in the evenings to acquire the experience I needed. That would have meant paying a baby sitter twice a week, and I had neither the inclination nor the time to do that. Rejected again – strike three.

In baseball terminology strike three would have meant I was out. But I wasn't playing baseball – this was my life. I would make up my own rules. I wasn't about to give up on my dream.

In the interim I returned to the data entry position, but by December of 1997 I'd had enough, and I made a decision. I told myself I would find something I liked in the New Year no matter what. If I couldn't be a formal teacher or teach ESL, perhaps I could use my HR background to find a position that would blend career guidance with ESL for adults. Somehow, some way, **I was going to teach**.

I quit my data entry job even though I didn't have another job lined up. That might not have been the most prudent thing to do, but I was determined to make it work. I wasn't eligible for unemployment insurance because I quit, but I had a little bit of savings tucked away. When my girls asked, "Mom, what are you doing?" I responded, "This is for the better. Believe me it will be better. Your mother will be happier. It will all work out." I replied as confidently as I could, but I was going on pure faith and blind determination.

I knew I had to cut spending, so I created a family budget. During this time, my kids learned to appreciate meatloaf and Kraft dinners. We all relinquished some perks, but my children were well cared for. I gave them my most precious commodity – my time. I worked my career schedule around them. As a single mom I had many responsibilities. I wanted to be responsible to myself in finding a career that suited me, and I wanted to be there for my children.

Working in HR had given me the skills to know how to look for a new career. First I went to the library to begin targeting companies. I was looking for places that had an adult program with ESL clients in the process of looking for employment, so I got a list of directories on community service. There were several neighbourhood centres and settlement houses for new immigrants that fit the bill, but there wasn't an abundance of opportunities. The Ministry of Immigration funded many of them, and they didn't have the budget to support many full time staff.

I sent my resumé to the local school boards because I knew they had ESL courses in their continuing education departments. Every week I looked over the classifieds in several newspapers. I was persistent. Then one morning I opened the *Mississauga News*, our local community newspaper, and saw an ad for a co-op placement officer. It required a BA, TESL certificate, and an HR background. BINGO! That was me. I almost tripped over the phone trying to call the number before anyone else saw the ad.

I had already sent my résumé to them two months earlier, but it must have been misfiled. I immediately faxed them my resumé with a cover letter. Within two hours they called to schedule an interview. After interviewing a few more people, they called me back. They offered me the job, telling me I was the best candidate they interviewed. I couldn't have agreed more. After striking out, I had hit a home run my next turn at bat.

My position at the adult centre has been the most fulfilling and personally satisfying position I have ever held. Over the last five years I have met over four hundred adult students, and they have truly been a gift in my life. Their enthusiasm, energy and genuine zest for a new, fresh life in Canada have been awe inspiring. Their positive energy radiates in the classroom, and stimulates a contagion for all their classmates. That energy follows them into the workplace.

I cherish the beautiful cards and letters my students have sent me. As a sensitive person they know that my eyes will not remain dry for long when I read their loving comments. Our long-standing joke in the class is, "You don't have to travel to Niagara Falls to see the waterfall, just come to one of Kim's classes." Ha!

What I do now incorporates many of the things I love – teaching, career guidance, counseling, and part-time therapy. I am much happier and fulfilled, and my students tell me they feel and appreciate my energy and passion for my work. Just as importantly I know I am being a good role model for my own two girls.

My children have seen the good and bad effects that work has had on me. They witnessed the boredom and low energy I felt doing data entry as well as my stick-to-it attitude by refusing to give up when the going got rough. They understood that I worked at the part-time job so I could be there for them at lunch and after school. They observed their mother go back to school at age thirty-three and my rejuvenation when I started my new career. They will understand you are never too old to do something new; that what you do in your twenties doesn't have to be what you will be doing in your thirties or forties. I hope I have shown them they have a choice, and to get into something they love. I believe I have taken this journey as much for them as for myself.

Dr. Gerstein's Comments

Rejection is good for you

Collecting rejection letters was not Kim's intent of a hobby. Kim realized, consciously or not, that rejection is just part of the success process. With each rejection she learned one more thing. The key was to use that learning and set a new course for herself. It was these small yet significant course deviations which eventually led her to discover her Dream Career. Unlike many people, she refused to allow those rejections to dissuade her from her goal.

When she was rejected from the Faculty of Education she went back and upgraded her degree to an Honours BA. Even so, she was rejected again because of stiff competition with people who had more qualifications. Undaunted she left that path and began knocking on another teaching door – ESL. She completed her courses in the evenings and was rejected again because of lack of teaching experience.

These attempts to enter the teaching field took her two years. Most people would have given up their dreams completely by then, but Kim was still intent on becoming a teacher in some form, and just shifted her vision.

Kim led by example. She has demonstrated the concept of "Never give up" better than most. She did it while being a single mom and raising two children. Most parents will advise their children to do something, but will act in contradictory ways. In the emergency department I once witnessed a mother imploring me to get her daughter off crack cocaine, and yet she herself was addicted to tobacco and alcohol. Kim is one lady who walks her talk and leads by example!

"Learning which involves the whole person of the learner, feelings as well as intellect, is the most lasting and pervasive."

Carl Rogers

John McAuley
President and CEO of Muskoka Woods

"One of my high school teachers told me I would never accomplish anything in life if I didn't stop going up the mountains and camping."

In Belfast I grew up in fear. As a Protestant I was afraid of being killed for my religion. Individually, I was afraid of being rejected if I failed to please others. I was afraid that I wasn't going to amount to much. What did I do? I gave up my religion and gave up my dreams. I found myself in a good job with a great income, but I was empty inside. That's when I began my journey back to my authentic self.

For my father, work was merely a means of freeing up time to be involved in our church, which dominated my life while growing up. I had a youth leader who loved the outdoors, and he took a group of us to the mountains every weekend. I loved it, and as a result, became an expedition leader myself.

I grew up in fear in Northern Ireland. I was raised in a Christian home and went to a church in a hostile neighbourhood. At the age of seven, I saw people being blown apart. In high school, I was threatened and brutally bullied. In order to better fit in and just survive, I slowly began to deny my own faith. I was afraid of being killed, and fear ruled my life. In addition, I also carried with me the fear of rejection. I had been conditioned to be a people pleaser. Mix those two fears up in the same person, and what you get is a recipe for burnout. It's a formula for doing what other people want you to do, instead of doing what is best for you.

I remember a story that clearly demonstrates those fears. When I was twelve I borrowed some nails from my neighbour, David, to build a soapbox go-cart. He kept his nails in a tartan tin. As he gave me the tin he looked in my eyes and said, "Do not lose these nails."

Well as luck would have it, my mother lent that tin out to another neighbour who came looking for nails. A few weeks later David came to pick them up but I wasn't home. When my mother told me he was returning to get them, I searched everywhere to no avail. My mom had forgotten that she lent them out. When I couldn't find them I ran to my room crying hysterically, locked the door and hid under my covers. Then I heard a knock on the front door of our house. It was him. When he heard the cries coming from my bedroom, he came and knocked on my door. I was terrified. What was he going to do to me?

My imagination ran wild. Over and over I recalled the look on his face when he told me not to lose his nails. Then, from outside the door I heard him say, "John, it's okay. They're just nails. They're just nails." I finally opened the door and he gave me a reassuring hug. I apologized profusely, explaining I had put them away carefully. Then he said, "John, it's all right. Your mom remembered she lent them out." I had felt so badly because I had disappointed someone.

I was such a sensitive boy, and often blew things out of proportion. I would worry about things that were all but forgotten a year later. I had to learn to develop the skill of shifting my focus away from things that weren't worth the worry.

Throughout high school I was told repeatedly I would never do well scholastically because I was preoccupied with climbing mountains. As it turned out, I was a below average student all through high school. I later realized I was merely pleasing the people who were predicting my poor performance. I allowed them to influence me – and made them right.

When I was sixteen, I applied to study forensic science but was turned down because I failed one of my classes. I went to my school's career officer – who also happened to be my uncle. He found me a job in a pop factory. Because of him I left school at sixteen, and immediately began working at that factory. I became so bored that every twenty minutes I walked down to the end of the factory floor to spin a machine that told me how many bubbles were in the lemonade batch we were making.

For me, that experience typified the meaninglessness and drudgery I foresaw if I stayed working in that environment for the rest of my life. I did it for two years though, because I didn't know what else to do. I was so busy trying to please others I had not taken time to know or please myself. I was told I wouldn't amount to much, and it was starting to look like my teachers had been right.

When I reached eighteen I applied for and was accepted by the police force. After walking the beat for a while I had the urge to be more active, so I joined the search and rescue team. This allowed me to work outdoors again. All along I could see this pattern of working outside and never wanting to be stuck in an office.

I was quite an effective police officer, and my file said I would likely excel in the future. I had good commendations and was earning good money. So why wasn't I happy? I began to feel that something big was missing from my life.

To avoid being different, and to save my hide, I had rejected God and religion back in school. That began to gnaw at me, and I went through a period of questioning everything in my life, who I was, and what I was supposed to be doing. I poured over the readings of the Bible. I sought help from mentors.

After all that effort I came to the conclusion there was a God after all. I made that decision myself. The one passage that stands out for me is Psalm 139, which says: *"I knit you together in your mother's womb. Before you were born, every day ordained for you was written in my book."*

This passage is never far from my mind. To me it means we were shaped with certain personality types and passions and our own individual destinies. One only has to search to find one's own calling. If it's true that all my days are already written in God's book, then I needed to discover, How do I get on the same page as God? How can I align myself with God's destiny for me?

I began to feel a calling to give myself to full time ministry. It took some courage to leave the police force, and other people definitely questioned what I was doing. But I had someone higher to answer to. I wanted to use outdoor adventures to help youth find God. Those trips had been a big part of my life, and I wanted to give back to others in the same way. I was excited by my discovery, and felt my path was beginning to become clear.

One day a former minister of our church returned to Belfast from Canada for a homecoming service. After the sermon I approached Reverend Little and asked if he would speak to the youth of our church. I told him then of my intention to leave the police force and go into the Christian camping industry. Looking at me with a smile, he told me it just so happened his son was the program director of a Christian, interdenominational, non-profit sports resort in Canada called Muskoka Woods. I couldn't believe it! **Someone told me that coincidences are where God has chosen to be silent**.

Reverend Little invited me to come to Canada for the summer. With great excitement I changed my summer plans, and within two weeks of my arrival in Muskoka, I knew I had found my destiny. It is also where I fell in love with the boss's daughter – my future wife.

There have been three dominant themes running throughout my life: My faith in God, my passion for young people, and taking people out of their routines to provide a life-changing experience outdoors. At Muskoka Woods I was able to fulfill all three.

When I finally got my passions aligned with my higher purpose, I began living a life without boundaries. When I found something I loved, I excelled at it. Other people began asking me to share my expertise with them.

However, I had not completely left my past behind. The people pleaser in me continued to say "yes" whenever others asked me for my help. I couldn't tell my staff when they were not performing up to expectations. I also had the feeling that I could never please God enough. I started to burn out.

I read two books that fundamentally changed my thinking in this area. The first was *The 7 Habits of Highly Effective People,* by Steven R. Covey (Fireside Books, 1990). Next to the Bible that has been the most influential book in my life.

The second book was *Managing Management Time: Who's Got the*

Monkey? by William Oncken (Prentice Hall, 1984). The author suggests that every day someone comes through your door with a monkey on his back. The monkey is a metaphor for a problem. They try to give you the monkey.

When I took over Muskoka Woods as director, I learned how to let the person keep his own monkey. Now when someone comes into my office and says, "John, we've got a problem." I say to myself, "*We* don't have a problem, *you* do." I keep a little statue of a monkey to remind me not to take on other people's problems, or their work, because of my own dysfunction and because it does not help their development.

I got quite a scare a few years ago when I awoke one day with six large ulcers in the back of my throat. It was a huge relief when the biopsy was negative for cancer. The ENT surgeon thought it was stress related, and warned me about taking on everyone else's problems. The message hit home, and I took the year off from all traveling and speeches. I returned to my priorities: all I did was be a husband, a dad and an executive director. By setting those boundaries I was able to regain my health.

I have found a life calling that invigorates me. When I go to bed at night I can't wait to get up the next day for work. I have found alignment and purpose in my life that is lived out in the very essence of my career. I spend fifty plus hours a week in my role as president of this large camping organization, so I made sure it was something I wanted to do.

We have three hundred summer seasonal staff, and an alumnus of thousands. I spend a fair amount of time talking with young people wondering what they should do after university. Some come to us in their twenties who are stuck in their jobs, in what I would call career depression. We help them to align their purpose, passion and personality. The transformation is remarkable. After the process they literally come alive again.

People's lives are changed here, and that is so fulfilling for me. I tell my family and friends, if I die today, don't come to the funeral and ask God why He let me die. For every day I have lived for Him, with Him and to Him. I learned that from Mother Theresa.

I had gotten back to God, the outdoors and to helping youth, and I was successful. I then began to wonder, could it possibly be that my demeaning teachers were wrong?

Well, I just completed a Masters of Science in Organizational Leadership. Now I have the opportunity of going on and doing doctorate work. Just the thought of doing a Masters degree was so intimidating because of all the negative feedback I'd received from my high school teachers. Comments like, "You won't be able to do it" and "You won't do well in school" were not uncommon jabs at my potential. In one of his reports my math teacher wrote, "John is very slow in grasping new concepts."

Looking back I realize that the teachers who made those comments were simply not good teachers. In their own poverty of spirit, they failed to recognize my abilities. It wasn't me – it was them, and that's the bottom line. I think I am one of only two students from that entire school that has gone on to do a Masters degree. I teach leadership across the country. I consult. I manage a large nonprofit organization and people come from other countries to visit. The education system didn't recognize who I really was and what I was capable of.

My arts and crafts teacher had me write out five hundred times, "I must not talk a load of verbal diarrhea." Think of the irony. I now make my living from speaking. Another teacher said I would never accomplish anything if I didn't stop going up the mountains and camping. What do I do now? I go camping! They had turned my natural potential strengths into weaknesses. But it was all about their weaknesses, not mine. I just didn't see it at the time. Everything they warned would be my downfall ultimately became my Dream Career.

$\diamond$

Dr. Gerstein's Comments

There are no such things as coincidences.
They are the manifestation of mutual intentions.

Thought is energy, and we attract to ourselves the same energy we pour out. Nothing is as powerful as focused, laser-like thought. Some people call that an intention. When people hold an intention in their head for a long period of time, they will eventually meet the manifestation of that thought in the physical world. To a passive observer it might look like a simple coincidence. From the perspective of the person with the determined focus, it is an expression of a scientific law.

There is an old saying that says, "Be careful what you wish for – it might come true." I don't believe in wishes. They are weak and vague, and have no true power. Now change the word "wish" to "intend," and I support it fully.

That's why it is *so* important to know what you want. If you don't, you are merely bumping into other people's intentions and you will be blown about like leaves in a windstorm. If you know your true path, *you* will be the one sending out powerful energetic thought-messages to which the universe must then respond.

"Experience is simply the name we give our mistakes."

Oscar Wilde

Jennifer Beale
Publicist

"It's not enough to learn something.
Applied knowledge is what separates the people who truly
know from those who only say they know something."

I was a pathetically shy teenager. I dropped out of high school and was heading nowhere fast. I didn't know who I was. I didn't think it could get much worse – but it did. Something tragic happened that was to change my whole life direction.

I felt like such a loser when I was younger. I was afraid of not being accepted and I was shy. I didn't believe that I could do what I really wanted to do. And I didn't know what I wanted to do. My solution was to drop out of high school. But, after that, I found few options available to me. I took a job at a bakery because, frankly, what else was I trained for?

Work at the bakery was boring and frustrating. I hated it. It was mindless and repetitive. I knew I could do much more. Then something happened that changed my whole life for the good.

At age 21, after drinking alcohol, I smashed a car into a tree and almost died. The reason I know I almost died was because the two people with me in the car died. The accident was pivotal. Not only had I fractured my spine and my knee, which required surgery and months of rehabilitation, I had to deal with tremendous guilt for my part in the death of two people.

That tragic event took me to the depths of shame, pain and guilt unlike anything I have ever experienced. I wouldn't wish what I went through on anyone.

Yet, I felt deep gratitude for being alive and getting a second chance. Remarkably, years of aimless living ended with a seemingly horrible experience. The accident forced me to grow up and become responsible. It wasn't my will. It threw me into a period of tremendous self-discovery that has not ceased for twenty years. I spun around and began heading in an entirely new direction – responsible, hopeful, and determined to live a life that made a positive difference.

I attended personal growth seminars and studied many pop psychology books. I did the exercises in the books. I got to know myself well and I owe a lot of my current clear decisions to that time in my life. I wanted more for my life and began believing I deserved it. I decided to go back to school and finished grades twelve and thirteen. Since then I've been striving to bring peace and harmony into my life. I am now forty-two and worlds away from where I was that fateful night.

I've been fired from almost every job I had. I've worked in various jobs. I came up with ideas and wanted to be heard. When people didn't listen to my ideas I voiced my frustrations. That didn't sit well with my supervisors. I now realize I am a true-blue entrepreneur.

I have always had a business of sorts. As a teen I had a paper route. I sold leather goods, I was a dog trainer, waitress, ESL teacher and network marketer. I was an editor and freelance writer. I was a contrarian. I didn't like getting a regular pay cheque. I liked being paid for what I contributed. I never was one to sit back and accept status quo. I looked to ways to improve any situation I was in.

In spite of my dubious work background I learned a lot in every situation. Most of all, I learned I had to be my own boss. My days as a waitress brought me out of my shell. My writing ability developed when I was editor for a health publication. As a freelancer I was assigned to write profiles of people who were experts in their respective fields. I learnt to find the exciting story in what they do.

It was exciting talking with these successful people. I would often suggest publications that I felt would be interested in their story. Many times they were surprised that a magazine or newspaper might be interested in them. They would usually come back and tell me they had no idea how to get published. They would ask me to do it for them. My Dream Career became a natural evolution of events.

If I was doing it informally I thought why not go to college and get a diploma in public relations (PR). I did just that and, upon graduation, began doing contract work with not-for-profit organizations.

At thirty-six I defended my thesis, "How we might get renewable energy in Ontario." At the end, though, I felt empty and burnt out. I was really staying at the not-for-profit sector so I could keep going to school. I always thought that I was going to become a professor because learning had become a prime motivator for me. Reaching my potential through academia was a logical way to proceed now that I loved learning. But it was not what I had imagined.

I spiraled into a six-month depression. Every day during that period, I woke up and asked myself, "What do I really want to do?" I didn't believe I was worthy of doing what I truly wanted. I reflected back on a lady I once interviewed as a journalist. She had a passion for black history in Ontario. I was envious of her. She was doing something she loved. I wondered if I'd ever have that but I didn't really believe I deserved it. I had hit a wall.

During this period of my life, I was barely able to eke out my writing for the few not-for-profit groups I worked for. The only saving grace that got me through that period was the time that I spent with a dog trainer on weekends. We took our dogs for long walks and as I accompanied him he would point out the different aspects of dog behavior and talked about distinctions that many other trainers did not make. I realized that I was talking to an expert in his field.

The publicist in me screamed to get his story out to the world. I got him a two-page spread in the *Toronto Sun*. Within a week he had received 350 phone calls and e-mails. Working for not-for-profits made me feel good about contributing to the world but it was an intangible. When I had this profound effect on one person I could see the difference I was making on somebody's life and how that helped many people. It was measurable, more personal and it had a greater effect on me. I essentially got him thousands of dollars of free publicity and helped catalyze his business. It felt good because that meant more animals would be helped.

I decided I was going to start a company where I would work for experts. Helping other specialists in varied fields excited me. That way I could help people truly solve their problems by letting them know about the experts around them.

I was in transition and needed help. Who should I turn to? An expert, of course. If I was going to take the big leap as an entrepreneur I needed a business coach. I contracted Paul Tindall. He taught me how to systemize my business. Before I met him I spent a lot of time with people who had no intention of becoming clients. He taught me how to quickly qualify people as to whether or not they were a real prospect. After that my business took off.

I made it a habit to only hire experts when I wanted to learn something. I may have paid a little more up front but it greatly reduced my learning time and time is money. Experts show me what the mind of humans is capable of doing. Learning is a core value for me and being around these kinds of people has motivated me to excel at what I do. I am amazed by what people can learn to do in their life. It's not enough to learn something. **Applied knowledge** is what separates the people who truly know from those who only say they know something.

To best represent my clients to the media I have to know their material well. By asking pointed questions, I become a mini-expert in their field. It's my university of real life. I'm the expert's expert in media relations. I unleash their expertise and help them communicate that to others. They, in turn, are able to bring their expertise to more people who need it. Spreading their message gives me great satisfaction. As a bonus, by surrounding myself with excellence, I can't help but become excellent myself. I will put in twelve to sixteen-hour days if necessary. I jump out of bed ready to go. Most of the time it's not really work. I would still do it even if I didn't get paid.

I hired a friend of mine to come up with a company name. She suggested, *Unleash PR*. At first I didn't like it. She said I could get the phone number, 416-UNLEASH. The double meaning of unleash was completely unintentional on her part. She knew nothing about my dogs and the whole time I was unconscious to the name's reference to dogs! When I appreciated that part, I realized it all fit so well. I was unleashing people to display their expertise to the world. By doing that I was unleashing myself. And ever since my dog returned from his training he heeds my call without a leash. It was a mystical fit. The name was a perfect metaphor for my life.

I loved *what* I was doing. I have confronted my shyness and today I have no problem walking up to a few people in a crowded room, introducing myself and asking them what they do. My passion for learning and my interest in other people motivated me to overcome my biggest obstacle – me.

Living through that tragedy of my youth made me appreciate the limited time we have to live our lives here on earth. By expressing my true self in doing what I love I am able to give a little something back to others. I am truly grateful for that.

Dr. Gerstein's Comments

It's always darkest before the dawn.

Jennifer was leading a self-admitted aimless life when tragedy struck. It shook her to her core. Riddled with guilt, she could have gone one of two ways. She could have spiraled into a world of self-pity and remorse or, she could attempt to do something with her life. She chose the latter. In doing so, she was able to find a purpose for living. She hit many bumps along the way, including some major depressive episodes, but she did not give up. In the end she was able to find her way through her pain.

You do not have to personally experience a major catastrophe to turn your life around. That is one of the reasons the people in this book want to share their stories – so you can learn key lessons without having to make the same mistakes. Heed the words of American journalist and TV host Sam Levenson, who once said, "You must learn from the mistakes of others. You can't possibly live long enough to make them all yourself."

If you feel that you are heading in the wrong direction or, even worse, wandering aimlessly throughout your life, use this opportunity now to change. Commit to begin your search for something meaningful. If you have experienced a tragedy in your life, it does not mean your life is no longer worthwhile. Your healing may begin when you begin giving something back. And you can give a lot more when you are giving from your heart, from your true self.

Myth-Diagnosis #4
Diploma Deficiency Disorder

✦

How *You* Can Bust This Myth

Do you feel that you weren't smart enough to do what you love? How long have you been carrying around that misconception? Who gave that one to you? Perhaps it was a family member or a misdirected teacher. Was it due to a failure or two? Because, as you will learn in Chapter Six, failing is a necessity in any success. Perhaps you didn't do very well because you were doing something outside of your true interest. Or it could have been that the way you were taught is different than the way you learn best.

Begin to consider that myth as merely a story that you or someone else contrived. It isn't true just because someone said so. Even more to the point, it isn't true just because you said it is.

Think of examples where you succeeded at something. How did you do it? List your unique talents. Again, do not restrict your list to career based skills. If you socialize easily at parties put that down. If you have a knack for getting great bargains, include it.

The standard IQ test is no longer the gold standard for measuring intelligence. Howard Gardner, a psychologist based at Harvard University, is one of the main principles who is responsible for a paradigm shift in how educators look at intelligence. In his classic work *Frames of Mind. The theory of multiple intelligences,* he outlines seven different types of intelligence: Visual/Spatial Intelligence, Musical Intelligence, Verbal/Linguistic Intelligence, Logical/Mathematical Intelligence, Interpersonal Intelligence, Intra personal Intelligence, Bodily/Kinesthetic Intelligence. He recently added an eighth, Naturalistic intelligence. The old IQ test is outdated and only applies to a few of the many intelligences abound.

Very few if any one is "smart" in all areas. Do not worry about what you are not good at. Begin to look at your strengths – this is where you will find your own Dream Career.

Myth – Diagnosis #5
Condition: Status Quo
"I can't do that. It's not me."

"What lies behind us and what lies before us are tiny matters compared to what lies within us."

Ralph Waldo Emerson

Cathleen Fillmore
Author, Speaker and Speaker's Bureau Owner

"I owe my life to books. I almost died discovering that."

I owe my life to books. Books have gotten me through so many hardships. Writing made me happy; it was a talent and my passion. And then I forgot. I forgot my talent, and my passion, and I forgot what made me happy as I abdicated my rights and interests in favour of trying to make others happy. Fortunately, I finally realized no one can make anyone else happy until they are happy with themselves. It was a tad late but I remembered.

I was born in New Brunswick and went to boarding school with my siblings. By the time I was five I could read and write. I could lose myself in fiction, and won prizes for my writing and poetry. In grade three I won a prize for a poem I had composed, and my music teacher used it as lyrics for a song. Then one day in grade four, my English teacher ridiculed my punctuation in front of the class. I was nine years old. I was deeply wounded, and so devastated I vowed I wouldn't write again.

My teacher's actions may not have had such an impact on me had I received any **encouragement** for my writing at home. But, alas, my parents showed no interest. That hurt too, and I didn't write again for years. At high school in Halifax, no one I knew wrote. The jocks I dated didn't even read. I foolishly allowed that one comment to deter me from writing for ten years!

But I had always expressed myself through my writing, and missed it so much. Then I moved to Toronto, and made a new start in a new city. It was the 1960s, the age of Aquarius. *The Beatles* were a household name, the sexual revolution was going strong and I felt free enough to write poetry. Slowly, I began to write again. It was all coming together for me.

I was working as a secretary, so to upgrade my standard of living I began volunteering as a teacher. I became an ESL (English as a Second Language) teacher, which made me feel good about myself, and initially elevated my self-esteem. Then, with some encouragement from the school board and a friend, I got my Bachelor of Arts degree. It took me twenty years. I was forty when I graduated, but I did it, and I was proud of it.

It was a brief euphoric feeling. The Toronto Board of Education insisted I teach by the book. That crushed any creativity and individuality I had, and sapped me of my energy for teaching. Board officials checked up on me and lectured me on the proper way of doing things. I never felt valued by them. They didn't appreciate me, and that mirrored my family experience. I felt exhausted to the point I had little energy left for writing. I really feel that this contributed to my becoming ill.

I had yet to recognize my worth. I found myself in one abusive relationship after the other, which simply reflected my own self-image. My financial situation was so bad in one relationship that rats cohabited with us. I had just had my second child and we had to close the kitchen door at night to prevent the rats from crawling on us while we slept.

Through all of it though, I always believed my situation would change. That belief allowed me to see possibilities that third generation poverty-stricken people never see. I wish I could tell them that secret. **Believing in something is crucial to the results you get in life.**

As an example of my poor self-image, I married a Honduran

refugee so he could get his papers and avoid deportation. Once again, I abdicated my own happiness and rights to others. It was just another abusive relationship. Soon I began feeling abdominal pains, and this went on for months. I was worried it might be an ovarian cyst or worse, but whenever I shared my concerns with my husband he would just disregard them as hysterical. He said it was nonsense and I was only telling him to upset him. And that was that. I had such low self-esteem I was actually foolish enough to believe him. So I ignored it for a couple of years, but the pain got worse, and I began losing weight and getting weaker.

I went to a counselor who told me to draw my life situation. I drew a person in the water with a hand on her head, but the head kept on bobbing back up. Someone was pushing it down but couldn't keep her down forever. That's what it felt like for me.

I had many special gifts, and what had **made me sick at work and in my relationships was not being valued**. There is nothing worse than effectively telling someone, "We don't want your gifts. We don't need you. Just give us what we want. You're a burden." However, I had to take some responsibility too. **I didn't value my gifts, so how could I expect others to?**

I suffered such abuse that I concluded all men were jerks. After a while I began to realize that was too harsh a generalization. All men aren't jerks – I was just attracting jerks. Then I had one of those "Ah-ha!" moments. I had to admit that if I was attracting jerks, there must be a jerk in me. My husband was merely expressing my inner image of myself. I believe that many women in abusive relationships are strong, but they have given up that strength to someone they believe is stronger than them. It's almost as if they couldn't handle their strength, and so abdicated it to a man. When my self-image changed my outer world changed too.

I sold my house and separated from my husband, who was ultimately deported back to Honduras. He later asked me for more money so he could return, but I wasn't about to give him any more. Eventually he made it back to Canada. I was in the washroom when immigration officials called to ask me to be responsible for him again. I was so glad I couldn't answer the phone. I didn't want to be the one to refuse his entry, because his living conditions in Honduras really were terrible. Despite the years of abuse, I still had compassion for his situation. The difference now was that my growing inner strength would no longer permit me to live with such a man.

I moved to an apartment and committed to begin taking care of myself for a change. I went to see my doctor for a full check-up, and that's when they found it. **I was diagnosed with ovarian cancer at age fifty. That was my wake up call.**

I realized there were two paths I could take. One path was inertia, disability and death. If I kept doing what I was doing, that was the inevitable outcome for me. My children were now twenty and twenty-four, and I envisioned them at my funeral. I was heartbroken at the legacy I would be leaving them. My whole life had been a combination of tragedies manifested by my own negative self-image, and I wanted to leave them so much more. I wanted them to believe they could be happy and enjoy life, and really express themselves. The other path was uncertain and unclear, but I knew it was my only chance.

Around this time I went to a lady who read tea leaves. When she looked at mine, she saw a woman sitting on the fence, and said: "I see a lot of tears and an early death if you don't realize the abuse going on in your life, and the need to get off the fence." She had no idea how correct she was. I can't say if it was just a good guess or not, **but I sure knew the truth when I heard it.**

After my cancer surgery, I finally quit my job teaching ESL, sold everything and moved back to Nova Scotia. I made a clean break, and it was very symbolic of beginning a new chapter in my life. This brought a sense of exhilaration, and I finally started writing again. It felt liberating to be doing what I had loved as a child. I see my return to writing as a metaphor for my return to health. I was returning to my passion – which is life. It was something that always felt good; it had just taken me a long time to see it.

A funny thing happened though. Writing is a solitary activity, and I found I missed contact with people. I realized I needed to begin a new kind of relationship with people, where I was coming from my strengths, and not my weaknesses. I was finally able to hear my real needs and wants, because for the first time in my life I felt a quiet calmness surround me. I began by becoming more active in the community, and giving speeches to church groups.

I even had the *chutzpah* to begin Nova Scotia's first chapter of *The Canadian Association of Professional Speakers* (CAPS). I was so energized in tapping into my newfound potential that I came across as a little pushy. In the Maritimes where modesty is the rule, it was not well received. After a year I resigned as president, but I feel good knowing that what I started is still running.

I learned several things from that experience. First, I could stand up for myself – I was beginning to value myself more. Second, I was able to leave a situation where I felt I was not being respected, and that took courage.

As a writer, I struggled to make money. I had no clue how to earn money outside an employee's pay cheque. There were times I had no money to pay my next month's rent, and I had more than a few sleepless nights worried sick about it. I felt so weak that one day while writing an article called "Leap of Faith" for a speech I was going to deliver about believing in yourself, I fell asleep. When I awoke I had a revelation. It may or may not have been divine intervention, but I knew then how I was going to make it. I was going to sell a newsletter.

I created the newsletter, and then sold it on-line to professional speakers for $29 annually. That income got me through the three remaining years of my stay in Nova Scotia.

When I returned to Toronto, I soon began earning extra income writing for trade magazines. I wrote a book, and taking all my savings I self-published it. It was an inner success for me, but when the distributor went bankrupt, it became a financial disaster. But it was okay, I don't get depressed when I hit the wall. The wall and I have become well acquainted over the years. I have learned that I am an idea person, I find solutions. When I come up against a block I find something to get me through. **That has made me realize my only security is internal security.** The thing is I can't lose my job; no one can fire me. I can turn on a dime. If one door closes in my face, I will find another door no one knew existed.

I began giving seminars on how to get paid for speaking, and then I opened a speaker's bureau called Speakers Gold. As yet I had no business skills, I was not in the corporate world, and soon found myself in trouble due to lack of experience in a very competitive market.

At this time I met Derrick Sweet, a professional speaker. Derrick always thinks so big, he is relentlessly upbeat, and he believed in me, something I have always needed and longed for. By showing me how to believe in myself, he was pivotal in helping me bring my business back from the brink. I think people need other people more than they need money. As Michael Gerber said in the *E-myth Revisited*, if people just give you money, you will just piss that away too.

Encouragement is a vital commodity so often overlooked. I am now giving to others the encouragement I lacked in my own life. I coach budding authors and professional speakers how to market themselves. In contrast to the stifling, government-regulated environment from years gone by, I am now teaching what I love my way. As an information junkie, I use my many resources to help my clients. I encourage them, and I believe in them. It was what I always needed, and I know it is what they need.

The outer world reflection of my inner world looks better and brighter now. These days, business is thriving, my coaching practice grows daily and my bureau is flourishing.

Dr. Gerstein's Comments

Your outside world will reflect
your inside world.

In my work, I often encounter people who go from one abusive relationship to the next. They lament their fate, citing bad luck as the culprit. What they don't see is their own filter. They use it to filter out all of the kind people that come into their lives. They are left with the abusers and then wonder what happened.

They don't see that their choices merely reflect what is going on inside their head. Many have grown up in abusive situations, and they learned to associate abuse with love. So they surround themselves with people who mirror that, and then try to change them. Their thinking is they can heal old wounds by trying to relive their childhood in the way they would have preferred. As most people discover, it is ten times more difficult to change someone else than it is to change yourself.

When we learn to value ourselves more, we attract people who reflect that back. If we want a life with more purpose and passion, we must first begin by believing we deserve it. Otherwise, we will just keep walking right by the doors with the big "opportunity" signs on them. When we begin to recognize and value our own gifts, others will too.

*"Every achiever that I have ever met says,
'My life turned around when I began to believe in me.'"*

Dr. Robert Schuller

Daniella Santana

Police Officer

*"I was becoming disgruntled as a nurse.
I didn't feel I was doing enough. I wanted to make
a bigger difference in people's lives."*

From a very young age I knew I wanted to be a police officer. But there was one huge problem – I didn't think I could do it. My friends told me I couldn't do it. My colleagues told me I didn't have a chance. Sadly, I believed them all. It took my father's death to toss all those doubts and doubters aside and go for it. If I knew then what I know now, I would have pursued my dream career ten years earlier.

My father had been a nurse in the army. Interestingly enough it was the military influence that affected me more than the medical one. I was always interested in the police profession. I really wanted to pursue it, but never believed I could do it. First of all, I was female and would be entering a male dominated profession. Second, I'm petite, and I just wasn't sure I could handle the physical requirements of the job. I didn't have enough confidence in myself and as a result, I sold myself short. My friends didn't believe I could do it. The list of obstacles went on and on, and eventually I gave up on the idea.

However, I still loved helping people. I am a very positive and happy person, I'm a good listener, and I get along well with most people. I still wanted to contribute, so I decided to go into the nursing profession. If I couldn't be a police officer I would play a part this way.

I graduated from nursing school in 1992. When I had difficulty finding a job, I worked for the Canadian Red Cross. I then went back to school and took the operating room (OR) course. I worked in the OR in London, Ontario, for two years.

At first, every day was very exciting and every case was different. After a while, I found it all started to become routine. I became unhappy, and was soon disgruntled with nursing. I began asking myself questions like, where do I see myself in ten years? Will I be happy? I knew I was making a difference as a nurse but I wasn't happy. **Once I asked the questions the answers started becoming clear.** I knew I simply could not do this for ten more years.

But what would I do? I wanted to be more involved with people. Nursing only allowed me to be a part of their healthcare needs. But I wanted to get involved in the other aspects of people's lives, in fact I longed for this. Making a bigger difference was a very exciting prospect for me. That's when I awoke to my old dream of becoming a police officer.

What if I *could* do it? Did I really have a chance? Questions like these began to bubble up from my subconscious. Yet every time I mentioned my aspirations to my friends and colleagues they would retort immediately with comments like, "You're too small," "You're too nice," or "You could never be a police officer."

All too eager to believe the doubters, I repressed my ambition again and again. I was now thirty-one, and rapidly approaching the point where the other factors would become irrelevant. I would be rejected on age alone. That sudden awareness was enough to start me doubting the doubters. What if they were wrong? What if I *could* get in, despite my size, gender and "nice" personality? But it still took three more years and a catastrophe to push me over the top to take action on my dream.

In 1999 my father died at the tender age of fifty-six. He had worked all his life as a nurse, and was looking forward to retirement. I also knew he had not been happy during the last few years of his career. As I watched him dying, I was very sad. Seeing him die so young and being unhappy and unfulfilled shook me to the bone. I didn't want to end up like that – stuck in a profession that no longer fulfilled me. I wanted to be happy at what I was doing. **I decided I didn't want to regret something I hadn't done; if I was going to regret something, I wanted it to be something I had done.**

I'd always said I was going to make a difference. Why did I continue to believe the doubters? What if I *could* make it, and never tried? It was moving time and I was the one who had to move. I was going to change my life.

It wasn't that easy though. I had a family – a husband and two sons aged nine and fourteen. I had a good job and a good income. To pursue my dream I knew I would have to rock the boat. And rock I did, making waves for everyone concerned.

The following two years were two of the hardest years of my life. While I was still just contemplating changing careers, my husband wasn't supportive at all. He would make comments like, "Policing is not really a profession. What if something happens to you? What will the children do?" But his attempts to manipulate me with guilt were transparent. He wanted me to play the role *he* wanted for me. He wasn't thinking of my wishes, my desires, my dreams, only his own needs.

There was also the financial aspect to consider. As a nurse I made a good income. To make this change, first I would have to go through the application process and then hopefully be hired. Once hired, there was police training, but what if I didn't make it through? And even if I did make it I would be taking a cut in pay. Should I just quit everything and follow my dream? I had no guarantees.

Then a funny thing started to happen. **The more I thought about it, the more my dream began to look like reality.** As I wrote it out, I began imagining the small steps I needed to take. All of a sudden it no longer felt like a big leap, but merely a row of baby steps I could easily maneuver. I went from not believing I had a chance, to questioning those beliefs, to finally being confident I could do it. In the end I believed that nothing would stop me from becoming a police officer. It was then I knew I simply had to go for it. I realized policing was what I wanted to do for the rest of my life.

Mentally I knew I would be okay. However, I wasn't so sure about the physical challenges of the job because of my gender and small size, so I began training very hard.

After training for about a year, I finally applied. After six months of interviews, physicals, testing and profiling, I was accepted on my first try in December 2000.

Cadet training followed, and for this I was required to stay at the police college five days a week. I had weekends off, so I was able to pick up a few nursing shifts to supplement my income.

This was very difficult for my family. I was away all week, and on weekends I was doing homework, working nursing shifts, or sleeping. My family began saying I didn't love them anymore. I realized a lot of that stemmed from my husband's negative attitude in a further attempt to make me feel guilty. My friends couldn't understand why I had stopped calling. My wallet was thinning. I felt like I was being squeezed from all sides. Something had to give or I was going to break.

What broke instead was my marriage, and my husband and I went our separate ways. He was unable to see me as a separate entity with my own aspirations and dreams. He only saw me as an extension of himself, and how I could help him and the family. I could no longer accept or live with his unsupportive behaviour. For years I had given so much, and it was just time I took something for myself. This transition also cost me some girlfriends who couldn't see themselves out of the role of dutiful housewife, and therefore could not accept or relate to me that way.

It also had a big impact on my children. At first they were confused as to why their mother was changing careers, and naturally, they were worried about the inherent dangers of my new job. I told them that if anything ever happened to me it was my choice, but I definitely felt guilty for following my dreams.

My oldest son, who is now seventeen, understands the value of pursuing your dreams. I know he is now very proud of me. It was tougher on the little guy, but now at twelve he just thinks it is the coolest thing. Both my boys now have a strong role model in someone who had the courage to follow her dream. I really believe this is worth more than all the encouraging talk I could ever throw at them. They know I'm happy, and they're happy for me.

When I began, I was no longer young relative to the other trainees. I trained with about four hundred and sixty cadets, most between the ages of twenty and twenty-five. I was already thirty-one. That made the challenge that much harder, but I knew I could do it because I wanted it so much.

I was determined to do it. Whenever a hint of doubt crept into my thoughts I would look around at more veteran police officers and say to myself, "If they went through it I know I can do it too. Once this training is all over I will be happier. When I am happier I will live longer." And that is how I became a policewoman.

It is not always easy. As police officers, sometimes the people we help vent at us. They criticize and express themselves loudly when they disagree with our decisions. I then have to go home and deal with those ill feelings. While everyone else is safely at home sleeping, I'm out there cruising around through alleyways, watching their backyards, and sometimes chasing people. People have no idea how much we do. They want to feel safe, but don't always want to know the gory details of what we deal with. That's my job.

Even with all these obstacles, I love my job. **Knowing I am making a difference puts a smile on my face.** When I go to work I think, "Oh my God, I'm going to work." I really think if you love your job, you never have to work another day in your life. I work ten hours a day and I love it. That's not to say I'm not sometimes exhausted at the end of a shift. Many days I'm just going from one call to the next, and it all happens so fast. When I sit down at the end of the day and review my activity log, I can't believe what I did in one day.

If I were to do it all over again I would do the same thing, except this time I would do it ten years earlier. I wish other people, even strangers, had told me I could change careers because they did it. I needed to have heard their stories. I needed encouragement. I needed people to tell me I could do it, with or without the support of my husband. What I got were people stepping on my dreams, and not a scrap of support from family or friends. It took the tragedy of losing my father to shake me loose from my own chains.

From all this I learned an invaluable lesson: Always follow your heart, and if you want it with all of your heart, then *just go for it*.

I wouldn't change a thing. I would put myself through the pain of every broken rib I suffered in training – again. I would endure the emotional heartbreak of my family breakup. There were months when I couldn't go to the movies or buy a new shirt, but I would go through all that financial hardship again. It all made me a wiser, more empathetic person. It made me who I am today – a very understanding, warm and caring police officer.

Following my dream wasn't easy but it was absolutely worth it. I now know I won't die wondering if I could have followed my dream. I did it.

Dr. Gerstein's Comments

Follow your Dream for your children's sake if not for yourself

Daniella's story is a perfect example of what I discuss in my seminars. The best gift we can give our children is to be their role model.

Daniella told me her children didn't at first understand why she was rocking the boat. Of course, at that time they were still heavily influenced by their father. This was very tough on her, yet she stuck to it and finally got into her dream career. Her children eventually learned the whole truth, and grew to appreciate what their mother had done.

By example, Daniella has demonstrated to her children what they can accomplish if they commit to their dreams. Anyone can give lip service to any topic – that's easy. That's why on Monday morning there are so many armchair quarterbacks who all would have done it differently during Sunday's game. Very few people actually get out of their comfort zone, to make their dreams real. Few have the courage to do it. Few have the backbone and strength of conviction to question the limiting dogma so pervasive in their world. So they watch and envy, and then bemoan the fact that they hate their job. They even have the nerve to call those who work hard to pursue their dream careers "lucky." We can learn from the renowned Roman philosopher and politician, Seneca (5 BC - 65 AD) who once said, *Luck is what happens when preparation meets opportunity.*

It takes work to pursue your dream, but it takes more emotional work to *not* go for it, and settle for less than what you are capable. If you don't have the courage to do it for yourself, then do it for your children. If you don't have children, do it for children in your community, and for your friends' children. They deserve to believe in themselves. What greater gift can you give them?

"To be yourself in a world that is constantly trying to make you something else is the greatest accomplishment."

Ralph Waldo Emerson

Shirley Koch
Gardener

"I went from being my parent's daughter, to my husband's wife and then to my children's mother. I hadn't yet taken the time to find out who I was."

Before I could find my Dream Career I had to find me. I didn't know who I was. All my life I had tried to please other people, and somewhere along the way I had forgotten my own needs. When we moved to the farm, I began to experience loneliness in a way I never had before. I was forced to come to terms with the truth – I didn't know who I was. I became depressed; I cried a lot and felt a huge emptiness deep inside.

One day I read something in my Bible that finally woke me up. It must have been a spiritual message because to this day I have not been able to find the same written passage again.

I grew up on a ten-acre plot of land in a rural community in southwestern Ontario. Mom and dad had their own small gardening business. We raised all our own vegetables and took our produce to market in Kitchener. My mother sold the skimmed milk cheese she made. My father also sold tractors and farm machinery. They did what was needed to raise a family, and I was expected to garden and pull my share of the load. It was a family affair.

When I was eight years old, my mom gave me my first package of seeds. I'll never forget it, they were Zinnias.

I loved learning, and I loved school, but after completing grade ten, my parents forced me to leave school. I was crushed because I had always wanted to be a teacher. Back then kids just didn't question what their parents expected of them. I was told to leave school, so that's what I had to do. I surely didn't have the self-confidence to challenge them.

I went to business school for six months, and then two weeks shy of my sixteenth birthday I began work at my first job in an office. I earned forty dollars a week as a secretary, about the going rate in 1962. I worked there for the next five years while I still lived at home.

Back in high school, I had met a boy named Allan. I like to say I chased him for six years before he turned around and caught me. By the time we married he was a teacher, and we were able to move into a home in New Hamburg with a handkerchief backyard. He dug that up so we could have a vegetable garden. It wasn't long before we were blessed with our first child and by the time he was four he had three siblings. We were busy making and caring for babies, while tending to our other love, our garden. We grew lettuce, onions, strawberries, peas, corn and beans. We did our own preserving and canning, and it felt good to be able to provide for my family.

We soon bought a five-acre property where I could have a huge garden in my front yard. We raised pigs for meat, hens for eggs, fresh fruit and vegetables. Seeing my fruit cellar in the fall was like looking at a rich colour picture of autumn leaves with the oranges of peaches, the reds of tomatoes and the greens of pickles and beans.

After ten years of teaching, Allan decided he wanted to farm full time. Naturally, I just agreed, and in 1973 we moved to a farm. This move was important to Allan, so I went, although it wasn't my dream. But I was still living unconsciously, and that fact eluded me back then.

Farms are relatively isolated, so while living on a farm with four kids was not quiet, it got pretty lonely for me. For the first time in my life, I was able to think about who I was and where I fit. I discovered just how lonely, lonely could be. I was so sad. Up until that point I hadn't given much thought about what I wanted or needed. The Legalistic Church taught me that if I did the right things, I would be okay. But I was doing the right things. I was a good obedient daughter, a dutiful wife and a caring mother. And I wasn't okay. I wasn't happy. The fact is I was often depressed.

In my life so far I had gone from being my parent's daughter, to my husband's wife and then to my children's mother. I hadn't taken the time to find out who I was. Having always identified myself with someone else, I didn't have much self-worth. It took a spiritual moment to wake me from this life-long slumber.

That moment came one day while I was reading my Bible. Having grown up in the ways of the Church I had always read my Bible, but I had never consciously used specific passages in my personal life. On this day, when I opened it up, out of the depths of my crying heart I suddenly found the peace I sought. In that moment, my heart told me how to make the Bible meaningful to me. In the beginning of my Bible were listed four steps:

1. Recognize your sinful nature.
2. Ask for forgiveness.
3. Recognize that Christ took over the burdens of imperfect people and gave them eternal life.
4. Walk into the awareness of who He is.

I had read that passage before but on this particular day it was as if I was reading it for the first time. Awareness came to me in a flash. For the first time I recognized who God was and what He did – He made me someone special and has a plan for my life. I realized that I DIDN'T HAVE TO DO ANYTHING TO BE SPECIAL. I was special by just being. I didn't have to be the perfect mom or wife or daughter. It was okay to be me. It took about a year for that message to sink in, but when it did, it was freeing.

The initial awareness happened quickly but the depth of the message ripened slowly. Afterward, whenever I found myself in a circumstance where I didn't feel valued, I would go to a safe place deep within myself to get the affirmation from Him. I would remind myself of His love for me, and that He has good plans for me. I would return to my life with peace in my heart.

I found meaning when I realized I could still love being a stay-at-home mom *and* could take the time to discover who I was. I started taking personal growth courses and reading other people's inspirational life stories. I noticed that gardening let me experience the beauty of creation and allowed my creativity to emerge. I found it interesting and ironic that such pleasure could be derived from something I had been forced to do as a child.

In the meantime everyone on the farm had a job to do. I picked up eggs from our 10,000 chickens. Over the next ten years I also worked other jobs to earn extra money for the household, including a stint in an interior decorator store and a bakery where I baked donuts. My spiritual awakening allowed me to enjoy all of these activities but I would feel even more fulfilled if I could find a way to earn income from my true passion – gardening.

Then one day I had an idea. I love people and I love plants, so gathering my courage, I approached a nursery owner near our farm and said, "Don, I'd like to supply your nursery with perennials from the garden on our farm." It was a big step for me. My newfound confidence pushed me in a direction hitherto unknown. To my delight, he agreed, and I ended up working at his nursery for seven years. It was a great job because I was dealing with people in an area I loved. I could only imagine one thing that could top it – going into business myself and working from my own home. That would certainly be a dream-come-true.

From my thoughts to God's ears – Don was retiring and he sold the nursery. To my surprise, the new owners no longer needed my services. By that time, both my faith in God and my personal confidence had grown strong, so I was more frustrated than concerned about my future. I practically ran that nursery – how could the new owners not realize they needed me? Being let go may have been the gentle kick I needed to get me out on my own, just another move in God's plan for my life.

Around this time, Wayne, one of Don's suppliers, had applied for a zoning variance that would allow him to set up a retail establishment on his property. Government officials were being difficult saying he needed six more feet of space from his greenhouse to the river. After thousands of dollars in legal and rezoning application fees, he gave up.

On one of my buying visits Wayne told me about all the trouble he was having with the zoning bylaws, and asked if my boss might be interested in buying his operation. I told him Don was actually retiring, and had already sold his nursery. Then Wayne asked me if I might be interested. "Of course," I replied, "But I don't have any money." I couldn't even consider it.

As the months went by, the question tugged on my thoughts. There had to be an answer, I could feel it. I was so close to fulfilling my dream. Around Christmas I called Wayne and asked if his business was still for sale. When he said it was, I told him I was interested, but reiterated that I had no money. And then Wayne came up with a remarkable proposal, and made me an offer I couldn't refuse. He offered to sell me 7,500 potted plants in one and two gallon containers for a very fair price. He accepted a low down payment, and a promissory note for the balance – at no interest! I almost fell down in disbelief. I instantly realized the opportunity I had been waiting for was being handed to me on a golden platter. I grabbed it.

I believe this opportunity was God opening doors and giving me an opportunity to do what I loved right from my home, and to make other people happy by helping them find the right plants and flowers for them.

Now I am fully involved in my business. I grow and sell my plants from our farm, and I'm involved with various gardening groups. I also give presentations to fellow plant lovers. In that capacity, I have become what I always wanted to be, but never thought I could be because I was forced to leave school. After all this time, I have become a teacher.

It all started one lonely day on our farm. With God's help I began believing in me. What's strange, is when I go back to my Bible, I can no longer find those four steps printed as such. They are there in verse, but not as steps. That day, thirty years ago, I read those four steps just as clearly as I read the daily newspaper. I believe I was able to read it then, because I was ready to receive the message. As stated in Jeremiah 29:11: *For I know the plans I have for you, says the Lord. They are plans for good and not for evil, to give you a future and a hope.* For me that means I pray as if it was up to God and work as if it was up to me.

Dr. Gerstein's Comments

Believing is seeing

Shirley found her gift of gardening at an early age. But, like so many things in life, she was not able to appreciate it until she began to believe in her own self-worth. For Shirley it was religion that helped her to believe in herself. For others it may be a mentor, a book, a historical figure or a life-changing event. I have found that the source of this belief in oneself is not as important as the belief itself.

I have worked with people who told me they couldn't even begin discovering their Dream Career because they didn't believe they were worthy of even having one! They had grown up believing mistruths. I then spend a great deal of time working with the client to dispel these myths before they can move on to their dream. First they have to believe that they deserve to have something good in their life before they can manifest that belief. As stated in the title of one of Dr. Wayne Dyer's books, *You'll See It When You Believe It.*

Once Shirley began believing in herself her eyes were opened to all of the gifts around her. She was able to see opportunities that might have previously been overlooked.

"To dare is to lose one's footing momentarily.
To not dare is to lose oneself."

Soren Kierkegaard

Brenda Barnes
Owner, Operator and Principal of
Martingrove Montessori School

"My power was unleashed when I divorced my first husband."

When I was a little girl, I often played teacher. My parents owned a bakeshop, and on Saturdays I would go with them to help out and earn my ten cents. After spending it I would go to the basement of the shop and pretend the sacks of flour stored there were my five and six-year-old pupils. I then proceeded to teach them various subjects. My brother would kid me and say my parents had three kinds of flour – white, whole wheat and smart.

My mother always told me I could do whatever I wanted in life, but I didn't have the same faith in myself until many years had passed. She would later be there for me in the darkest hour of my dream.

As a teenager, I really had no direction, so when I left high school I just went out and found a job. When I was twenty-one I enrolled in university as a mature student, but left after two years. Then I got married, had children and became a full-time mom. I had a wonderful time playing with and teaching my kids, but I was on a boat without a rudder, going wherever the wind blew me. Then one day I saw something that changed the direction of my life.

I was out walking my son in his stroller when I came upon a big beautiful old church. There was an archway leading to the side entrance, and I remember it as a magical little path. I walked down the path through the archway, under a large tree and arrived at a door displaying the sign: "Welcome to Hamilton Montessori School." I had never heard of it, so I opened the door and was awestruck by what I saw. The sun streamed through the stained glass windows and lit up the classroom. It was a magical moment for me. I didn't know anything about the school but I'll never forget the incredible connectedness I felt for the place. **Something just clicked inside me.** I enrolled my children there immediately. When I was ready to make more definitive choices in my life I would remember that moment.

In the meantime, my marriage was not going well. I had always been independent and my young husband was trying to stifle that. Our small children were just two and five, I was a full-time mom and once in a while I needed a break. To get away for a bit, I signed up for a local baking course that involved attending class one evening a week. I just wanted one evening a week for myself. In the second week, my husband had the audacity to call me at the class and demand I come home because he couldn't get the baby to stop crying. This is a man who went out to play hockey three evenings a week. He was holding me back. He didn't support me in any of my ventures. He wanted total control.

It was a turning point for me, and I made the decision to end the marriage.

Divorcing him unleashed my natural self and allowed me the freedom to pursue my own dreams. I had thought about it for quite some time, but fear of the unknown had stopped me from doing anything sooner. The hardest part was dealing with my fears around money. How would I support myself? I would be a single mom and I had no support from family. What if I couldn't make it on my own?

My ex-husband fought it hard and refused to allow us to remain in the family home. The divorce did provide me with a financial settlement and good child support payments. I picked up and moved with the children to Toronto to start over, and there my life began to fall into place. Interestingly enough, almost as soon as we moved out another woman moved into what had been our family home. It seemed that all his issues around controlling me had stemmed from his own infidelity and negative behaviors.

It's ironic. In the time of my greatest worry, I found my strength. For the first time in my life I began developing the same faith in myself that my mother always had in me.

Recalling that magical feeling I had at the Hamilton Montessori School, I made up my mind to work at one in Toronto. At that time you needed a university degree to do the teacher training. During my interview I said to the founder of the Montessori school, "You're telling me I have to go back to school for a year. What if you don't accept me after I earn my degree?" She calmly remarked with a patronizing tone, "Well isn't it lovely dear? You'd have finished something that you started." Begrudgingly I concurred.

I took a year off work, went back to university and finished my BA When I was done, I applied and was accepted into the Montessori school teacher training program. It was very intensive. There were no textbooks. As trainees we wrote and illustrated our own books. I learned by doing and using all my senses, and they were modeling their teaching philosophy to us. During this time I met a wonderful man and began a new, long-term relationship. It turned out to be everything my marriage was not, and eventually we married.

Once I finished the year-long program, I began work immediately teaching three-to-six-year-olds. It took me a couple of years to feel comfortable, but I loved it. For the next seven years I taught, never staying at one Montessori school for more than two years.

I grew weary of all of the rules I had to work under. It felt confining, and I wished the administration would be more flexible. The business of running the school was something I never really had a full appreciation for. Because it was a private school, sometimes there was favouritism. If I came down hard on a particular child, I would be reprimanded for no other reason than her parents' influence on the owners. The bosses I worked for took away the fun of day-to-day teaching. I soon realized I wanted to work for myself and make my own rules.

Around that time I heard that the Second Cup™ coffee shop

franchise was placing a cappuccino café on campus at the University of Toronto as a pilot project. It was the break I needed from teaching. I applied for the managerial position, and during the interview told them I was the right person for the job. I was very confident, and I guess they liked that, so they hired me. **I was creating something new and nurturing it.**

The Second Cup™ experience made me realize that I loved to create and make things happen. I realized what I really wanted was to start my own Montessori school. It would be a significant challenge financially. For the first year, I would have no income; we would have only my second husband's income as a carpenter to support us.

In spite of everything, I had a vision of what my new school would look like. **For six months prior to the opening I took a half hour every day to envision every detail of my new school**: How the rooms were going to look; the furniture I would have; how I would develop the back garden.

Visualization was a powerful tool for me, but I had difficulty getting people to understand my vision. I found some space to rent in a church, and had open houses even before I had painted the place. But people didn't see what I saw. So I borrowed materials from other Montessori schools I had worked for to exemplify the kind of things we would have in the classroom. They still didn't get it. I knew exactly what it would look like, and I just needed one person to buy into it so I could demonstrate my vision into reality.

My newfound faith in myself spurred me on. With no income, I borrowed $15,000 from my parents and gave my word I would pay it back. With that, I renovated the one room and ordered all the materials for the school. When I was done, it looked just the way I had envisioned it.

When I first began marketing I got a call from a woman at an advertising company offering to put my ad on grocery carts. She told me it would reach all the mothers I wanted to reach, and there was only one space left. I believed her, and signed on for six months. After three months, I hadn't received even one call. I wanted to cancel but I was told there was a no cancellation clause until the contract expired. From this I learned to be less gullible in future contracts.

My own marketing campaign involved biannual advertising in the local community newspaper and holding open houses twice a year to introduce the school to families in the neighbourhood. Ultimately those two strategies were a lot more effective than the one I paid a professional to do. Most of my growth has been through word of mouth.

I had started advertising my school a few months before I left Second Cup™, but it was now the end of August on the cusp of my first school opening, and I still had no enrollments. I was afraid I was going to fail. I had put up flyers all over the neighbourhood and had advertised the new school locally. During this period my mother had been diagnosed with cancer, and my father suffered a stroke while visiting her in the hospital. Even though I still had no enrollments, I felt an obligation to be at the school for any potential inquiries. So much was happening at the same time. Sometimes it felt as if I was losing it, yet I was determined to carry on with my dream.

One day I sat in the church crying with my head in my lap. I thought I had made the biggest mistake in my life. I asked myself, "What if this doesn't fly? What if no one shows up?" "How am I going to pay the loan back to my parents?"

At that very moment I heard a car pull up and the door close. In through the school door walked a woman who enrolled her child into my school on the spot. She was the first. It was too much of a coincidence. **At my most despairing moment I met with opportunity.** I told her there were no other children in the school yet. But *she reassured me* they would come. She was a Godsend. A week later a Taiwanese family who had just immigrated to Canada enrolled their two children. For the first half year, that was the total school body – two children who spoke no English and a little girl. Three children – three glorious children.

I did not set a deadline for the school to be successful. There was no minimum quota needed to avoid packing up and leaving. I would use sheer will and determination to make this thing fly. Even though I was afraid of failure, I wasn't going to let it beat me. I used that fear to motivate me to go forward. **I was sure I would have children in that classroom before Christmas.** It was going to happen. I would make it happen. Then, at Christmas two other children joined the group. I was running the school by myself five mornings a week. In the afternoon I would go out into the neighbourhood and drop off more advertising flyers.

By the following September we were up to eight children.

Because we were licensed under the auspices of social services, our mandate was a maximum ratio of one teacher to eight children. I now had to hire an assistant, and synchronicity knocked again. A good friend of ours had a friend who would be perfect. I hired her, and she has been with me ever since.

I was now teaching preschool during the day as well as handling all the administrative duties. Always looking for a new challenge in the school, I added an elementary program to the curriculum. Then I had to train to teach that course in the evenings. It wasn't easy to juggle all my roles, but then again I had gone through more difficult times before, and it seemed to give me the strength to face this challenge. Eventually I hired an assistant to handle the dreaded daily administrative duties, and that freed me to have fun doing everything else.

I now know I can do whatever I want. My mom knew it all along; it just took me a few years to catch on. Thank you mom for having faith in me.

Dr. Gerstein's Comments

Don't be afraid of the dark –
it may be holding your key to your dreams

Mulla Nasruddin was a Middle Eastern Sufi visionary who lived during the thirteenth century. He tells a story of a man who is looking for his keys outside his house. Another man walks by and seeing this man on his hands and knees, asks if he is looking for something.

The first man replies, "My keys."

The second man asks, "Where was the last place you had them?"

"In my house." was the reply.

Bewildered, the second man inquires, "Then why are you looking for them out here?" The first man looks up and says matter-of-factly, "Because the light is better outside my house!"

So many people are afraid of the dark – literally and figuratively. They are so afraid of the unknown they remain stuck in a poor situation just because it is familiar. They would rather stay in the comfort of the light, and let the answers remain hidden. They say "the devil you do know is better than the devil you don't." I think the devil himself made that up, because it is a complete lie. Many people who want you to stay in a bad situation have a vested interest in your staying.

Over the years, in the ER, I have treated the injuries of many battered women. They usually come up with a multitude of reasons to go back to their abuser, even though I supply them with immediate resources if they chose to leave.

Brenda was not in that bad a situation yet she endured this controlling husband because she feared leaving. Those fears turned out to be a bogeyman. They did not exist in reality, only in her mind. Soon after her divorce she unleashed her true self.

Dr. Gerstein's Comments

She discovered her real power and began having the same faith in herself as her mother always had. She had a dream, set a goal, visualized it and made it happen. She was in her power. The real Brenda was hiding for many years. Her greatest fear – being on her own – turned out to be her greatest strength.

Twice in her life Brenda summoned up the tremendous courage to walk into the dark unknown. Both times she was rewarded for her strength. The first time, she divorced her first husband. The second time, she persisted in taking the bold steps to open her new school while everything around her was falling apart. Some people might have completely given up at either point. But not Brenda. She had faith in herself, and in her dream. She was there for her parents when they were sick, she continued to advertise the school despite zero enrollments and she maintained her daily practice of visualizing her dream. Just when she was at her lowest, crying in an empty decorated school, her first student pulled up to the front door with her mother.

People aren't broken. If they are unsatisfied with their lives it is because they have not yet found the right fit. That could mean the right career, the right mate, the right friends or the right environment. If and when they finally tap into their strength, watch out. It will be like striking oil. They will overflow with powerful energy and focus.

To get to your strength you may have to first walk through the dark. Don't be afraid of the dark. You really have nothing to fear but the fear itself. In fact, the answer to your yearnings may actually be in the dark. Think of the dark as a veil hiding your dreams. Bravely take one step at a time and trust your heart to lead you in the right direction. Let faith and persistence be your guiding lights and just when you begin doubting the direction you are going, that is when you will find your keys.

◇

Dr. Gerstein's Comments

What fears are you allowing to hold you back? What small step can you take in the direction of the unknown? You will not likely find the keys by searching where the light is best.

"Keep away from people who try to belittle your ambitions. Small people always do that, but the really great make you feel that you too can become great."

Mark Twain

Judy Suke
Motivational Humorist

"If you love someone, you don't ask them to give up their passion in life. That's what my husband asked me to do."

I grew up in a house full of laughter. I loved to laugh, and I loved to watch people who made others laugh. I really wanted to pattern my own life that way. Then I took a long detour. Looking back, I wonder why I had to go through all the hardships I endured. The joke was on me.

As a kid I had three role models – Lucille Ball, Carol Burnett and Red Skelton. I wanted to be just like them. If you asked my mother when I started giving speeches, she would say from the time I was five years old I would tell a story if more than four people walked into a room. As a child, I won several speaking contests.

My mother raised us in financial poverty, but spiritual abundance. We didn't have a lot but we always had laughter in our house. My mother is an incredible woman with lots of energy to spare. She is one of my mentors, and the greatest gift she gave me was the gift of laughter.

My dad died when I was ten, so along with my two older sisters, I had to start working to help out with the expenses. Not working was not an option. I began working at my aunt's nursing home and continued doing so throughout high school. I would find out what my class covered that day, and then do the homework in the evening. It didn't seem to matter if I showed up for class, as long as I passed the provincial exams at the end of the year.

By example, my mother also showed us the importance of volunteering. From a young age I canvassed for the Heart and Stroke Foundation. I was brought up to give, and that has not changed to this day.

In high school I was a powerhouse, winning beauty pageants, participating in the drama club, becoming yearbook editor and president of the student council. I often came up with ideas and themes for parties, and would be the one to organize baseball games and picnics and other fun events. I was unstoppable but when I graduated, it all changed.

After high school I married a man who sought to control me. For some reason I was complicit in this dubious exercise. Little by little I lost my autonomy, and with it my enthusiasm for life. If you had met me at the end of my first marriage (which lasted nine years) you would have thought I was the quietest, most introverted, unconfident person you ever met. I allowed my husband to change me from my high school persona to the point where if a bank teller looked at me the wrong way, I would cry.

Work wise, I couldn't see how all my leadership and speaking skills from school could be used in a career. I sold myself short both personally and professionally, and didn't set the bar very high. My first job out of high school was with Bell Canada because they had jobs and I needed money. I became a customer service representative.

Bell Canada often spent a fortune sending a group of us to out-of-town training seminars. When we came back, I would be flying high with all the new stuff I had learned. The others generally had trouble incorporating the learning into their work, so Bell often asked me to retrain them. They noticed I was good at training – I had a way of explaining things to people that made it easy to understand.

Bell soon discovered they could save a whole stack of money if they just sent me out of town for training, and then had me train the whole office when I returned. They said I was a natural. It was a funny thing – I just fell into my niche. I had no background in training, but Bell made it a part of my job. When I came to Toronto, I kept doing this work. They had me training sales people, and I was enjoying it.

After nine years I finally managed to extricate myself from my first marriage, and landed in a slightly better one. Despite my second husband's negativity, I gradually built up my confidence. "He allowed me the freedom" to do the volunteer work I so cherished. The very phrase, "*he allowed me...*" indicates my state of mind at the time. It has been a very slow process, but over the years I have learned to *never* put a man in that position of control again.

Around this time I had my fourth baby. At birth he weighed a mere two pounds and had breathing difficulties. I'd had so many miscarriages that I understood just how precarious and precious life can be. Not trusting anyone else to look after him, I decided to leave Bell, and started a day care centre out of my house, which I ran for the next fifteen years.

During this period of my life I didn't want to lose my training skills, so I volunteered at various organizations. I joined Beta Sigma Phi, a women's sorority, which got me into community work. I volunteered for The Canadian Cancer Society and The Heart and Stroke Foundation. It's interesting that the same charitable foundation I enjoyed helping as a kid led me to my human resources job.

In my volunteer work I recruited people, trained them and really got to know them. I encouraged them to better understand and use their unique talents and skills. When they became confident enough in themselves, I trained them for executive positions. Soon people began approaching me to come into their company and do the same for their employees. I was taken aback and thought, Wow, you mean I can get paid to do this? I did earn a small amount for my services in this area. Then, to improve my poise and self-assurance as a public speaker I joined the Toastmasters™ International Speaking Club.

After you complete ten speeches, Toastmasters™ awards you a certificate. The night I was to receive my award, I invited my family to watch. My kids saw how much enthusiasm I had for it and really supported me in my quest to become a professional speaker. And my husband? Well, let's just say he was less than enthused.

After fifteen years of running a day care from our home, I was ready to return to the corporate world. I had big plans of how I could make it all work, but my husband could only see I was leaving a stable income. He was afraid I wouldn't get a job, and even if I did it would be a secretary at best.

Taking it a step further I told him about my idea of negotiating a contract, which would give me time to develop my speaking career on the side. His response was; "Judy, don't be silly. If you say that to them, they won't hire you." When I told him how important public speaking was to me, he would come back with, "You can't tell people these things." Luckily by this time I believed in myself enough to stick to my original idea.

I applied to be an HR manager because understanding people would help my speaking career. I told the managers that I could give the company 37.5 hours a week for a minimum of five years. In return they needed to allow me to go out and do independent half-day or full day seminars so I could build my professional speaking career. They knew they were getting a great ambassador for their company when I was training because I was always introduced as an HR manager at Dial One Wolfedale Electric Ltd. It was a win-win contract, and they agreed. When I came home with the job, my husband was one of the most surprised people on the face of the earth.

Then in one moment, my life changed. On New Years Eve of 1998 I had a heart attack. I was forty-eight years old. I sure wasn't drinking any champagne that night! Afterwards, I remember lying in a hospital bed feeling frightened and very alone. So I counted my blessings. I had four wonderful children. I had done so much more than I had ever dreamed possible. I decided that if I died that day, I'd be okay with it.

This health crisis made me reassess my priorities in life. I asked myself, "What legacy have I left to the world?" The answer hit me in a flash. **I had brought humour into people's lives.** I recalled the walks I had taken with a neighbour whose husband was dying of cancer. We'd talk and laugh, and the laughter brought her some relief from her stress. I was best at making people laugh and making them feel good about themselves. **In that moment I decided that is what I would do when I got out of that hospital bed. Professional speaking was going to be my career. It was my mission, and I was not going to allow anyone to stop me.**

When I returned to work, the plan was to nurture my speaking skills while earning an income at Dial One Wolfedale Electric. However, I ended up working fifty and sixty-hour weeks. I had to turn down many speaking opportunities because I felt I was needed so much in my HR role. I cared about the people I worked with, but I ended up pushing myself too much.

Meanwhile my doctors tried a new drug for my heart, which ended up shutting down my kidneys and then flared my fibromyalgia. Once again, I was unable to work. My only relief came in sleep. Looking back, that might have been the only way I would have stayed away from work. It was God's way of whacking me on the back of the head and telling me to slow down. It gave me a chance to pause and think. Do I really want to go back? My doctors told me I couldn't handle that kind of frenetic pace. I figured I could schedule my needed rest time if I concentrated solely on my speaking. Slowing down has been a difficult lesson for me to learn.

When my kidneys shut down there was a good six weeks when I couldn't concentrate or drive a car. For the first time in my life I had to accept help. I had to allow people to pick up groceries for me and drive me to doctor's appointments. Young apprentices at the company called to ask if they could do anything for me. It was a very humbling experience but good because it allowed me to see the love others had for me. I had felt unloved in both of my marriages, so it was hard to ask for help. When I finally did, I was startled to find it was there in abundance. I was overwhelmed by the love around me. That experience made me realize I could quit my job and do what I really wanted, because I had incredible support in the world. I had never tested it before because I was so busy helping everyone else.

It felt like I was now caught in a three-ring circus, and I was playing in all three rings; my marriage, my financial situation and my ill health. I had to cut some of my acts or risk death, and I couldn't postpone it any longer. The first one I dealt with was my marriage.

My husband was one of those people who would go around telling people to "be realistic." This is a euphemism for "Stop thinking about your silly dreamers. I'm just trying to prevent you from getting hurt because you're going to fail anyway." He'd get upset when I shared my ideas of becoming a speaker. He'd then tell me I couldn't do it. He thought he was being realistic, when in fact he was really being very negative. He was projecting his own limitations onto me, and I had been accepting his limits! **If you love someone you don't ask them to give up their passion in life.** When I finally realized he had no idea who I was, I was gone for good.

I could hear the ringmaster crying out, "Ladies and gentlemen! Please turn your attention to ring two now." When I left my husband, I moved in with my eighty-eight year old mother. I was in a financial mess because I had given up that power to my husband. I had no credit, no car, and I even had to get my company to co-sign my cell phone contract. My mother asked me, "Judy, are you stupid?" I said "yes." I just thought the marriage would last forever. When the HR Association offered me a MasterCard with a $5,000 limit, I grabbed it.

I was exhausted, and I felt other women in similar situations might be feeling the same. I decided women needed a retreat. Using my new credit card, I paid $5,000 to book the retreat, and then started telling people about it. As the money came in for registrations, I paid off the credit card debt.

Two months later I put another $5,000 on the card for the conference, and paid it off as more applicants registered. By the end of the conference I had built my credit line to $10,000. I never advertised it – it was all word-of-mouth marketing. Many of the participants had family who were suffering or dying from cancer, and it gave me great pleasure to help them. My heart melted when people came up afterward to thank me, saying they thought after what they had been through they would never laugh again. I was becoming more confident that my life was finally on the right track.

Six months later I repeated the process with even more participants. I was building a good credit rating. But I still felt I needed help – a push in the right direction, so I joined a mastermind group. I also bought a new car so I could get to my speaking engagements. I had to do this before I went out on my own because I knew no bank would loan me money as a stand-up comedian. They are too conservative to see the potential in that career. Then I quit my job. I didn't burn any bridges though, because Dial One became my first client.

I am still working on ring three, my healthcare needs. I am learning to put balance back into my life and spend time focused on this area. I know good results will soon begin to show.

I am clear of what my mission here on earth is: to bring hope to people through humour using workshops and stand-up comedy. I want people to see that their lives can be better. When I hear people laugh, I see their whole body relax. When I feel their hearts lighten, it lightens my heart. I liken myself to people like the late Erma Bombeck and Loretta LaRoche. They deliver serious messages using humour. Because of who I am, I can't help but be funny.

Sometimes I get letters and cards from people many months after a workshop, telling me I saved their life. I save those letters in a file called my Hard Day File. When I am feeling so down and out I think I can't even go down to the lake for my hour long walk, I pull out that file and remind myself why I want to be healthy. It helps me sustain my belief in myself.

It has taken a long time for me to get back to my childhood dream of becoming someone like Red Skelton. Why couldn't I have just realized it then? Why did I have to go through all of this? I am a very spiritual, but not religious person. I believe in fate. I believe there is a reason we meet the people in our lives, and I just have to look for the lesson God has for me in each experience, and leave my trust in Him.

I guess I had a lot of lessons to learn. I use all of my experiences as the source of my humour. I look at it this way – if I hadn't gone through all those hardships, I wouldn't have had as much material to work with. Now that's funny!

Dr. Gerstein's Comments

To all the givers out there I have
an important message – It's OK to take.

Judy is a people pleaser, which is not a bad thing in and of itself. But like anything in extreme, it became an obstacle for Judy, who has a classic case of 'giving-itis.' Perhaps because they are the mothers of the world, women especially suffer from this condition. Symptoms include overwhelming feelings of empathy for other people's situations; forever taking care of other people's needs; and, continuously saving people (like husbands). Self-denial is a way of life for those inflicted with this ailment. Pleasing others is tops on their to-do list. Typical physical signs include chronic bags under your eyes, sore arms from reaching out to others so often, and a speech disorder – not being able to say the word, No.

Let me illustrate by using Judy as an example. Judy had a heart attack at forty-eight. I have since become friends with her through our mastermind group. About a year after our interview for this book, Judy wrote me an e-mail in which, unbeknownst to her, she described the classic symptoms of another heart attack. I didn't get home until late that evening so at midnight when I read her message, I was alarmed.

I phoned her immediately and told her to go straight to the hospital. Typical of someone who takes care of others, but who doesn't do such a good job on herself, she downplayed her symptoms. I reminded her I was an Emergency physician who treats this kind of illness every day. Again she said the pain was almost gone. We went back and forth like this for half an hour. I implored her to go. I even volunteered to drive her, but she refused. Finally she agreed that if the pain was not completely gone in the next half hour, she would go to the hospital. I relented but told her she is very precious, and I wanted to have her

Dr. Gerstein's Comments

around for a long time.

The pain did not subside, and Judy did not go to the hospital that night despite her promise. When she did see her doctor the next day, he told her she'd had another heart attack, and she was lucky it was not fatal.

I was very upset. That's when I told her she must start thinking of herself or her efforts to help the world will be in vain because she won't be in this world much longer.

Treatment of *'giving-itis'* is tough. You have to learn to look after – dare I say it – **yourself.** Yes, to the sufferers of this disease, that is a dirty word. But let me tell those of you who suffer from this illness something. IT'S OK TO BE GOOD TO YOURSELF.

Think of your life as a bank account. If you continually dole out money to everyone around you, your account will dry up and you will have nothing left to give. Sound familiar? You must take time to replenish your funds so you'll be able to continue giving to others. Yes, giving in itself does replenish some of the funds in your account. But there is a limit. You are a spiritual being in a physical body, and you have to take care of that body. Your spirit may be infinite but your body is not. **It is very finite.**

Set aside time to take care of your physical health. Write your health disciplines into your schedule. That way you can tell the person asking for your help that you have a prior commitment. And you do – to yourself. Do it with love, knowing you'll have more to give after you tend to your own needs.

To her credit Judy has begun taking better care of herself. She is getting rest, exercising, and meditating weekly. This is not easy for her. It is a challenge just as tough as the other ones she has faced and overcome. I know she will overcome this one too. She is an amazing person who has so much humour to share with others. I want to see her sharing it for at least another fifty years.

Myth-Diagnosis #5
Condition: Status Quo

✦

How *You* Can Bust This Myth

Your past does not equal your future. The people in this chapter inspired me and reminded me of that fact. Just because you are poor, dissatisfied, in a bad relationship, sick and tired does not mean that you will always be that way. For that matter it does not mean you have to be that way tomorrow. Many people around you have grown accustomed to the way you act around them. They even have a vested interest in keeping you that way because having things people can count on gives them a sense of security. It also means they don't have to look at what's lacking in *their* own lives.

What if you don't like what you are doing at work or how you express yourself? What if you are not really expressing your true personality? Have you ever felt that people around you don't actually know the real you? Have you ever thought that if you were to ever let the cat out of the bag and reveal your true nature and shared your passions with the world, your family and friends would be shocked?

Well what are you waiting for? Right now, get out a blank sheet of paper and write down what you would do if you could just be yourself. Would you sing? Would you dance? Would you express your own opinions more? What would you say or do differently? Then go out and do one thing on your list and be aware of how that makes you feel. (Notice how other people react to you. Don't judge it, just notice it. Be cognizant of the fact that their reaction is more about their issues than anything to do with you.) Let your feelings be your guide. If it makes you feel centred and whole and brings you inner peace, then do it again. This is yet one more way to get you back onto your true life path.

Part 2
Your Outer World

Myth – Diagnosis #6
Future Shock

"I can't leave my stable job. What else will I do?"

"I was always looking outside myself for strength and confidence but it comes from within. It is there all the time."

Anna Freud

Noel Gordon
Cook

"I can cook, I can bake, I know that it will work!"

I grew up in Jamaica in a large, very poor family of four brothers and five sisters. We all had to pitch in to make ends meet. Even as a ten-year-old I was expected to do my share of the household cooking. I had no idea this would be the source from which my latent interest in life would grow.

I always wanted to be a doctor. In Jamaica we made our own healing home remedies, and the whole field of medicine intrigued me. It cost money to see a doctor, and we had none. Here in Canada when you step on a nail you see a doctor and get a tetanus shot. Back in Jamaica we would heat up an extract similar to aloe vera, put it on a stick and place it on the wound, which would then heal within a week. Our home remedies consisted of folklore, myths and half-truths, but sometimes they were accurate.

These home remedies were all we could afford. You had to be on death's door to indulge in the privilege of seeing a doctor. I always looked up to the doctors in our city, and that's probably why I set my heart on becoming one.

When I was nineteen I moved to England to explore greater opportunities, and find my place in the world. It was exciting living by myself in a new place. When I was twenty-one, I sent for my girlfriend. We had known each other in Jamaica from when we were fourteen and we wanted to get married. Very soon we were expecting a baby, and with that reality my dream of becoming a doctor died. We needed money, and I needed a job. And so I became a lab technician.

Do I regret not becoming a doctor? No, although I certainly had the academic marks. I realized I was often devastated by people's illness and death. Perhaps I had glamorized the physician because it was so difficult to see one in my own town. My respect might have been partly due to a lack of direct contact with the profession. Would I have made a good surgeon? I'll never know the answers to these questions. My priorities were now different. I had a wife I adored, and soon I had a wonderful family.

We moved to Canada in 1966. I found work as a lab technician with the Ontario Ministry of Health. I was doing exciting research in various aspects of medical testing. For the most part, over the course of my twenty-three-year career, I enjoyed the work. I loved doing things with my hands, and seeing the results of my experiments. But, after a while, the research became tedious. I was spending sixty hours a week just keeping abreast of the latest research papers in my field. It took time away from my family and I began getting headaches. My joy at work began to wane.

I am an active member of my church and I loved cooking for the various functions. A turning point came when I met an English chef at one of the church's events. Together we prepared many different dishes including turkey, roast beef, Yorkshire pudding, apple pie and wedding cakes. I was impressed with his cooking skills, how organized he was in the kitchen and how easy he made it all seem. I really began to take notice when I saw the satisfaction on people's faces after eating his meals. I wanted to see that reaction to my own cooking. My early childhood passion was coming back to me. In actual fact it had never left; I had just turned my focus elsewhere.

The idea of opening my own restaurant began to attract me. I wondered if it was possible. I had no idea I'd be able to scratch this itch sooner than I thought. It turned out my sister knew someone who owned a Mr. Jerk restaurant franchise, and after a bit of thought I made an offer to buy it. He was willing to sell, and we agreed on the sum of $140,000.

I couldn't keep my job with the Ministry of Health and start a restaurant on the side because both involved sixty-hour weeks and more. I asked the ministry for a severance package, and they agreed. I received $23,000, but I would need a lot more than that to purchase and fix up the place. I put a second mortgage on my home for $80,000 and my former boss at the ministry loaned me $20,000.

I still needed another $30,000. There was a federal assistance plan called a Venture's Loan. The government would loan me the money if I could come up with thirty per cent of the needed cash. I went to a bank to ask for my share, but grew concerned when I did not hear anything for several weeks. My future was on the line and I certainly wasn't going to let it ride on a phone call.

My wife and I both went down to see the loan officer at the Royal Bank of Canada. She told me the bank had considered my application, but discovered there were already three West Indies' restaurants in the area I wanted to locate. The bank didn't think I could succeed.

I straightened up, and looked directly into her eyes. Then, very calmly, and with absolute confidence I said: "I can cook, I can bake, and I know I can do better than the others. I enjoy it and I am going to make it work!" It wasn't what I said, but the way I said it that caused her to second-guess the bank report. She changed her mind because she saw the confidence oozing from my pores. I wasn't wondering if it was going to work. I knew it would work. I just had to convince her, and I did, because she approved the loan.

Opening day was scheduled for May, but our new stove had not yet arrived. It looked like we would have to delay a month, but I couldn't afford to wait. Our only income now came from my wife working part-time as a nurse. Our financial situation had become desperate. We had to open now.

I brought in a small propane stove, stayed up all night cleaning the place and we opened on time. When my first customer walked in he ordered rice and jerk chicken. Watching a paying customer eat and enjoy my food gave me an amazing feeling I will never forget.

I had lots of help. My wife and son, my sisters, nieces and friends all worked at the restaurant for a while. Even my ten-year-old nephew lent a hand.

Within five years I had paid back all my loans and then some. I did better than I had projected in my bank's applications. Then, in 2003, a fire decimated part of the kitchen. The city inspector told us we had to put in a $100,000 exhaust system, and we had to close for six months to do that. When we reopened many people told us how much they missed our cooking and how glad they were to see us again. That's when I knew we were doing really well.

They say you can take the scientist out of the lab but you can't take the lab out of the scientist. As a lab technician, I generally looked for the method that was easiest to reproduce. That way I could be more confident of our quality assurance. If anyone else used the method I was confident the results were true, because the process was easily duplicated. Because I believe that cooking is a science, I began to apply the same practice in my recipes.

I measured and recorded every ingredient I used in each recipe so that my staff could reproduce my results. This was one of the reasons for our success – of course using only the best ingredients helped too. Employing this method provided another benefit – it allowed me to reduce my work week from sixty-hours in the first years to sixteen-hour weeks now.

I thought I wanted to be a doctor because of what I saw around me as a child. Doctors held a lofty position of respect in my home country, and I looked up to them. Instead, I became a cook because of what I felt within me. It was what I did from the time I was a little boy. When I became a cook and opened my own restaurant, I felt like I had come home.

Dr. Gerstein's Comments

People are attracted to people who are confident in themselves and their work

Confidence is a quality that is difficult to quantify. It is what makes a leader a leader, and you just know it when you see it. People like to follow people who have confidence, and they will often buy from people who demonstrate this trait. Where do you get confidence? Some people believe in the "fake it till you make it" method. It has its merits because no novice can expect to have great skills. However, if you truly believe in yourself and have a great passion for what you are doing, you will get there a lot faster.

Noel cooked for most of his life. As a child growing up in a large family, it was a necessity. As an adult he did it as a hobby, cooking for his family and for his church. When the opportunity came along to make a career out of cooking, he had total confidence in his success. He believed in himself and he had a passion for what he was doing. He couldn't even envision the possibility of failing. Noel said, "If you really want to do something you will find a way to do it." Below is a success formula.

> ### Confidence = Faith in yourself
> ### and
> ### Confidence + Passion = Success

Confidence will attract people to you. Confidence is the intangible quality that could make a difference between a successful business, and one that isn't. Noel's self-confidence is what influenced the loan officer at the bank to change her mind and approve the loan – the final piece of the puzzle needed to kick-start Noel's successful restaurant venture.

"Creativity requires the courage to let go of certainties."

Erich Fromm

Tsufit
Singer, Actress and Coach

"I never gave up my dream of being a singer.
Law was going to be my waitress job."

When I was five, I wanted to be an actress. My mom hoped I'd outgrow it but I never did. I was blessed with a good singing voice, I was funny, and I enjoyed the attention. My teenage years were spent on stage and I was progressing smoothly on the road to my dreams. So what did I become? A lawyer, naturally!

It could have gone either way. I was an outgoing kid, or so I'm told. I don't remember the childhood incident but at a high school reunion a few years ago, I approached a woman I recognized as the older sister of one of my classmates. When I said she probably wouldn't remember me she replied, "Are you kidding? Of course I remember you. When we moved into the neighbourhood you were eight. You walked up to me and said, 'Hi. I'm Tsufit. Welcome to the neighbourhood.'"

In high school, another side of me began to emerge. I joined the debating club and was even made a debating judge, critiquing others my age. People began telling my mother that I would become a lawyer.

Actress or lawyer? Which path to choose? For my parents, this was an easy choice. My mother told me that being a lawyer was more practical than being a singer – and that everyone wanted to be an actress. My parents told me to find a solid career, like law or medicine, and make a living for myself. They never had any doubt that I'd be a career woman. This made sense to me because I didn't want to ever have to depend on any guy to support me. So, I listened.

I used to watch Perry Mason on TV. I thought he was so cool, and criminal law did interest me. I had a soft spot for the underdog and wanted to see justice done. I never did become a criminal lawyer, but I did go to law school, and became a lawyer in 1987. **But I never gave up my dream of being a singer. Law was going to be my waitress job.**

I never stopped performing, and even when I was studying law I was in shows. I brought my administrative law books to rehearsals and while everyone else was hanging out, I was busy highlighting. A few days after completing my year of articling, I flew to Expo '86 in Vancouver to sing with a group of performers.

I became a litigation lawyer at a small boutique firm but I didn't feel like I could be myself in the office. I had long hair and enjoyed wearing casual dresses. One day, my boss called me into the office and told me to put my hair in a bun and wear a suit. I had graduated fourth in my class at the most prestigious law school in the country. *Canadian Lawyer* magazine had even called me, "One of the super achievers across Canada." I thought they were buying my brains not my appearance, but I was mistaken.

A colleague came to see a show in 1987. She couldn't believe that the person on stage was the one she saw at the office every day. She commented that I had the audience eating out of my hands on stage, whereas at the office I seemed shy and more reserved. The truth is that I was never comfortable with the politics of practicing law.

I moved to a more low-key firm and started a family. During those years I would see people performing on stage and say to my husband, "Why her and not me?" "We're starting a family," he would say, "It's just not your time yet." Looking back he was probably right. There is a time for everything and you can't have it all at once.

Unlike the other lawyers at the firm, to me law was just a job. I wanted a life outside of law. I rarely worked weekends. I had children and was on the mommy track. With that one phrase I was relegated to be the junior lawyer *ad infinitum.*

My family grew and I became busier with my law practice. I allowed my performance career to wane. Along the way, I also lost my confidence. Then, in 1995, a friend of mine heard me practicing a song. She knew I hadn't performed for a few years, but she asked me to perform for a benefit she was involved in. That request rekindled my fire. I felt it was finally time to fully embrace my dream.

Except for my young children, my family didn't understand my desire to change careers. Why would I want to leave law for something as flaky as performing? It didn't make sense to them. I even found some of that attitude in the entertainment business. I had never broadcast the fact I was a lawyer because I feared I wouldn't be taken as seriously as a performer. One night, when I was performing in a comedy club, a fellow comedian saw a newspaper article about me entitled, *"Litigation Lawyer Leaves Law For Limelight."* He thought I was crazy and said to me, "If I were a lawyer, there's no way I would be doing this!"

Those attitudes didn't derive from spite or jealousy. They saw law as a stable, respected, well-paying profession and in stark contrast to the unpredictable world of entertainment. Only my kids understood, although it must have been a bit confusing for them when they were young. I remember my three year old, who was just learning the meaning of words, asking me, "Mommy, is being a lawyer singing on stage?"

There were times when I allowed the lack of support to get in the way. Other times I used it as motivation. I once showed a video of my live performances to an entertainment lawyer at my firm for his feedback. He told me I had a great voice but the video would never get me any work. I said to myself, "I'll show him." That video *did* lead to me getting work in comedy clubs, and next thing I knew I was doing comedy on national TV.

Giving up my law practice would make a change for us financially, but not a huge one. It is difficult making a decent income as an entertainer. Someone once said, "In Canada you can headline at Maple Leaf Gardens and still have to take the subway home." Money *was* a concern, but I wasn't going to let it stop me. After articling, I chose to work at smaller firms so I never had a large income to begin with. I had taken maternity leave four times in the past, so our family had learned to manage on less. I enjoyed bargain hunting, and we drastically limited our vacation and other leisure expenses. We were very frugal anyway, so it wasn't an enormous change.

I have been performing full-time for several years now – on stage, on radio and on TV. I've released a CD and a live recording. Being able to fully express myself at work has allowed me to genuinely enjoy my life. When I'm on stage, I am the "ON" version of me. I am very direct with my audiences. They like it and I like it. It just works.

I enjoy the applause but it's not what I live for. It's easy to get caught up in that scene and forget what is real. I can't allow myself to be too affected by what people say about me – good or bad. People tell you not to read your own reviews in this industry, but I do. Most of reviews have been amazing but two or three times a sharp tongued reviewer has taken a bite out of me. It hurts for as long as I let it but now I've learned to snap out of it. You can't take them seriously. You have to let it go. When my children run to greet me at the door after a show I realize that is the real love. Sometimes I need to be reminded of that lesson.

I have developed broad shoulders. I don't get my hopes up too high on any one engagement or audition. It really is just a numbers game. If I go to twenty auditions, I figure a few will choose me, but I don't know which ones they'll be. I just throw myself out there, and see what comes back but I don't fret about it. I am also surrounding myself with more positive people. As time goes by, I have less and less patience for negative people.

I am continually searching for that balance of public recognition and privacy. I've been lucky to have a lot of international media interest and while I like the public attention when I'm on stage or promoting myself as a performer or coach, I don't want my picture taken when I'm in my t-shirt and sweat pants taking my garbage out to the curb. Fortunately, or maybe unfortunately, that problem will probably never become a huge one in Canada.

Because I have done it, other people started coming to me for help discovering their dreams. So now, I am a coach, coaching people to follow their dreams and earn a living doing it. I don't have any coaching certification but they come because they know that I've done it. What gives me credibility is that I've walked my talk.

My clients tell me that they appreciate the two sides of my personality. There is the creative, theatrical side that comes alive when I brainstorm with people about their future possibilities and how to best present themselves. Then there is my cautious lawyer side, which interrupts with practical, down-to-earth advice.

I still perform but I'm much more selective about what I take on. A good part of my time is now spent coaching and speaking to business audiences about pursuing their dreams and how to draw media attention for their businesses. What once seemed like diametrically opposed choices have now been merged. I have the best of both worlds, and have come full circle.

Dr. Gerstein's Comments

Take note of your portable skills that can enhance your Dream Career.

If you find yourself in an unsatisfying career, don't fret. It doesn't mean you have wasted your time. You can use the skills you acquired along the way, as you follow your dreams. Most of the time, you won't have to start over from square one.

Tsufit had the musical talent and aspirations to be an entertainer from a young age. But she was encouraged to do the sensible thing and get a good, "respectable" job. She followed that advice, and became a successful lawyer.

Practicing law allowed her financial stability and flexibility while raising a family. It also provided skills in negotiating contracts for her entertainment career. The experience she garnered from practicing law gave her the rational wherewithal to help her coach clients to overcome practical obstacles. She has used her experiences as a lawyer to jump-start and continue her Dream Career.

Take a sheet of paper and draw a vertical line down the centre of the page. On the left side write your **Current Career** as a headline, (i.e., accountant) and on the right side, write down a career of your dreams (i.e., bush pilot). On the right list all the things you see yourself doing in your Dream Career. When you're done, think of all the ways you can use the skills from your current and previous career(s) to help you follow your dreams, and list them on the left side. Have fun with it. Brainstorm. Don't analyze as you are doing it, just write down as many ideas as you can. You'll have plenty of time to think about the details later.

You'll be surprised at how many of your skills are transferable, and how your previous experiences can help you in your new life direction.

"The pessimist sees difficulty in every opportunity. The optimist sees the opportunity in every difficulty."

Winston Churchill

Brent Rogers
Business Coach

"To find my new career I began to focus on the fun parts of my old one."

I was becoming irritable and others were starting to notice, too. Sleeping was troublesome so I would stay up thinking that I was not doing what I was supposed to be doing. This whole process began to nag at me for several years before I did anything about it. A quiet, inner voice probably began to whisper even two years before that, but I wasn't ready to hear it then. I was earning over $90,000 at the bank yet I still wasn't happy. I wondered if perhaps I might be having a mid-life crisis. The reality of the matter was that changes at the bank had taken the joyful part of my job away. Increasingly, I felt I had to do something about this untenable situation.

My father, one of my biggest mentors, was an executive at IBM. My mother was a teacher. They both encouraged me to experience life first hand. I learned more by trying things and through experience rather than by being taught. When we were young, my brother and I received new skis for Christmas. My father dropped us off at a ski hill to try them out. He said that he would be back in a few hours. I didn't know how to ski and had to learn by trial and error. I probably got much of my business acumen from my father. I was always a natural communicator. Other people interested me all through high school. Between that and the business courses I took, it laid the foundation for my present career.

When I got out of school I started a small contracting company. We used to build fences and decks. I was twenty-something, drove a Jaguar convertible and was living the high life. The first year of business was dynamite, the second year a little tougher and by the third year the challenges of running the business had me joking that if you gave me $20 in the third year I would have given you the key. I had a lot to learn about running a business. I was good at producing and selling the product but I was weak on administration, managing people and financially planning for the future.

So I decided to learn how to run a business. I turned to financial institutions for my education. In my first year of the "program" I was hired as an assistant credit manager for a customs and import broker. I did that for a year. Next I landed a position at a commercial finance company. After a couple of years there, my personal bank manager suggested I apply for a position at her bank. They made me a management trainee at one of the "big five" Canadian banks. I followed my interests into commercial and business banking with my goal of becoming a commercial bank manager. I stayed in that industry for twenty three years.

During my financial career I was exposed to and participated in thousands of different, real life cases of businesses striving for success. I often thought of the experience as a poor man's Harvard MBA with case study learning in real time with real risk, real dollars and real consequences. I learned different aspects of running diverse types of businesses and witnessed why some companies do well and others flop. It was a fascinating learning experience. For the first seven years I was enjoying my education. I took pleasure in the interactions and in helping people with their business. Others noticed my skills too. I saw rapid promotion and additional responsibilities. This meant I could skillfully practice business by wheeling and dealing with someone else's money.

As I became more knowledgeable in my position clients began

seeking my advice. Unfortunately, banks weren't geared to give that kind of advice. They were set up to sell loans to businesses. There was no paradigm set up to sit down with a client for two hours and discuss his business strategy. The only way this might have happened is if the bank thought it necessary in order to protect its loan exposure. I recognized the need for providing advisory services to clients but we had no way to charge for it. I could only give it on an informal basis and that frustrated me.

Over the years, banks formalized their processes so dealing with clients became more robotic. If the numbers didn't work out in the formula financial assistance was denied. This took much of the flexibility and challenge out of my job. I had been in the banking industry for twenty some years. In that time I had amassed a wealth of valuable knowledge and experience that allowed me to successfully use my discretion and judgment with individual clients. When that flexibility was eliminated, it left mostly administrative work and bureaucracy – the aspects of the job I most disliked. All the challenge and fun was being weeded out of my position.

I became ill tempered and that started to affect other aspects of my life, including many sleepless nights. I was faced with an intolerable situation at the bank but I refused to lower my standards. When the bank started to move in what I considered a less client-friendly direction – away from the principles we once both shared – I realized it was time to get out. I believed in myself and knew I was smarter than what my job had become so I began to search for my own way out.

I had always contemplated returning to a business of my own and began actively thinking of ways to do that. I had dinner with a friend who had a lot of experience and success in business. He saw how frustrated I was and suggested I try consulting.

I began by making lists of things I liked and disliked about my position at the bank over the years. From these lists I obtained a clearer picture of who I could best serve in my role as consultant. Over the next several months, my next career began to crystallize. I was slowly developing my plan but I needed to source some clients.

They say the definition of luck is, "when opportunity meets preparation." This was true for me. Through a strange twist of fate, I got a chance to practice my future career.

One of my hobbies is piloting small planes. A friend of mine was attempting to sell shares in his plane and asked me to demonstrate it and screen the people who were interested. After one such flight, the prospective purchaser thanked me but said he didn't think he was in a position to buy yet because of what was happening in his own business. He was classically stuck between a rock and a hard place. He wanted to grow his company but didn't have enough staff to take on more business. Alternately, he couldn't hire more staff because he didn't yet have the additional business to pay their salaries. He said he would call me back about the airplane in a few months, after he tried to work things out. At that point I told him I was commencing my business advisory practice and could help him out. He said that he would give it some thought. The very next evening, at 6 p.m. he called my office.

He was in crisis. Overnight his staffing problems had become much more critical. One of his employees had just quit and he didn't know what to do. I walked him through that crisis and the next day sat down with him to discuss the importance of developing a longer term business management strategy. He needed to replace the "management by crisis" method he was following.

When I looked at his books I immediately recognized several significant problems. I wondered to myself whether his company would even make it to the end of the month. He engaged my services and we tackled the critical issues first. In a few months we had his company back on track. His business is running much more smoothly now. It's working for him, rather than the other way around. This year alone he has successfully doubled his revenues!

Meanwhile, during my "career crisis" deliberations, my bank had begun yet another downsizing. I had seen it coming for half a year. This time around they were planning to even get rid of some front line managers – people who were actually generating revenue! I suspected I was a marked man because I had always been regarded as a sometimes outspoken, out-of-the box, entrepreneurial-type of thinker. My co-workers sometimes told me that I might be better off working for myself. My first conditioned instinct was to hunker down, keep quiet and work harder. After a few months I realized that I was getting more frustrated because that wasn't me and I wasn't willing to sustain that act much longer. Instead of ducking the issue, I made a conscious decision to stand in front of the bullet. I asked for and received a fair severance package.

The day I met with my manager to finalize the termination I came home and caught my spouse just as she was heading out the door to play tennis. I told her "I have some bad news and some good news. The bad news is that I no longer have a job. The good news is that I have a severance package and am going to start my own business practice full time." She said, "Okay, it sounds like you are okay with that." Telling me she was running late, she left for her game. She has always been supportive of me and that has helped me immensely along the way.

The severance package allowed me some breathing room to build up clients. Had the bank not been downsizing when it did, it would have taken me longer and would have been a more difficult transition to another career. Once I announced my departure to my clients at the bank, one of them called to inquire if I would consider doing some financial and banking advisory work for him. Once my notice period at the bank expired I accepted the engagement. I was off to a good start. Today my practice is doing quite well and growing, and I am enjoying working for myself. I called my new company, Strategic Advisory.

There have been some bumps in the transition period. My clients pay on a monthly, flat-fee based on a specific number of hours from me. Once, I unwittingly put in a lot of extra, uncompensated time into helping a client with his interview and hiring process. Since then I have learned to tell my clients up front that I have the discretion to charge for any service I render above and beyond our agreement.

In another instance I began to talk about some of my own problems after a client casually asked how I was doing. I caught myself after a few moments. I realized that my clients aren't paying me to hear about my problems. They want me to produce and improve their business situation.

However, looking at my career with a larger lens, those "bumps" were all minor annoyances compared to the aggravation I was feeling at the bank in the last few years.

Now my central activity is my passion. I no longer have to waste energy on administrative paper-shuffling and can concentrate on applying my knowledge and experience to improving my clients' businesses. By taking the time to develop my new venture I proactively eliminated those things that irritated me at the bank and built on the aspects of the job I truly enjoyed. My only regret is that I didn't do it sooner.

Dr. Gerstein's Comments

Use your current career to get a glimpse of your Dream Career

Brent did like some of his duties at the bank. He grew disenchanted when those activities were whittled away. To remind him why he once enjoyed it he created the following table:

What do I enjoy?	What do I dislike?	Who could I best serve?
Helping people build businesses. Giving advice. Wearing different hats when dealing with my clients – accountant hat, lawyer hat, psychologist hat, marketer hat etc…	Administrative work.	Independent businesses (revenues = $5 to 10 million.) They were bigger than mom-and-pop businesses yet smaller than the mid-marketing firms to which I was accustomed. (I often dealt with the lawyers in the latter scenario.)
Being bold and taking risks.	Losing ability to exercise discretion with clients.	Entrepreneurial mindsets where the owner knows his product cold but is weak on the management skills i.e., bookkeeping, managing people.
Dealing with owners.	Meetings! They probably cost me 30% of my time at the bank.	Businesses not bound by a multitude of corporate rules.
Dealing with people one-on-one.		A market where I wouldn't be competing with big accounting firms.
Having many irons in the fire at any one time.		A market where there is an abundance of business. The ratio of independent businesses to mid-marketing firms is probably around 100 to one in Canada.

Dr. Gerstein's Comments

To find your own pearls amidst the grains of sand in your job, create your own table. Begin looking at what you like and dislike. After a few months, if you take the time to do the exercise and think about it, the situation will become clearer. I can guarantee one thing. If you do not take the time to think about your future nothing will change. You may get some satisfaction from complaining about your work. People may appear empathetic but, in the end, dreams only come to those willing to work for them.

All of the people interviewed for *Live Your Dreams: Doctor's Orders* had many things in common but two of the core similarities were their ability to **dream big** and then **act** on it.

"Dreams without action are fantasy.
Actions without dreams are empty.
Dreams combined with actions manifest one's destiny."

Samuel Gerstein

*"There is nothing in a caterpillar that tells
you it's going to be a butterfly."*

R. Buckminster Fuller

Phil Solomon
Justice of the Peace

*"Once I realized I had control over what was
happening to me, my world changed."*

For many years I wasn't being myself. I feared change and the unknown but I was completely unconscious to this. I was forced to face reality when my business was failing. I became depressed and sought out help from a psychiatrist. He made me realize that I always had the ability to control my life – I just never exercised it.

After several difficult months of introspection I took back my life. My direction changed and with it all the other areas began to change. My career was only the tip of the iceberg.

My father managed a lumberyard. As a child I worked there every Saturday and some summers. I liked it but didn't necessarily want to follow in his footsteps. I had no idea what I wanted to do.

I joined a theatre group at sixteen. I did some acting but became intrigued by the work on the sets and doing scenery. I enrolled in the fine arts program at York University in theatre set construction and design. Upon graduation I belatedly discovered a problem in the field. There were very few jobs in set design and those jobs were only seasonal. I would also be required to join the union, which would, in turn, tell me where I could work. This wasn't a viable option for me.

I broadened my horizons to TV and film and was an extra in a couple of movies. I enjoyed the technical aspects of TV and film production. At nineteen, I was offered a position as a videotape operator when *Citytv* was in its infancy. I turned it down. That's a decision I regret because I may have become a director or producer had I accepted the challenge. But, at that time, I wasn't ready for the opportunity.

I chose to go back to my construction roots. Because I had previous experience hanging doors in set construction, I was hired at a door manufacturer where I eventually became a partner. I enjoyed many elements of the business, especially anything that involved talking with people – from marketing to getting the contract to getting paid for delivery.

After eleven years, I started another business with another partner. We manufactured wooden door components. That venture only lasted four and a half years. After working fourteen-hour days, seven days a week we simply could not turn the business around. The banks were on our backs and we were feeling the pinch.

For months we knew we ought to close the business but I wasn't able to face that truth. I feared change and didn't know what I would do if this business went under. In short, we were so low on cash we couldn't pay the employees. We finally closed the doors for good. Interestingly enough the day we closed up shop was the day I felt a giant weight off my shoulders.

During those final months my extreme stress resulted in my becoming depressed. I sought assistance from a psychiatrist. He helped me to realize I did have control of the situation. **I believed I did not have control of my life. In reality, I was just not exercising my control.** Having gone through this made me realize I wasn't stuck. I did have options.

I ended my 19-year marriage shortly thereafter. I had become a very negative, angry person. I kept emotions bottled up and then I'd fly off the handle as a release. I wasn't who I am today. Going through the business closing helped me feel that I could handle the change I needed in my personal life. I was single again and unemployed but I didn't feel stressed. I felt lighter and freer than ever before. I was starting to manage my life.

My fresh start began at a home inspection company. I was hired to do marketing and quickly became a general manager. I had fun doing that. Within four years the company became the second largest home inspection firm in southwestern Ontario.

I found that I enjoyed facilitating the homebuyer seminars. I drew on some of my early theatrical roles to help me on stage. I was quite good at it. I felt I was on track.

While working at the home inspection business I went back to York University with thoughts of doing an MBA. My first two courses were micro- and macroeconomics. It didn't take me long to realize that an MBA was not going to further my career. Instead, I began looking at courses I enjoyed and courses that would help me in my new business.

Historically, I had always hated school. I never saw the reason for it. It's funny. When I started taking these college courses I had a purpose and a positive attitude. I sat in the front of class – a big change from my high school days – and had some of the highest marks in class. For the first time I was actually interested in what I was taking.

I took courses in home appraisals and real estate law because they intrigued me. I was enjoying the journey and not necessarily committing to one destination. My path could have led me to become an appraiser or marketer for a large real estate company. I was very good at selling intangibles at the home inspection company and I reasoned I could always transfer those skills to real estate. I had no idea I would end up where I did.

The owners of the home inspection company were ready to sell and I was interested in buying the company. I thought their price was unreasonable. When I decided not to bid for the company, my contract was terminated.

In and around the same time, a friend of mine, Charles Harnick, then the Attorney General of Ontario, told me that he had to appoint some people to the Assessment Review Board because they were falling behind in their reviews. He knew what I was doing and he thought it would be a perfect fit for me. He was right.

I was appointed to a three-year term as an adjudicator to look after property assessment appeals. I found the cases fascinating. I got to travel all over Ontario to hold hearings involving car dealerships, hotels and shopping plazas. I found it challenging sifting through financial reports, listening to both sides and then deciding on a value for the property.

It turned out to be a great training ground for my next career move as Justice of the Peace. A friend I worked with at the Board was appointed Justice of the Peace. His appointment opened my eyes to a world I had not previously considered. He piqued my curiousity.

If I had to cite a common enjoyable characteristic in all of the careers I have been in I would say it was dealing with people. It was a thread that brought me satisfaction in spite of some of the challenges I faced along the way. In the door-manufacturing sector I liked dealing with purchasers, buyers, and customers. In the home inspection business, managing employees brought me satisfaction and leading seminars with the public was a kick. In the Assessment Review Board and as a Justice of the Peace my role was to listen, mediate and assess issues people bring forward.

Initially I sought help because of my career. Control of my professional life had a domino effect on all aspects of life. I learned about what interested me and I transitioned into careers I loved.

Epilogue

My work life was satisfying but my health was still suffering. I was overweight. I was taking a cholesterol-lowering drug and another medication to control my acid reflux from my stomach. I took 45 pounds off and kept it off. I no longer needed the medications. Because I was feeling so good in other parts of my life **my physical body no longer represented my mental image of who I was.** I have literally and figuratively become a different person.

Dr. Gerstein's Comments

Become your own role model - when you change one part of your life your whole life will change

Many people wonder how one area of your life spills over to affect other areas. We are who we are. We are not one person at work, another at home and a third with our friends. If you are attempting to be someone you are not in any role of your life you know how much energy you have to spend to keep up the charade. You can only be one person – yourself.

Phil is a good example. He was in a business that wasn't working. It was making him feel stressed, which led to his depression. At the time he was not enjoying his marriage or his life. He was overweight and had little energy. You'll notice that it was all congruent. The weight matched his depression, which depicted the state of his marriage and his business. Deep down he knew he wasn't being himself. However, he endured all of this because that was his conditioning. It wasn't his fault. He was doing the best he could with what he had learned along the way.

To change he had to break out of his patterns. The initial break is the hardest. As Phil himself says, fear of the unknown is a big obstacle. During the treatment for his depression, the psychiatrist helped Phil to see his options. Phil realized he had a choice in his life. The business closure forced him to change at work. Within a year he ended a marriage which was not working. He was now moving in the right direction for him. He started doing things he enjoyed.

One day he looked in the mirror and saw this obese person looking back who was no longer congruent with who he had become. He had grown and was more in control now. His overweight state no longer fit who he was. He now had leverage

Dr. Gerstein's Comments

over himself and it became easier to lose the weight. He had turned the momentum in his favour.

Doing what he loved helped Phil overcome some health issues because it was a natural progression of his new journey. When you are moving in the right direction you get into a flow and everything gets easier. Conversely, when you are moving in a direction that feels uncomfortable to you, everything seems harder than it has to be. It is the classic virtuous circle versus vicious circle effects.

I witness similar effects in medical care. When someone does something healthy, like losing weight, they often enjoy other benefits such as improved cholesterol levels, lowered blood pressure and less acid reflux.

Begin with one small change. But make sure it is what you love to do because you will build on that. As you strengthen this area of your life, you will be motivated to improve other areas that no longer fit with who you are. You are in effect acting as a role model for yourself. So stick with it. Never underestimate what you can learn from yourself.

Myth-Diagnosis #6
Future Shock

✦

How *You* Can Bust This Myth

The status quo feels secure and comfortable. That is why it is so hard to change it. It is a survival instinct that fears change and wants to keep you safe and sound. It may make sense if you are hunkering down inside somewhere warm and dry while waiting out the storm; it no longer seems as sensible if you only imagine an incoming storm.

Think back to the times when you forced to change any situation. It could be when you changed school as a kid, moved away to attend university or visit a foreign country. It could be when you divorced, moved homes or lost a job. How did you cope? Did your life fall apart or, did you manage? Chances are you adjusted to your new situation and maybe even thrived. And that was when you were forced into it.

What if you had time to plan it? What if you could try out your new ideas before you actually took the leap? Do not throw in the towel on your future even before you start. Try on your new life direction while you are still working in your present career. Do it on weekends or one evening a week; even one hour a week will get you moving in the right direction.

Plan ahead. Create an exit strategy for how you will slowly (or quickly) move out of your current career, if that is what you want to do, and into your Dream Career. Look at potential challenges and the worst case scenarios that may arise and make contingency plans for each one. By practicing this you will in effect be practicing your future now.

Myth - Diagnosis #7
Fatal Failure Phobia

"I'm not good enough."

*"You must learn from the mistakes of others.
You can't possibly live long enough to make them all yourself."*

Sam Levenson

Orlando Bowen
Professional Football Player

*I said to myself, "that is the last time in my life when
someone is going to say I can't do something."*

My family immigrated to Canada from Jamaica when I was young. Both my parents broke their backs to give me a better life, and a chance to do what I wanted. My father drove a taxi and then worked for a tool manufacturer. He liked neither job. My mother worked at odd jobs and then used her love of caring for people to become a nurse. By then I was eighteen. I truly appreciated all they did for me, and wasn't about to squander their hard work. I wanted to end up doing what I loved. I wanted it to be special, and I was determined not to settle.

I loved football, but my parents always told me not to focus on it. They stressed the importance of education and reminded me that no one could take that away from me. How prophetic those words would become.

I grew up in a rough part of Toronto. The drugs and violence were pervasive but I was too young to understand what was happening. From the time I was nine years old I held onto a dream of being a professional athlete.

I enjoyed shooting hoops with my uncle, who immigrated to Canada with us. He taught me a lot about the game and even more about life. He was a superstar who dominated in high school basketball, and he was my idol. Whenever I visited his home I gazed in awe at his all-star plaques on display. But despite his athletic prowess, he made one big mistake – he declined a university basketball scholarship because he didn't want to leave home. At the time he didn't understand the opportunity he was passing up, and I had no intention of making the same mistake. **I always reasoned if I could learn from someone else's mistake I didn't have to make the same one myself.**

The turning point in my life came in grade seven. My gym teacher and basketball coach was considered cool by the other kids, but I saw a different side. At the time, I was not a very good dribbler. During a tournament game a teammate passed me the ball. When I began dribbling, the ball hit my foot and went out of bounds. Then I heard my coach yell at my teammate, "Don't pass him the ball. You know better than that!" He didn't even yell at me. That hurt, but more than that it made me angry because it meant he had given up on me.

My interest in basketball led me to read about the life of Michael Jordan, probably the greatest player in the history of the game. I discovered he had been cut from his high school basketball team, but he didn't give up. He would sneak into the gym after school and practice by shooting hundreds of baskets a day.

If he could do that why couldn't I? If I could just identify what it would take to make me successful, there should be no reason I couldn't accomplish it. If I didn't possess that skill it was more than likely I could develop it. So it came down to how badly I wanted it. Once I made up my mind to pursue something, I paid no attention to any discouraging remarks. **All my dissenters sounded like the muffled voices of the grown ups in a *Charlie Brown* film.**

Determined to become an excellent dribbler, for that entire summer I dribbled everywhere for at least three hours every single day. I dribbled while listening to music. I dribbled in my garage. I said to myself, **"That is the last time in my life when someone is going to say I can't do something."** When I returned to school in the fall my progress was obvious, and the coach and the rest of the team were shocked. Suddenly, I was the guy the coach wanted to take the ball up court.

In high school my passion for the game continued. In grade nine I would catch the 5:39 a.m. bus to the YMCA, which opened at 6 a.m. I would then practice from 6 a.m. to 8 a.m. I did that four mornings a week throughout grade nine, and for part of grade ten. My dad didn't believe what I was doing so one day he drove to the Y to see if I was telling the truth. He only told me that story when I reached university. I was single-minded in my commitment – I would never ever be the weak link again. Never.

I have learned a lot of life lessons, many from other people's mistakes. I never knew when these lessons would appear. One of them came when I was a teenager.

When you're fourteen, image is important, and I wanted fashionable clothes. To earn some extra cash, I got a job in an assembly line. The scruffy middle-aged man next to me hated this job. On the first day I asked him to pass me a box of nails. If looks could kill I would have been six feet under right then and there. During our break I went up to him and said, "I'm sorry for whatever I did wrong. I didn't mean to offend you." That's when he told me something I will never forget.

He said, "I have a son a little younger than you. I have a car and a house and the bills have to be paid. I work here twelve hours a day, four days a week and I hate every minute of it." Then he continued: "When I was in high school I goofed off. If I could do it all over again I would focus in high school. If I had, it would have allowed me to do something more with my life. I don't have an option now, and I sure don't want my son to screw up like his old man did."

That story was the first in a long line of stories I heard in my life. *"If only I could do it again..."* became a recurrent theme. I was determined not to end up bitter like that man. I used that lesson as a reminder to focus on whatever I wanted – be it in school, professional sports, or just life in general.

At sixteen, a buddy of mine suggested I play football. I was big for my age, and he said I would do well. The idea lit a fire under me, and I decided to try it. Being from Jamaica, at first I didn't like playing in the cold weather. However, when they put me on defence I started to feel comfortable. When I played basketball I took pleasure in covering people, and this felt very similar to that. Then I got to tackle people, and that sure felt good. I was hooked.

I started out as a corner, then moved to safety, and then became a linebacker. I made the regional all-star team, and then in my senior high school year I was selected to play on the All-Canadian Dream Team. That helped me climb the Canadian ranking scale and attracted some American football scouts.

After the scouts tested my skill and saw my game films, I was offered three football scholarships. Some of my teammates advised me not to take a scholarship saying that once I signed they would own me. "They will tell you what to eat, when to sleep and when to get up" they warned. My teammates didn't see the possibilities, only the limitations.

Ignoring them, I chose Northern Illinois because it was located close to a big metropolis like Chicago. I thought it would give me the best opportunities for life after university for both inside and outside the football arena. I was thinking ahead, I had a scholarship at a renowned university, I excelled in academics and I was a starter as a freshman. My high school coach said, "I've coached a lot of good players, and you've got a rare combination of size, speed and academia. You take care of your business academically and everything will work out on the field."

Before starting college I wrote out my goals. I identified potential obstacles that may arise and then came up with plans of how to handle each one. These included time management, the physical demands of football, and excelling in my academic studies. It was the unexpected obstacles that were to become my true test.

In 1995 in my second year of college, I was diagnosed with a lower back spinal condition. I was miserable and in so much pain I couldn't even sleep. I got partial relief by lying on the floor and putting my legs up on the bed. For three months I wore a plastic corset and had to sit out the entire 1995 season. The doctors told me I might not play again.

But in 1996 I came back. During the off-season the university fired most of the old coaching staff and brought in new coaches with a tough attitude towards many of the players that they hadn't personally recruited. They were hard on all of us right from the get-go, telling us we weren't putting enough attention on football. I thought I was in university to get an education. When I studied for my courses, I gave them all of my attention. When I practiced football, my total focus was football. But the new coaching staff felt otherwise. They claimed that I wasn't putting enough into football. We locked horns, and they turned up the pressure. In practice I found myself doing extra drills and facing bigger guys in front of me. They pushed me hard, but I wasn't going to break. I wasn't going to give anyone the satisfaction of beating me.

I hadn't prepared for this challenge, but I knew if I let them knock me off my feet I was done. I had come too far to let anyone deter me from my goals. By now I had heard too many stories of people regretting what they didn't do; of people wishing they had another chance. This was my chance and I wasn't going to let it pass me by.

I wasn't backing down. I was in school to get an education AND play football. Their opposition only seemed to drive me, and I became more determined than ever to graduate at the top of my class. I said to myself, "No one is going to study harder and no one is going to beat me on the football field." To some of the new administration's dismay, as it applies to its influence on the football team, I earned my starting position that season. I had earned my way back onto the field, and as much as it frustrated them they weren't about to shoot themselves in the foot by having me sit on the sidelines. They figured I would help them win games. And I was happy to be back out there with my teammates.

When I graduated with my Masters in Information Technology (IT) I was equally as proud. I had succeeded on my terms. I might not have gotten a lot of publicity to showcase my football talents but I had something my parents told me no one could take from me – my education. I began working as an IT consultant in Chicago in January 2000.

Then, just when I began to grow accustomed to my other dream career outside of football, I got a call from the director of scouting of The Toronto Argonauts. Many CFL (Canadian Football League) recruiters follow players who had received scholarships at US universities, who were not drafted by an NFL team, to look for any potential candidates for their team. He may have also seen me in some pre-season games the year before when I was drafted by the Edmonton

Eskimos before I was released.

My hard work in both areas was about to pay off. When asked if I was still interested in playing ball, I said, "very much so." Taking a leave of absence from the IT job, I went home to Toronto, made the team, and became a professional football player.

I have accomplished what I wanted, both on and off the field by excelling in my education and in football. You could say I had two dreams and I followed them both. I learned that if you want something badly enough, there is no obstacle that can stop you. I had watched so many people let opportunities pass through their fingers like the sand at the beach, and I wasn't going to be the guy who would look back on his life and wonder, "What if?"

$\diamondsuit$

Dr. Gerstein's Comments

Don't live in regret.
Learn form other people's successes and mistakes.

As a boy Orlando listened well – an unusual quality. If only more people would listen and learn from the mistakes of others, they would save themselves a lot of disappointment and grief. He was quite mature at a young age. When he read about his boyhood hero Michael Jordan, he learned Michael had been cut from his high school basketball team. But Michael didn't give up. He would sneak in to the gym to practice and improve. Orlando took that lesson to heart and improved his own basketball skills through sheer determination.

From the disgruntled worker on the assembly line he learned not to take high school for granted. That man, many years his senior, reminded him of what was important. It was a gift and, unlike many teenagers, Orlando accepted the gift by receiving and understanding the message.

His very talented uncle and mentor had missed a great opportunity by passing up a university basketball scholarship. Orlando remembered that lesson, and took advantage of both the academic and athletic opportunities offered by the scholarship he received. Orlando did not want to end up with the coulda-woulda-shoulda syndrome. He saw that so many people live in regret, their lives filled with stories that begin with, "If only I _____"

We have all made mistakes in our lives, but the key is not to dwell on them. If you are bemoaning your fate, then you are missing new opportunities arising for you right now. Learn from your mistakes and take action now.

If you don't go after what you want now, how will you feel in five years? In ten years? Don't live in regret. This wisdom applies to

Dr. Gerstein's Comments

you at forty, fifty and sixty years old and older, as much as it does when you are twenty. What are you putting off until tomorrow? If you don't know your dream, find a coach to help you uncover it. Don't wait another five years. You will only be five years older and even more resentful.

Alternately, no matter how old you are now, imagine how you could feel in five years if you pursued your dreams. Feel the satisfaction you will derive from accomplishing something you've always wanted to do. What will you say to yourself then? What will other people say to you when you do it? How will it make you feel?

Now go and start!

"When one door of happiness closes, another opens;
but often we look so long at the closed door that we do not
see the one which has been opened for us."

Helen Keller

Normand Bouliane
Streetcar Operator

"When I call out the stops I forget my problems."

I do everything fast – I drive fast, I eat fast and I make love fast – that's probably why my first wife left me.

From the time I was very small I had a fascination with cars. When I was three my father and I often sat on our front steps watching the cars go by. At six years old I built and raced go-carts. Speed excited me.

My school guidance counselor advised me to become a driver in the army. Later, an aptitude test actually agreed with that advice (although it also suggested that I go into computers). At thirteen I became an army cadet, and by sixteen I was driving armoured carriers. One day we held a program with the air cadets. When I took a ride in a glider, I immediately fell in love with flying. Flying in the air, I could go even faster than driving.

In grade twelve I dropped out of school and became a car jockey, making deliveries around town. Later, I fell in love with a girl who was studying to be a teacher. She convinced me to follow my dreams, and the first step was to go back and finish high school. This allowed me to get accepted into pilot school. I followed her to the Indian reserve where we got married. We lived there for a few years while I took my aviation flight management course. In my off time I took flying lessons, and eventually got my private flying license. I was on my way to my dream.

On the day I flew my first solo flight, I had two other "solo flights" waiting for me afterward. The second one was a dunk in the creek by my flight classmates – a rite of passage event. The third one came from my wife. When I got home that evening, she had the Justice of the Peace serve me with divorce papers. I was in shock. I had just made a giant step in my life, a step she had encouraged me to take, and now she was leaving me. I was heartbroken. How could she have done that to me? And on that special day, to boot?

Now I was really flying solo. When she left me I lost all motivation for flying, and then I dropped out of aviation school. That was a big mistake, but at the time I felt so low I couldn't see a way to make it happen. I was depressed, and needing a break I headed off to become a beach bum on the west coast. It was great for the summer, but when the cool, rainy winter arrived, it shook me out of my stupor.

It was time to come back to reality. I was out of money, and I needed a job, so I used my last $100 to buy a bus ticket to Toronto. I didn't even have enough cash to eat on the way home but I still enjoyed the ride. I took a test to enter the air force as a pilot, but my score was only good enough to land me a co-pilot position. I turned it down. If I couldn't be a pilot, I didn't want it. Later I discovered that had I accepted that position I would have been able to move up to pilot if I proved myself worthy. In hindsight that was another mistake, but I don't live in the past. I always say, what's next?

I turned my attention to another career involving motion – buses. I did enjoy the ride from Vancouver, and I have always loved driving. First I became a school bus driver. The company paid for my class B license, but all the noisy kids rattled me. So I drove delivery trucks for a while. Once I almost took the top off a truck. Another time I forgot to secure the pop bottles, and many fell out on the floor. I learned to be more patient and cautious. I learned to be keenly aware of the big picture, of all that was happening in front of me when I drove. Thank goodness I made my mistakes early and learned these lessons before landing what would turn out to be my dream job at the Toronto Transit Commission (TTC).

I submitted my application to all the major bus companies, and the TTC accepted me. Soon I was driving a streetcar on the midnight shift. My last ride was 4:27 a.m. out of Long Branch and I had to be in the yard by 5:27 a.m. There was very little traffic at that time so I was able to motor it. Flying along, I really felt like a pilot on wheels, and was able to make both careers come true! I even tattooed "The Rocket" on my arm – a picture of a TTC streetcar with 747 wings.

My career has been a saving grace for all of my personal strife. After that first divorce, I remarried, and am now again separated. I fought for, and won custody of my children. Then I opted to exchange the streetcar position for a spot as a bus driver. From here I am better able to look after my kids. The lawyers and my ex-wives have put me $35,000 in debt, but the TTC is like a family. They take care of their own.

When I go to work I am able to put all that behind me. When I call out the stops, I can forget my problems. When I put my foot on the gas time whizzes by. I love to drive, and I'm never bored. I enjoy interacting with the customers. When I first started driving the Queen Line people would ask me where certain Toronto landmarks were. One day I decided to incorporate all the answers into my stop calls. For instance, I lower my voice, speak right into the mike and belt out, "Citytv, MuchMusic, etc…" like a tour guide. The riders are amused and I enjoy hamming it up.

Do I have any regrets of not becoming a pilot? Not really. I found something better. Now I drive the rocket.

Dr. Gerstein's Comments

Do not regret your losses.
There is always another opportunity up the road.

Normand could have folded up like a cheap suitcase after twice giving up on his piloting career. The first time he was still reeling from the shock of the unexpected divorce. After taking a break for the summer, he came back looking for a job. The second time his pride prevented him from taking a lower position as a co-pilot, which he could have eventually turned into a full pilot's license. But still he didn't give up, and set out again to find a job.

He didn't just grab any job. He stuck with his personality of requiring mobility and started as a school bus driver, which ultimately led to his Dream Career. Normand beams with pride about being a pilot on wheels and proudly shows off his TTC "Rocket" tattoo.

So many people think they have only one or two chances in life. When those pass them by, they give up, bemoaning lost opportunities for the rest of their lives. It makes for great pity-me stories in a bar somewhere, but it doesn't help them find their Dream Career. The people in this book continued to search until they found or created their own opportunities.

If you have suffered a loss or a setback, take some time to grieve it, but not too long. When you're done, get back on the bus and renew your search for what you want to do. Just like busses and streetcars, if you miss one, the next opportunity will be along shortly. Just ask the driver, Normand Bouliane.

"To get what you want, help other people get what they want."

Zig Ziglar

Avraham E. Plotkin
Rabbi

*"I realized they were not going to buy into my dream.
After all it was my dream not theirs."*

From the beginning I was in the high-risk category of becoming a rabbi. My grandfather and my father were both rabbis. Knowing what I wanted to do was never my challenge. But finding a congregation to lead in this spiritual desert? That was the tough part. After all, being a rabbi was my dream. I had to find a way to make "having a rabbi" someone else's dream too.

I grew up in the Jewish Chabad-Lubavitch movement where the ultimate expectation for every boy is to become a rabbi. In that culture everyone is pointed in the direction of community work. But within that spectrum there are a lot of choices. You could become a rabbi, a Gabbai[3], a Shamash[4], a youth director, a teacher or an administrator.

3. In Hebrew a Gabbai is either a person who assists in the running of a synagogue and ensures that the Jewish prayers run smoothly and that other needs are met, or an assistant to a rabbi.
4. A Shamash is also a Hebrew word for an attendant, caretaker, custodian, or synagogue janitor

During Sabbath services it is customary for the rabbi to follow right behind the Torah when it is returned to the ark. However, during my Bar Mitzvah when my father was carrying the Torah back to the ark, the rabbi nudged me forward to follow my father. I like to say it was a metaphorical nudge that directed me towards my unique path, my destiny of becoming a rabbi too.

I fully embraced the Chabad philosophy. We are on this earth for seventy or eighty years, and our only goal is to give service to others. That is really what life is about. It is not about expanding our own ego. **It is about giving and sharing.**

I was parachuted in from New York to an unaffiliated neighbourhood in Toronto around 1989. There are Chabad representatives in all the major cities of North America, and those people identify the communities in greatest need of a rabbi to the leaders in New York. They offered me a few choices. After doing my due diligence, I chose the one where I felt I could be most helpful.

A few days after we moved into our new home and community, we learned a lady was sitting *shiva* (The Jewish custom of mourning for the dead) on our street. A neighbour thought it would be a good idea if I went over to comfort her. When I walked in the young woman said, "Rabbi, did the rabbi from Hong Kong send you?" I had no clue what she was talking about.

When she saw my quizzical look she explained that her mother had actually passed away in Hong Kong. They brought her back, buried her in Toronto, and were sitting *shiva* here. While in Hong Kong they got to know a rabbi who came regularly to their house during their mother's illness. When she finally passed away he told them to get in touch with his cousin, a rabbi, who would surely help them in their time of grief.

Then she said, "In fact, I have the name of that rabbi scribbled on a piece of paper in my pocketbook." When she opened up her pocketbook, there it was in black and white. It said, "Rabbi Plotkin." There was no phone number or address on that paper, just my name. And here I came walking into her house three days after I moved into the neighbourhood. Talk about a **coincidence!** That might have been a sign from God that I made the right move.

I discovered I had landed in a fledgling new neighbourhood in Toronto, a Jewish spiritual desert located a good distance from the known religious community. I had my challenge set before me. I went door-to-door just to get a *minyan* – a group of ten men that Jewish law requires as a minimum to conduct prayer services. We started out running services from my house. On one Sabbath evening we had only nine people. We were short one.

It was Halloween, and predictably the doorbell rang. When I opened the door I saw some young people dressed in costumes. I turned to one of them and asked, "Are you Jewish?" When he said yes, I brought him in to be our tenth man for the service. He wasn't expecting that treat when he went out trick-or-treating!

The biggest obstacle we faced in our new community was indifference. One day when I sat down with a group of people, they asked rhetorically, "Rabbi, what are you doing? Why do we need all this?" They continued, "We're happy with our lives as they are. We don't need you. Go back home. You're wasting your time here. People in this neighbourhood are not very religious, and not actively spiritual."

I had a big dream for them, and here they were rejecting my dream. After hitting this brick wall of apathy, I became a little depressed. I never felt like giving up, but I had no idea where my help was going to come from. I couldn't logically see the route to take.

However, I had faith that it would work out somehow. My rabbinical teachings taught me that I have the resources to solve problems. **The bigger the problem, the deeper I have to look into my soul for the answers.** Spiritually I know the answers are always there. I had the will to persevere, and I knew I just had to work a little harder.

I felt the picture of the area needed changing. **Instead of forcing others to change the picture they had drawn for themselves, I painted a new picture and invited people to come and look at it.** I had to find a way to show them why it was important to them, and that required that I get out of my head and into theirs. I had to motivate them from their perspective not mine. I had to show others I had something to offer that could enhance their family life and their meaning in life.

My wife and I thought of where their biggest needs were, where they were having trouble. We found a real need in their children. Families wanted to educate their children in Judaism, and perhaps they might feel we had something to offer in that regard. So we started some children's programs. We began a nursery school in our house until we were told that wasn't allowed. We gave parenting classes. We showed how Judaism could enhance family life.

I also had to get over their stereotyping of me – "the rabbi." At first people weren't able to see me being part of their lives. They thought I was some kind of missionary coming to turn them into orthodox Jews. I needed to show them a different picture, so I set out to show how what I was offering would compliment lives, not detract from them. To break a lot of the stereotypes, I had to totally rethink my approach. I began by reassuring people that my purpose was not to change them completely, but rather to give them something that would add meaning to their lives.

Before I could have any influence on this community I had to become part of it. I needed to build trust, and I began by building friendships. We went on picnics with families. We had a few drinks with them and shared a few laughs. They started to see that in many ways, I was just a regular guy. I had to show them I didn't speak in a Biblical tongue with "thous" and "untos," and I wasn't going to come to a picnic with a tome under my arm.

For the first two years it was a struggle. We built our synagogue one person at a time, taking baby steps. **As it turned out the biggest protestors became our biggest supporters.** I learned that people who care about things will speak out. If they are shown the advantages of belonging, those same passionate people will speak out in your favour. I have learned not to prejudge anyone who loudly protests my beliefs. He may be reaching out and actually yelling for help. Or, he may be testing me.

I believe any goal can be achieved. When you are traveling down the road and you see an obstacle, you have a few choices. You can let it stop you. You can deal with it head on. Or perhaps best of all, you can jump over it or walk around it. The latter will take a lot less out of you. If you are coming from your soul purpose, you have a strong sense of where you are going. You know your unique path and are coming from a higher plane. With that conviction, nothing can stop you if you tap into your soul – your inner resource that is higher than anything else.

That is not to say I never get down. Sometimes the politics of my job weighs me down. When that happens I usually sit down with my wife and we remind ourselves of what we have accomplished – of the individuals and families we have helped. We have been instrumental in turning lots of families around including families whose children were abusing drugs and are now role model families, children we've assisted in getting an education, and families we've helped to buy a house. Soon after we do this, we feel reenergized.

I live and breathe this job twenty-four hours a day. Most people's jobs are a means to an end. The means is miserable but the end is either the end of the day or the end of the week, where they hope happiness resides. The synagogue's life, my family's life and my life are all intertwined. Much of family time is spent with other families in the community. **I do give up some private time but the benefits offset the sacrifices. My children are raised in a giving atmosphere, which is a role model for the way of life I want them to emulate.** In the long run I think it is a lot more powerful way of life.

I learned a valuable lesson in giving when I came to Toronto. When I first arrived here people did not want my gifts, yet giving is what a rabbi does. I had to first seek to understand the community's needs. Only then was I able to give them what they wanted.

Dr. Gerstein's Comments

How to get yourself out of a funk
when you face an obstacle

Rabbi Plotkin has a good method of changing his mood. When the tedious parts of the job begin to get to him, he doesn't tackle it head on. Instead, he sits down and thinks of the more fulfilling parts of his career. With his wife, he recounts all of the families they have helped and the lives they have changed. Soon, without him consciously being aware of it, he feels better. Happiness is often like a mirage, disappearing when you try to grab it directly. Happiness is not a goal in itself, but rather a byproduct of your beliefs and thoughts; a result of your choices and actions.

You too can use this method to get you out of a funk. Think of what you can do to elevate your mood. Make the list when you are feeling good because you will have a difficult time focusing while in the midst of a sad state. The list can include activities that normally make you feel better like taking a bath, playing your favourite music, watching a funny movie, and talking to a supportive friend. You could also think of your original purpose for being in your Dream Career and the people you have helped along the way.

No matter how meticulously you plan your future you will face obstacles. There are politics in every job, and even Dream Careers involve activities that are not dreamlike. You may come up against complaints, broken promises, late shipments and bounced cheques. At times you will feel frustrated or depressed. Rest assured you are not alone. Everyone has obstacles in their lives. What separates successful people from the rest is the effective ways they deal with these challenges.

Make your list today before you come up against a roadblock.

"Just as a small fire is extinguished by the storm whereas a large fire is enhanced by it - likewise a weak faith is weakened by predicament and catastrophes whereas a strong faith is strengthened by them."

Viktor E. Frankl

Joan Barrington
"Bunky" The Therapeutic Clown

"At the cottage I had dreamt of a clown. In the morning I told my father, 'I know what I'm going to be…I'm going to be a clown.' I was married with children. I had no idea where this came from."

As a child I had to go to The Hospital for Sick Children (SickKids) for an appendectomy. It was the first time I was away from home, and back then parents were not allowed to stay. There were so many firsts during that hospital experience. I had so many fears that I never forgot. It became a negative imprint on my memory.

Fast forward to the summer of 1985. By now I was married with two children. We were at the cottage, and one morning I awoke from a very vivid dream of being a clown. When I came down to breakfast I said to my father, "I know what I'm going to be…I'm going to be a clown." I had no idea where that came from.

I was about to discover how those scenarios would come together.

Before the birth of my two boys I had a miscarriage. This experience made me realize how precious my sons were and I decided to stay home as a full-time mom. In 1987, I was having lunch with my youngest son. After watching the morning cartoons I switched to the noon news. Valerie Pringle was interviewing Karen Ridd. They showed her clown persona "Robo" working as a therapeutic clown at the Winnipeg Children's Hospital. As I watched her interacting with critically ill children, the lights and bells went off in my head and I said, **"Yes – that's the kind of clown I am supposed to be."**

The pull was so strong that I sensed this was my destiny. I knew I had to speak to Karen Ridd, so I immediately phoned the CBC to discover how to reach her. I left a message, and she returned my call. We spoke several times, and when I read her paper on therapeutic clowning, I wept. My journey had begun. I wasn't sure how or where I was going to do it, but I was sure this was my destiny. **I knew it from my heart not my head. I was being pulled along this path.**

Karen advised me to get involved in clowning in any and all ways I could find. I had some experience in acting. It seemed so natural to me. My aunt, Josephine Barrington, was a well-known actress in Toronto and Stratford. It was in my genes, but I guess I wasn't ready yet. I didn't have a degree and I was afraid I wasn't good enough. What did I know about therapeutic clowning? I needed more experience to bolster my confidence.

I took a clown class at Seneca College in the evenings, which focused on applying clown make-up and learning tricks. I did some improv comedy at Second City, and acted at a local theatre. I was a party clown for birthdays, and events like Big Sisters and The Children's Aid Society Christmas parties. I wanted to see where I fit in this profession. Karen was right. Getting involved in different aspects of clowning led me to my next step. **Doing things helped me know where to go next. My purpose was to be a therapeutic clown. I couldn't have gotten that from a textbook.**

I was still not feeling ready, so I chickened out by taking a safe position in administration and sales. I feared failing if I followed my artistic side, so I focused on the business aspect of theatre. Getting a degree in Arts Management was my next step, which led me to volunteer with the Young People's Theatre. By producing two plays at my son's public school, I saw how theatre opened up even the shyest and most awkward child on stage. This inspired me, and I realized I was finally ready to embrace my path.

Gathering up my courage, I approached SickKids with a formal proposal and offered to begin a Therapeutic Clown Program. I first looked at becoming part of the women's auxiliary or the volunteer resources department. However, I felt if therapeutic clowning was to be a respected profession, we should be part of the multi-professional team and, as such, be on staff and paid accordingly. I looked for another department.

A doctor friend suggested I approach the child life department of SickKids, which looks after the psychosocial aspect of care. In my pitch, I described the importance of gentle play and humour in relation to the psychosocial needs of sick children, and how our partnership in this mission was an important part of their recovery. The director of child life told me she had heard of the Winnipeg therapeutic clown program and Karen Ridd, and thought it was a noble cause. Unfortunately, she told me, there was no money in their budget. Undeterred I asked, "If I raise the funds for this program will you allow me to run it?" To this she said, "Yes."

I believe in the saying, "If you can dream it, you can do it." You just have to keep experimenting. I knew this was my destiny, and I would find a way to make it happen. This turned out to be the most difficult part of my career.

In 1990 I flew to Winnipeg and shadowed David Langdon, "Hubert," a truly inspiring gentle therapeutic clown at Winnipeg Children's Hospital. For the next three years I wrote out fundraising proposals for this new program I passionately believed in. It was extremely hard work to raise awareness and funding for my position. I could have made a lot more money in private practice as an entertainment/party clown, but I stuck with it because I believed strongly in the methodology of therapeutic clowning and what it could do for these chronically ill children.

Then Karen *Robo* Ridd, whose father was a United Church minister, put me in contact with her United Church friends in Toronto. They administered the funds I raised. Pioneering sponsors included The Tippet Foundation, The Rotary Club of Toronto, and Levi Strauss.

In the spring of 1993, six years after laying eyes on *Robo* the therapeutic clown on TV and realizing what I wanted to do, I launched the therapeutic clown program at SickKids. I had done it. I realized my dream. We opened with one clown, *Robo*. After mentoring with "Robo"

Karen and child life for six months, my own vulnerable clown persona, "Bunky" was born in hospital. This was the authentic me, the clown who comes out to play from the inside out – the soul whisperer.

Now I wear several hats. I am a therapeutic clown, therapeutic clown practitioner and senior manager of the therapeutic clown program at SickKids. I still fundraise and I am the co-founder and now past director of *Therapeutic Clowns Canada*, which raises money to seed therapeutic clown programs in other hospitals.

What I most love about my work are these children. They are my true heroes. Our team of therapeutic clowns are on all five inpatient floors and out in the day clinics two days a week. I love it when "Bunky" happens upon some young friends from years ago and they come running over for a big hug and a high-five to catch me up with their lives. Once I worked with a seven-year-old boy who after his heart transplant was afraid to move after such a major operation. He was petrified when he saw the large scar on his chest and thinking he might stop breathing again. He cried silently and often. The child was totally frozen, so his nurse asked "Bunky" to go in and get him mobile again.

When I got to his room his parents were with him. But he just lay there staring straight ahead. When I was still just out of sight, I gently rang my bell so he could first hear me. Next, I gently blew bubbles across the doorway then into the room. The bubbles caught the little boy's eye, but he still didn't move. Bunky asked permission to enter into his space. After being accepted and still blowing bubbles, I began riding my tricycle, following the bubbles inch by inch through the doorway – not too close. I handed his parents the butterfly net and I gently encouraged them to begin catching my bubbles. Still nothing from my little friend. "Be patient Joan," I told myself. "It will come." I moved onto a child's chair and gradually blew bubbles a little closer towards him. I brought out some wind-up toys and with each turn I put them on the floor heading them towards his bed. I gently coaxed him to take a look to see who or what was coming his way.

Then it happened…he started to move…slowly at first, then a little more direct. His total focus was now on the bubbles overhead and as he was trying to catch them in his hands, his feet glided over the edge of the bed. I was ecstatic! I had taken his mind and attention off his operation, his scar and this hospital space and into another world of magic. When he began walking I could hardly control myself. But I had to stay "in nose" – as my persona, "Bunky." My heart was bursting with joy.

His nurse smiled happily and later told me how much she appreciated what I had done for him. That kind of gratitude from parents and staff just reinforces my belief that this career is where I'm supposed to be.

Therapeutic clowning is about building trusting relationships. Bunky is present to humanize a stressful time and place and offer up choices when there is no choice. Patients have no choice over their illness, who comes into their room, what medication they have to take, how long they have to stay, etc. Bunky's presence alone brings pure silliness to this highly structured environment. I am not there to entertain but to travel along beside them in their journey through illness. These are chronically ill children and often in the hospital for a very long time, sometimes all their young lives. I hope to normalize their lives as much as possible by offering a safe play space – to be children first, *then* sick children. Now, patients book their clinic appointments around the therapeutic clown days. They develop a comfort level and trusting friendship with *their* clown. Being in hospital is a necessity for these children; being alone in their ordeal is not. I go straight to what is working for them, not to what isn't working. I never forgot the feeling of abandonment of that little girl fifty years ago, who had to stay all alone in the hospital when she had her appendix out. Because of therapeutic clowns like Bunky, children today do not have to feel that same sense of abandonment. I am humbled and privileged to travel along side these children in their journey through illness.

Dr. Gerstein's Comments

Joan was out of her mind.
When are you going to get out of yours?

So many people choose a career for the wrong reason. Some do it because it is popular at the time. Some relent to pressure from parents or significant others. Others do it for money. And some do it because it seemed logical. The problem with all these reasons is the reasoning. If you have a logical reason for a career, it is coming from your mind, and it is probably not your passion. Dreams don't come from your mind – they come from your heart.

Joan did not have a life-long dream for a vocation. When her children were old enough she went into sales and fundraising because that is what she knew. She took a job as an administrative assistant because it was close to home. Those are hardly moving scenarios for entering into a career, yet it is how many people choose their life's work.

It was only when she saw the TV show that it triggered her traumatic childhood memory of having to stay alone in the hospital. She was so deeply moved by it that she knew it was her destiny. That sudden awareness and declaration did not come from reasoning things out. It didn't come from her mind. It came from a place inside of her heart, and it felt right. The key word here is FELT. If your career came from THINKING it probably is not your Dream Career.

Your Dream Career will move you. There are tough days to endure in any career so you had better love what you are doing to get through them. On a lighter note, when you are coming from your heart you feel energized. Joan wears five different hats at work and I am truly moved by how much she does. She would not have that kind of dedication if she had merely thought up this career. She had to know it was for her.

Dr. Gerstein's Comments

Finding one's Dream Career is not about filling out a bunch of psychometric tests and getting a computer to print out an answer. It has to be personal. You are unique so look at what has moved you in your life. Look at what has made you laugh and what has made you cry. Look at what has pulled on your heart strings and you will be looking in the right direction. Get out of your mind. Get into your heart.

Myth-Diagnosis #7
Fatal Failure Phobia

◆

How *You* Can Bust This Myth

Most people fear failure but, the people I interviewed for *Live Your Dreams* had a totally different perspective. Not only did they not fear failure, they often didn't even recognize it as such. As a group, they had a tough time recalling their failures because they saw the experiences as learning opportunities for growth. I began calling them "flopportunities" (every flop has embedded within it an opportunity) so the interviewees could better relate. I do not believe that it is a coincidence that people living their dreams do not allow "failure" to stop them. In fact it is embraced.

List the "flopportunities" you have experienced in your life. Write down what you learned from each? The bigger the failure, the bigger the lesson. How did it change your behaviour? If you are embarrassed by your so-called "failures," use this as an opportunity to learn something new. Some say that it is our mistakes, more than our successes, that help us grow – but only if you learn from them and stop running from them. Use this time now to write down the lessons you will take away from the "flopportunities" in your life. Plan how you will act, think or feel differently when faced with similar circumstances in the future.

Take solace in the fact that every successful person you see has failed at something sometime in life. And often the bigger the success one has had the bigger the failures she has overcome.

Myth – Diagnosis #8 Empty Pocket Stress Syndrome

"I don't have enough money."

*"Initially invest ten times the effort and energy up front,
for one times the return. Later you will get ten times
the return for one times the effort and energy."*

Ken Vegotsky

Mark Gelgor

Operations Director of Sportball™

*"For the first three years I was working until 2 a.m.,
seven days a week solid. What sustained me was the love for
the work, and the children's enjoyment of our program."*

Changing countries AND changing careers was not a small challenge. It turned into a ride I wish I had begun a lot earlier.

I grew up in South Africa. As a child I was fairly artistic, and enjoyed sculpting and painting. My artistic nature, coupled with living in a country where jewelry is a large industry, led me to believe I could succeed creatively in that field. I began making jewelry, and by 1983 I was managing a jewelry workshop. After a big retail chain bought us up, a series of robberies followed, and our insurance premiums skyrocketed. The stress became too much for me. While driving to work, I sometimes found myself banging my head on the steering wheel with dread. To say my job satisfaction was in decline would be an understatement. I began hating every minute of it.

The stress and dread began affecting my health. I would wake up in the middle of the night completely drenched in sweat. Convinced there must be something seriously wrong with me, I sought medical help. But when the doctors ran tests, they came up empty. They neglected to ask me about the effects my work stress was having on me. My only reprieve for the week was coaching kids' sports on the weekend. I loved it, and that turned out to be a clue for my future Dream Career.

In the middle of winter, in 1991, I came to Canada to visit my cousin. Because of my interest in sports, I asked him to take me to a hockey game. What I saw at that game blew me away. As I watched the kids on the ice, a father began yelling at his five-year-old son. As he berated him, I saw the look of disappointment on the child's face. The berating continued after the child came off the ice. I was already shocked by the cold climate in Canada, but it was the cold climate inside the arena between that father and son that truly rattled and distressed me. I decided to come back one spring to see if things had warmed up in *all* areas of Canadian life.

When I returned in early 1994 I took a deep breath of the warm spring breezes that were blowing. People were no longer bundled in their winter wear, and already I was more optimistic about what I would find in the sports fields. When I attended a soccer game in a nearby field, this time I witnessed a different scenario. It also cried out for attention, but of a different nature. As I watched, I saw children who simply lacked the skills to play the game. **Immediately I recognized a potential niche in this country – children who needed to learn the skills of sports.**

I had always loved playing sports. I was quite proficient in gymnastics and enjoyed playing cricket, tennis, squash and soccer. With this background I reasoned I could teach children the skills required for various sports. I had coached children in South Africa, and I could do it in Canada. Sports are sports. I am also a kid at heart, and I decided it was a dream match for me. Now came the hard part – making that dream a reality. It turned out to be even harder than I thought.

When my wife, Carmella, and I immigrated to Canada the next year, my fears got the best of me. In the space on the immigration form asking for "career" I wrote in "jeweler." Even though I now had another dream, I rationalized that a fresh start in the jewelry business in a new country might rejuvenate me. I couldn't have been more wrong. After only four days on the job, I quit! I walked away but would return for a short while out of necessity.

The sale of my assets in South Africa had not netted as much as I hoped because of the poor currency exchange rate. Once we converted our money we were left with only enough to live in Canada for about a year. What was I going to do? How would I get started in my new career?

Someone suggested I get a book called, *Help, We've Got Kids*. In a search for potential customers for my services, I called every business in that book. Carmella and I were determined to make this work. We made hundreds of cold calls. We often showcased our program to interested parents who would call later to find out more about it. Our ratio of calls to appointments was about twenty-five to one; however, when we started doing face-to-face selling, that ratio dramatically improved.

We had only enough money to lease one van in which we carried around all our sports equipment. For the first nine months we made a pittance working at schools, community centres and sports clubs. We were struggling badly, and I began to seriously grow nervous about our financial situation. In a bit of a panic I opened the job section of the paper and looked at some jewelry ads – the industry I thought I had walked away from for good. I ended up making copper bracelets for three or four hours a night for several months, and this brought in some badly needed cash.

In the middle of that tough first year we sometimes wondered if we should go back to South Africa. Things just didn't seem to be working out. If we went back, at least we would have a way of earning an income that was familiar. But neither of us wanted to do that, so we made an agreement to give it 100% for two years and promised not to consider any alternatives until the two years were up. Only then would we reassess our financial situation.

For the first three years Carmella and I both put in seven-day weeks. When some friends asked us to join them at an *Earth, Wind and Fire* concert that would have set us back over $100, we passed, thinking of how we could use that money in our business. It was three years before either of us could relax on a weekend. I often worked until 2 a.m. I'd go to bed exhausted and wake up at 8 a.m. to lead another group of children. What sustained me was my passion for what I was doing, and the kids.

Despite all the hardships of starting the business, it was the kids that kept me going. One day I wasn't feeling too well. Coming to a new country and playing with children all day long meant I contracted all of the colds and viruses they brought with them. I had no immunity to any of it. That day I woke up vomiting. I couldn't call in sick because I was running the program, while my wife was handling the marketing and logistical arrangements. The kids could see I wasn't feeling so well. Then, one of the little ones in my morning class came up and asked, "Mark, if I sit on your lap will that make you feel better?" How could I not be motivated with that kind of love around me?

I love what the program does for children. For example, one day a three-year-old boy named Lou came into one of our classes, wearing his mother's hat. I guess she dressed him in it because she thought he looked cute, but all it brought him was ridicule from the other children. Lou was introverted and overweight – a recipe for disaster if left unchecked in his early school years. I wanted to help turn this child around and give him some confidence through athleticism. At the beginning of each class I quietly removed the hat. Then I slowly taught Lou the fundamental skills of sport. Eventually, he became more coordinated in all areas of sport. At the end of three years Lou sported a baseball cap turned backwards, and the other kids were saying, "I want to be on Lou's team." It was quite a change for this child, and I felt great knowing I had a hand in helping him, not only in sports, but in life.

All of our hard work finally began to pay off. At the end of our first year, one of the schools we worked for gave us our first long-term contract. It was the first time we'd had any kind of security at all in our business. To this day we still go out and do programs for that school because of our gratitude; they believed in us when we were just starting out. By the end of that first year we had earned about $2,000. Not much, but it was a start.

We continued to market our program to the public, learning as we went. On one occasion Carmella and I worked diligently to set up a demo for families at a local cricket club. On the day the demo ran, we had not yet secured a facility to run the program. We ended up taking the parent's phone numbers, assuring them we would call them shortly with the location. But these parents were excited enough by the demo that most of them didn't bother to wait for our call. Instead, they enrolled their children in a competitor's program. We did the marketing and another program got the sale!

I was depressed for about five days. So much effort gone to waste. On the fifth day I woke up and said to myself, "Learn and move on," And that is what we did. We learned to always secure the facility before we do the demo so we can sign the children up on the spot. In addition, we developed the habit of waking up every morning at 8 a.m. no matter what time our programs start that day. It gets us going, and I believe that when we are moving and connecting to people good things will happen.

After eighteen months we decided we had to start charging per child in order to have any chance of making this program work. We got out of the school programming and began offering our services independently. By the end of the second year we had a hundred and twenty children enrolled in Sportball™ classes around the city. Additionally, we each hired one assistant to help us with the growing business, and one of those became our first coach. It was the first time I realized I could teach someone else to do what I did, freeing up my time to expand the business. It was a turning point for us. While I discovered that I can teach others to coach my way, I cannot teach them the passion I have for what I do. Making sure our coaches have that passion comes through careful selection in the hiring process.

In the first year we began with three children in our first independent class at a country club. Now we have 2,700 children enrolled per week, employ twenty-eight coaches and are still growing. The financial success is great. But I know I would never have gotten this far if not for the pleasure I experience when working with the children.

Dr. Gerstein's Comments

Hard work early on in your Dream will pay big dividends later.

Mark didn't have a lot of money to start his Dream Career. He had fewer savings than what he had expected because of the poor exchange rate between his South African rand and the Canadian dollar. When his company did not take off immediately Mark did not quit. He persevered until he saw the results he wanted.

At the beginning Mark reluctantly worked in his former industry to earn some needed cash to stay afloat. He learned from mistakes, and redirected his efforts to begin independent sports programs instead of affiliating with schools. He also decreased his spending in the first few years of his startup, watching carefully to not fritter his cash away on anything superfluous. He knew any savings at this time would make a huge difference later.

Today we live in an immediate gratification society. We want things and we want them now. From the people I interviewed I learned that if you invest a lot of work in the first few years of your venture, it will pay dividends later. This is a key piece of wisdom that they passed on to me. There is no magic short-cut to your dream, and if there is I haven't found many people who took it. I will go one step further: If you did happen to find and take this mythical magical short-cut you would probably not be as satisfied when you got to where you wanted to go. Part of the satisfaction comes in the struggle to follow your unique path. Did you ever notice how you appreciate those things in life that were the most challenging to acquire?

Your path is a lifelong journey, not a destination. So put in the time and effort now, and you will see the benefits of your work down the road.

*"Our success has really been based
on partnerships from the very beginning."*

Bill Gates

Robin Tapley

Creator and Leader of Nature Tourism programs

*"I was flabbergasted...I had no idea there could be
this kind of interest for what I considered a hobby of mine."*

I was born around nature and grew up in nature. It comes as no surprise to me that my Dream Career is in nature. But I had no inkling that I would find it the way I did.

As a young boy, I was always interested in nature. I grew up on the edge of Canada's famous Algonquin Provincial Park. When I was eight years old, I crossed paths with a rough grouse. I suddenly found myself staring at this bird about the size of a chicken. I had no idea what it was, but I was totally intrigued so I followed it through the woods in the dark. Already I was in my element.

As I got older, I became a bird lover and continued to track them just to see where they would go. In order to do this, I learned to always keep my eyes and ears open. This habit turned out to be the key to discovering my Dream Career.

In university I majored in business and marketing, and when I graduated, I got a position at The Minaki Lodge, a fishing lodge in northern Ontario. Then I got my pilot's license, so I was able to fly fishermen around to various fishing hot spots. From my vantage point in the air, I could see where logging was being conducted, and I became very concerned about the welfare of the rare birds in those areas. That's when I started recording the nesting sites of bald eagles, which I could also clearly see from my aircraft.

This began as a special interest hobby for me, but it turned into a part-time job. When I called the Ontario Ministry of Natural Resources and told them about the work I'd been doing, they were very interested in receiving my research on a regular basis. I would first locate the nests from the air, and then visit the sites by boat. We counted the number of eggs and baby chicks and recorded survival rates in the area. The ministry took that information and was able to divert loggers away from areas of any endangered species.

One day, a couple of guests were on the dock when I returned. We chatted as I tied up the plane, and when they learned what I'd being doing, they asked if they could join me the next day on my route, and I agreed. So I flew them around, gave them a bit of a narrative, and they enjoyed it immensely. In fact, they found their little excursion so interesting they told their friends about it at dinner. Lo and behold the next morning I was greeted by twenty-five eager people waiting for me to take them on my "natural habitat reconnaissance trip!" I was flabbergasted, and excited at the same time. I had no idea there could be this kind of interest in what I considered to be a hobby.

I couldn't possibly accommodate the whole group that day. But it got me thinking about how many other people might be interested in nature, and the environment. I decided to tap into this interest, and began at once to develop my Nature Trails program. I would use it to introduce the public to nature in a soft wilderness environment.

I began conducting bird-watching tours in Ontario, and more adventuresome nature tours in Cost Rica. During this time I became the program director at the Wye Marsh Wildlife Centre, an education research centre in Midland, Ontario. My dream was coming together.

I really wanted a home base from which I could lead all my programs, but I didn't have the financial resources to do it myself. For this I needed help, I needed a partner. I wanted someone well-established who could supply me with an immediate and ongoing flow of clients. After pondering this for a while, I thought maybe I didn't need a "who," maybe I needed a "what." If I could hitch myself onto the back of a popular resort, I could be in a positive cash flow situation immediately, and continue to develop new programs.

I chose the perfect location for me – the Delta Grandview Resort near Huntsville, in the heart of cottage country in Ontario. It had everything I wanted. Now I just had to convince them I had everything they were looking for, even though they weren't yet looking for anything like I was offering. I had to show them how they would benefit from my program, and this meant doing some homework before I approached them. I knew I would have one shot, and I had no intention of squandering it.

I worked out all the logistics. I thought of every possible question they might ask during my proposal, and came up with at least three answers to each question. I racked my brain for any holes in my plan, and when I found one, I quickly filled it in. Finally I was ready. I had worked out a turn-key operation where I would do all the work, and they would get most of the benefits. I would run it under their name. I made it easy for them to say yes, because I had already worked out all of the kinks beforehand.

When I presented my plan to the general manager, he immediately liked it. What attracted him most was the added value I would be offering his guests. As I had hoped, he agreed to fund it. I had gotten the job that was never posted in any headhunter office!

My new job included a full salary, with incentives to continue to develop new programs. My expenses were paid whenever I went on an out-of-country expedition, and I had full use of a vehicle at their expense. I was totally free to develop my program as I saw fit so I was working independently, but at the same time I was working for someone else.

I still use the same method that got me my position with Grandview to introduce new programs in Nature Trails. First I do my homework. I anticipate all the obstacles I can imagine that might crop up, and then deal with each one. That way, when management questions me about my new idea I already have the answers to most of their queries.

My biggest obstacle has also been my biggest strength. I am always thinking of new ideas and new adventures to plan. Sometimes my ideas are a bit of a stretch; in fact, some would say they are way outside the box. People like to come up will all kinds of reasons why a particular idea won't work, but that just motivates me to prove them wrong. I become determined to make it work no matter what, and then spend even more time working out the details to convince them it will.

One of those ideas came from a corporate team-building retreat. Nine independently-thinking CEOs came together for a weekend to learn to work together. Needless to say, coming up with a strategy that would meet with their high expectations was a challenge.

The program was designed to gel the group in a high-pressure situation, and allow them to use their own unique skills to assist in a tense situation. But the plan we came up with had a little twist. We told them we were going to take them into the bush at night. They believed that was the experience. But the real experience would unfold before them.

My two assistants were my partners in crime. My assistant Kendra, made her way out to a river bank with a canoe about an hour before I was to bring the group to that point. She would be alone, and pretend to have fallen on the rocks and suffered a broken leg. The other nature leader was the bus driver, whom the CEOs thought was just coming along for the ride.

As it got dark, I led the group near the target site. By the light of the moon, one of the CEOs noticed an overturned canoe in the river. As I smiled to myself, we all ran to see what had happened. When we got there we found Kendra lying face down on the riverbank giving an Academy Award performance of someone exhausted and in pain. When the team looked at me they only saw the concerned look of their guide. I was acting too, and they didn't catch on.

By escorting these CEOs into a remote area at night we put them in the unusual situation (for them) of not being in control. To successfully navigate this circumstance they had to rely on someone else – first me and then each other. With apparent concern, I told them we had to transport this woman to a parking lot about two and a half kilometers away to get more help. But I allowed them to make the decisions to get us to safety.

One participant took a few others and started to assemble a stretcher out of tree branches and rope. Another one calmed the so-called victim and another made a splint for her leg. It almost all fell apart when one guy pulled out a cell phone to dial 911. I quickly grabbed the phone, shut it off and told him calling now wouldn't do any good. I told him we had to get her to the nearest clearing before we could get help, and we would call from there. The group successfully evacuated the victim using the available resources.

When we got to the clearing, Kendra stood up from the stretcher miraculously healed, and I revealed this was all planned as part of their team building exercise. The entire thing had been a staged event. **As I spoke, my heart was beating a mile a minute; I was well aware of the emotional and physical stress I had just put them through.**

The experience had been traumatic, yet uplifting. It was everything you would experience in a real life-threatening situation. One person was a little upset at first, but most agreed the next day that it got them to work together. It made them realize that as individuals, they might not have all the answers to every question they each face, and they might have to rely on each other at times.

It was such an emotionally powerful exercise I get goose bumps even as I speak about it today. It is an experience those CEOs will never forget, and it was a lesson they appreciated.

I don't always win these battles, nor should I. My passion for my work has led to me being known locally as *Father Nature*, or more humorously, *Muskoka's Nature Nut*. Some of my hair-brained ideas need to be reigned in. I've had some all-out shouting matches with Kendra as we argue over a program's feasibility. We have a great relationship, and I'm thankful to have her on my team. She is sensible and keeps me in check and on budget. I am not a detail person. I can't do that, and I need her for this. My challenge has become to make my programs exciting and fresh yet keep them doable in a timely manner.

Nature is the key behind my Dream Career. Nature led me to serendipitously discover it and nature keeps me inspired. I may be doing my thousandth guided trail, but it may be the first one a guest has been on. I have to be excited about *that* one, and fortunately that is easy for me because I am simply in awe of nature. Every time I go on a nature trail it is new for me. If I ever lose that feeling, I just have to bring a child with me and see it fresh through his eyes. That allows me to slow down and regain the magic of the moment.

Dr. Gerstein's Comments

The Yin of your Dream Career

There is one tool the people in *Live Your Dreams* use, that most other people don't. It is so powerful that just stating it at the beginning would diminish its magnitude. It uses the power of our imagination but is much more than that. Can you guess what it is?

Most people want a guarantee in life. They want to see the results before they do the work. They want to see the cash. One of the biggest problems with our society today is the fast pace at which we live. We want the lottery win, the quick buck. If we don't see, hear or feel it immediately, we dismiss it. We have become impatient in our need for immediate gratification. It was thought that as cell phones and computer technology speeded our communications, our work would be streamlined allowing us extra time to relax. What really happened is that it only led to more demands in a technologically driven environment. Now we can't even get away because of the capabilities of the new communications. We've been duped!

Most worthwhile things are not easy, and they take time. Discovering your dream often involves our female energy, what the Chinese refer to as our Yin. We can't go out and grab it. We have to look inward and allow ourselves the time and space to feel it, and then create it. We need to nurture the concept of delayed gratification.

If you are one of the fortunate few who actually knows what your dreams are, you may still want it now. Again that is a twenty-first century mindset. It is like trying to squeeze a handful of water. The more tightly you squeeze, the more water slips through your fingers.

Dr. Gerstein's Comments

Follow your dream path, but try not to do it in a rigid way. Many of the people featured here started out by volunteering in the area of their choice. They allowed the circumstances to develop on their own, and this brought them in contact with situations or other people who guided them further along their path. They couldn't have seen the opportunities while just sitting at a desk. They had to get out and do it. One of the easiest ways to get into the flow of your dream is to volunteer in that field.

While transporting fishermen to their hot spots, Robin engaged naturally in his lifelong love of birds by noticing bald eagles, and then keeping track of their nests. He also recorded how close the logging areas were to these nests. He created his first job by calling the Ministry of Natural Resources and asking if they'd be interested in his work. He created his second job by taking a guest along on one of his reconnaissance flights. That led to other people becoming interested in joining him on future flights. He created his third career when he realized there was an interest for nature tours. He developed his own program, and then sold the idea to a large resort.

None of this would have been foreseeable if he'd stayed in the privacy of his home. By getting out and volunteering, he made things happen. Doors opened, opportunities arose. He was living his dreams and not just dreaming about it.

Volunteer to do what you love. You will be surprised by the opportunities that may come your way.

*"Some people make things happen, Some watch things happen,
While others wonder, "What happened?""*

Proverb

Gregory Kaminsky
Founder & Owner of Sign Store

*"I was fascinated the first time I saw an engraving machine.
Where I came from back in Russia, I had never seen a machine like
that. I immediately wanted one for myself."*

I grew up in Russia and went to a merchant marine college. By trade I was a ship's engineer, and worked on Soviet boats. I also had an untapped creative side. I was a good draftsman and enjoyed calligraphy. But that side of me lay dormant until serendipity allowed me to discover my niche.

As a Jew, travel outside mainland Soviet Union was prohibited. Working on a boat was my only opportunity to see the world. We were located in ports in Canada, Europe and Japan. Whenever I traveled I didn't want to return home, but I was afraid of repercussions to my family if I did not. In 1975 I received permission for my wife and I to come to Canada.

When we arrived I found a job with the Canadian Steamship Line. The company started me in the engine room as a non-union worker. Because I spoke very little English, they underestimated my abilities. Then one day the engine totally broke down. I got to work on it as soon as it happened. I fixed the pistons, reengineered the cylinder and got it running again. After that my supervisors understood I was not just a grease monkey. They promised me work, but only until the end of the winter. Sure enough when spring came, they told me they would be hiring union people again. I had no desire to join a union so I told them I was walking.

I found a job across the road with The United Steel and Metal Company. For the next two years I worked in the scrap yard cutting metal, and welding and repairing trucks. I was gaining experience and providing food for my family, but I always hoped that one day I would get a better opportunity. At one point, I sensed that my foreman was threatened by my apparent potential because he started making my work life difficult – so I quit. Within three weeks I landed a job with the Union Boiler Company of Hamilton. The new job meant an increase in income and an upgraded benefits package. I did that until I began seeing some layoffs. I was afraid I was going to be on the chopping block next.

I have always been an independent person. I have never liked unions where uniformity is the rule and creativity is all but dead. I enjoy making decisions on my own – thinking for myself, and in Canada you are free to do that. I don't want someone else to tell me I can't have this job because I don't have the proper seniority. I believe rewards should correspond to your talents and the effort you put into your work.

There was only one way to solve my dilemma. I realized I had to start my own company. So I bought a truck and started my own scrap metal business. I was excited and nervous about going into business for myself. When I needed some help, it came from a man I had met at our synagogue. Goldal Silver gave me both financial backing and advisory assistance in selling my services. I will never forget what he did for me. That experience would later help me when I got into another business.

After my truck was vandalized a few times, I figured that someone in a union felt threatened by my presence. It dawned on me that I didn't have complete freedom in this country either. This frightened me, and I became concerned for my family. We had a newborn son, and my wife's parents had just emigrated from the Soviet Union. I decided Hamilton was not the best place for me, so I packed everything up and moved to Toronto.

In Toronto I found a job doing maintenance work at CIBC head office. It was a big step down, but we needed money. The events in Hamilton had scared me off, and I was licking my wounds.

At work one day I noticed they had an engraving machine, which produced nameplates and labels. I was fascinated by this device. I had never seen anything like it before. Earlier I had made an $800 investment in precious metals, and when I sold it I was delighted to walk away with $5,000. Using some of that money I bought a small engraving machine and began my own hobby. I was working the evening shift (4 p.m. to midnight) at the bank so I was happy to find something to do in the daytime.

When friends got wind of what I was doing they would ask me to engrave things for them. They wanted office desk nameplates, and jewellery engravings. They told their friends, and people were literally lining up for my services in our tiny apartment. What started out as a hobby began earning me pocket money. After seeing the looks of appreciation on people's faces I began thinking more creatively. I asked myself, what else can I do to be creative in this industry? What other materials can I use? How can I expand my services?

In what turned out to be the first of several relocations to garner more space, we moved from our apartment to a semi-detached house. The house had a separate walkout from the basement so I could run my little business without affecting my home life. Increased demand forced me to add two additional engraving machines, and a vinyl machine. Then I had to hire some part-timers to work with me in my basement.

Meanwhile the maintenance company that supplied workers to the bank was bought out, and once again I was not part of the union. Unhappy with the new work conditions, I quit. That was pretty tough on our family's income. But my wife was always supportive of me. She began teaching piano and for awhile we lived off her income. I only withdrew $100 a week for groceries from what I took in. I needed to create something bigger that would support my family. I decided to go into the signage business.

In 1981 I borrowed $10,000 from my father-in law and bought a small 1,500 square foot industrial unit in Toronto. That is where I officially began my sign shop. There's a downside to owning your own business – you have to stay until the job is done! There is no such thing as overtime for the owner. The upside is I got to create the kind of work I wanted. I was able to achieve a lot with my own hands. With growth came the need to hire sculptors, designers and painters to take it to the next level.

Bill Taylor with the CIBC gave me my first big break. He was in charge of purchasing and facility management at the Commerce Court location in downtown Toronto. I knew him from when I was a maintenance worker. He initially hired me to do small nameplates for broker offices. When he recommended me to a securities company, they contracted me to do large signs. They liked my work.

Over time I developed a solid reputation for good work and dependability. As a result, I never had any trouble getting supplier extensions or bank loans. Once I needed a special tool only available in the US. When I called the company they asked who my suppliers were. I told them, and the next morning the needed tool was at my front door with a bill attached. My suppliers had vouched for me.

I enjoy the creative part of the business, and I've had to learn to manage the financial aspects. Much of that learning came through the school of hard knocks. I have been duped into making signs for people who have then reneged on the balance. I've learned to get all the terms and conditions on paper right from the start.

In 1989 we were doing so well that we relocated to a 10,000 square foot facility. I have a staff of fourteen people, and my wife and son are valued partners. Every sign is different than the last. It's a learning process. Some people who do this use only a few materials. In contrast, we use a couple of thousand materials in our signs. The technology we use is all up-to-date and I am just as committed to my customers now as I was when I first began in my tiny apartment. I got into this business because I enjoyed the creative part of it. Twenty-two years later I am still able to be creative.

I was never a union man. I have always enjoyed doing things my own way. However, that doesn't mean I've done it on my own. There are many people who have helped me along the way, and I am grateful to all of them. Without them I might not be where I am today – doing what I love.

Dr. Gerstein's Comments

Overcoming obstacles

Gregory Kaminsky faced numerous obstacles to success in his Dream Career. Coming from the Soviet Union he had a language barrier. He was trained as a ship's engineer, not what he loved but what was available to him in the Soviet Union. He arrived in Canada when he was twenty-eight with little formal education, and he wasn't given his due respect for his engineering training and experience. He lost several jobs in his early years in Canada because of his refusal to join a union. He was even chased out of Hamilton because of it.

He only found his future path by accident while working as a maintenance worker at a major bank. The engraving machine gave him something to do in his spare time. Many people would call him lucky and say "He just happened to be in the right place at the right time". My response to that is, "Hogwash."

We are all surrounded by hundreds of opportunities every day. Most of us are so busy complaining or hoping for a lottery win that we don't even notice them. Gregory Kaminsky noticed. However, if that were all he did he would still be dreaming about his own business. What made him different from most people? He ACTED on his wishes.

Taking action is what separates people who only hope things will happen from people who actually make things happen. *Dreams without action are fantasy. Actions without dreams are empty. Dreams combined with actions manifest one's destiny.* The power comes when you combine the two:
DREAMS + ACTION = PERSONAL POWER.

The odds were stacked against Gregory Kaminsky. If you had added up all of his potential obstacles when he first started his venture, you would likely have given him little chance of success.

Dr. Gerstein's Comments

Yet Gregory wouldn't have cared about that. He was doing what he loved and was building his business one step at a time.

What first began as a hobby eventually turned into a 10,000 square foot, professional, quality driven company whose owner still believes in creativity.

What do you believe in? What do you love? Which of your hobbies can you expand? Ignore those who talk about the odds of success. They can't see your heart – the key ingredient in following your dreams.

"The mice think they are right, but my cat eats them anyways. This is the point, reality is nothing, perception is everything."

Terry Goodkind

Greg Brophy
President and Chairman of Shred It

"The more I knew the less I talked and the more I listened."

The number one thing preventing my company from moving ahead was me. I was so enthusiastic about what my company was selling that I wanted to tell the whole world about it. But I was running a company, and I wasn't in it alone. About ten years ago I realized the most important part of my company were the people. If I wanted exponential growth, I would have to give more control to the people who worked for me.

At first it was tough to just sit there and be quiet. I was accustomed to leading by words. In meetings I had to write down on a piece of paper in front of me, "Shut up; Be Quiet" because I had all this energy. I just wanted to share my ideas. The best thing I could do was to be quiet and listen, and that was a huge change for me. It's ironic – **the more I knew the less I talked and the more I listened.**

I grew up around business. My father was a businessman. He owned several companies and always seemed to enjoy it. While growing up my three brothers and I often pitched in and helped, and overall it was a positive experience. I had a gift for selling creatively that may stem from my attitude that all problems are solvable. In due course making a deal became a passion for me.

It seems like I was either in a business or thinking about one all through school. In grade eight I watered lawns for new model homes. Beginning in grade eleven I sealed driveways for seven years. Eventually I became the supplier of a driveway sealant to other driveway sealing companies. In first year university I read *Cane and Abel* by Jeffrey Archer, and that motivated me to get into real estate. I bought older houses, renovated them and then sold them for a profit. My parents weren't in a position to lend me money, so I used my savings to put a deposit down. Then I'd go out and get a mortgage. I scratched money together to take a risk, and then I took more risks. It turned out that the experience of taking risks was more valuable than the money I made. That prepared me for my future business.

Both my older brothers were studying engineering at university so I enrolled in engineering as well. Then, just two weeks before I was set to begin, my brothers took me aside and questioned my choice of a major. They told me I was never the academic type and reminded me I was always into some sort of business. Being the youngest I just assumed I would follow in their footsteps. It took their caring and openness to help me see the light. They suggested I change to a bachelor of commerce program, which was more suited to my business aspirations. I listened, and I'm glad I did. Listening to others turned out to be a key part of my future.

By my second year of college I knew I wanted to run a business. I often stayed after class to pester my professors for advice on starting a business. When I asked one of them about an idea, he suggested I hire a board like they have at public companies to give me continual business advice but one that wasn't held liable for their role. It was a novel idea, and one I used after starting my own company.

After receiving my commerce degree I went on to complete my MBA. I now had the degrees, but I still wasn't sure what I wanted to do. There were so many businesses from which to choose and I wanted to make the right choice. **Statistically, more people spend more time**

choosing a sofa than they do a career. I didn't want to make that same mistake. I didn't want to get caught up in the idea of a new business because I was an excitable emotional person. I wanted to keep focused. To help me do that I drew up a list of the top ten things I was looking for in a business. These would be my criteria from which I would choose my ideal career. Some of the criteria on my list included:

1. **I wanted to be proactive in going out and getting business.** I didn't want to wait for people to come to me, like in a retail situation.

2. **It had to be focused on the business week.** I love spending time with my wife and children. I didn't want a business where I would have to work a lot of evenings or weekends.

3. I wanted the product to be **environmentally friendly**. I didn't want to do something that would hurt the planet. I wanted to do my part.

4. **No client could make up a big percent of the business**. I didn't want to be too dependent on any one client. In that scenario, should that client go under, he would drag me under with him.

5. I wanted a business that had the **potential for global expansion**.

6. **I wanted a business that sold to business.** Selling to individual customers was too difficult. I learned in the driveway sealant business that individuals don't always respect time. If they spend ten minutes to save five dollars they will do it. Business people won't. In addition, you can sell larger quantities to businesses and they will keep using you as long as you give good service.

When I finished the list, I prioritized it according to importance. With my list in hand I began looking at all the business opportunities I could find. It became my game plan for choosing my future business. It wasn't long until I discovered Shred-it, a company that shreds confidential paper for other companies. It was perfect. It met all of my criteria, and I became excited about the future.

At this time I was twenty-six and already married with one child. To raise capital I took the $100,000 I had earned from my real estate business, and then used the equity in my house to raise another $140,000. I needed the money to purchase the trucks, the large shredding machines and to hire my first seven employees in the first two years.

I told my wife it would take two years of hard work to make it over the hump. **Well it actually took five years of sixteen-hour days to get my company into a good financial position.** I had a lot to learn in those early years.

In the beginning I had these dreams and ambitions of how I would build my company and keep my employees happy. Then reality hit. I had fewer clients and more expenses than I predicted. Revenue didn't come in as fast as I'd thought it would. Trucks started breaking down. It became a real grind. After the first four months I spent every day finding ways to keep costs down and my staff paid. It was like prolonged boot camp. I was tired and stressed. **What kept me going was my belief that all these challenges had solutions.** That period taught me a lot about running a business though. I dug deep down to continually come up with creative solutions to keep my business solvent.

The first two and a half years were the toughest. After that, the challenges were just as great, but I got used to it. It was sort of like swimming. Moving from the shallow end of the pool to the deep end is tough, but once you are there it no longer matters if the water gets any deeper – you still have to keep swimming to stay afloat. I wouldn't give up, and my wife was very supportive through those early years. Too often I brought my worries home with me. My doctor advised me to leave the stress at work, and suggested I focus on my family when I got home. My friends listened to my stresses, and that meant a lot to me. I sought advice from other business owners and anyone else that could help. I began to exercise regularly, and that helped me better cope with the extreme workload. All the while I held on to my dream for my company. That definitely helped me through the lean years.

After only eight months our cash flow began to falter and the bank became tough to deal with. But after all that hard work I wasn't about to give up. I believed in what I was doing and the future of my company. Instead of allowing myself to be in the weak position of going to the banks to plead for help, I decided to turn the tables. I put out a call to the five big banks, telling each one I would meet with them at *my* office. I intentionally did that to make them treat me as a potential valued customer. I wanted *them* to sell *me* on accepting their bank as the one who gets the opportunity to invest in my successful company. Also, sitting behind my own desk gave me the power position usually reserved for the loan officer back in his office.

The strategy worked. I got an offer bid for twice as much money as the loan that I had with the previous bank. I paid off that loan and now had more money to continue to invest and grow my company. I figured I was on my way out of this hole.

But I needed to do more. I had started my business selling people on what my company could do for them. Once I got in their office, I was off and running trying to sell them on why they should buy from me. I was still running my company that way, doing most of the talking and leading. I had to learn to listen more. I had hired good managers, but I was telling them what to do. I was still doing their jobs. I realized if I allowed them to come up with the solutions they would feel more valued, and more like part of the company. You would think that the more you know, the more you should share what you know. I discovered it was the opposite – the more I knew the less I should say.

I started to let go of the reigns. I encouraged my people to take on more responsibility and then I praised them for their efforts. I began noticing people becoming more confident with their job when I stopped trying to be an expert in every area.

The turning point came when I read two books by Jim Collins – *Good to Great: Why Some Companies Make the Leap... and Others Don't* by Jim Collins, (HarperCollins Publishers Inc.) and *Built to Last: Successful Habits of Visionary Companies* by Jim Collins and Jerry I. Porras (HarperCollins Publishers Inc.). Collins talks about who should be on the bus, who needs to change seats and who has to get off the bus. It finally sank in that the people I hired – *my employees* – are the most valuable assets of my business.

That became evident during what turned out to be a colossal breakdown in my company. I had changed to a new vendor to build the shredders in our shredding trucks, which are worth a quarter of a million dollars each. Within a few weeks of the installations all forty trucks began to break down simultaneously in different countries around the world. Logistically it was very difficult to get people out to repair them in all of those areas. It was a nightmare.

I later discovered the new vendor didn't have enough quality controls in place. Their shredders were poorly manufactured and couldn't tolerate the workload. It was my own fault – lack of experience and lack of due diligence. I tried to sue the vendor but quickly discovered they didn't have enough assets to cover the cost of the shredders.

I learned some valuable lessons from this fiasco. One is to make sure the people I deal with have more to lose than me if something goes wrong. Another was to have people around me who can cover my weaknesses. I now surround myself with people who have the skills I lack, like the detail people I have who are now responsible for quality control.

I learned to trust and rely on my own people. I don't blame them for mistakes as long as they don't continue to make them. Likewise, if I continually made the same mistake I wouldn't deserve to run the company any more. **I've always believed it's not how long you stand that counts, it's how many times you are willing to get back up when you fall down.** I have trouble remembering my mistakes because when I make one I don't beat myself up. I don't recall being blamed for things growing up, and that gave me a lot of freedom.

I also took my professor's advice and hired a private board, which has been instrumental in my company's success. My only regret is not hiring them right at the start – my pride was still in the way. I waited four years thinking that I needed to be bigger before people would be interested in helping me on a Board of Advisors. I lined up people with backgrounds that would complement the strengths of my company. We still meet every two months and I pay them for each meeting for their learned advice. They have no liability, and I have learned to listen carefully to their wisdom.

I keep listening. I continuously seek advice from different experts, and I keep taking courses. I believe if I keep seeking new knowledge I will earn the right to remain president of this company. I will never become complacent in my position because if I do I will surely miss something. I am convinced that the moment I start thinking how good I am, my demise is just around the corner. I am proud of what I've built, but I am not so arrogant to believe I did it alone.

One of the keys to following my dream was a willingness to ask questions and listen to the answers. I believe that every problem has a solution and if I don't have the answer someone else will. I believe that people want to help, and the world is there to support you. **If you asked a hundred people on the street for help I believe that ninety would be willing and eager to help.** Ask. Ask. Ask. I keep asking, listening and learning. I found my dream because I listened to my brothers. I developed my dream by continuing to listen to the valuable input of others.

Dr. Gerstein's Comments

Approach your financial challenges
from a position of strength

Greg ran into a financial obstacle in his first year of operating his business. The bank called in his loan creating a serious cash flow challenge. He still needed to pay his employees and keep his trucks on the road. He could have panicked and run to the banks looking for assistance, but instead, just as he had done in choosing his Dream Career, Greg formulated a plan. He decided to operate from a position of strength rather weakness.

How many times have you looked across at the loan officer at the other side of that big oak desk in the bank or other financial institution, looking for a loan to help with a car or house payment? How did it make you feel? Did you notice that you usually sat in the smaller chair perhaps looking up to him literally and metaphorically? You probably felt even shakier when he told you he would get back to you with his decision.

What they don't tell you is that they need you as much as you need them. Loaning out money at healthy interest rates is how they earn more income.

By having the banks come to him instead of the other way around, Greg turned the tables at this imbalance in power and put the odds in his favour. He dealt from a position of strength and confidence, and then *he* got back to *them* with *his* decision. It certainly helped that he had an excellent business plan, but don't ever underestimate the image you present. It is as important in getting a loan as it is in sales and marketing.

Whenever you are dealing with people, perception is reality.

"You have to find something that you love enough to be able to take risks, jump over the hurdles and break through the brick walls that are always going to be placed in front of you. If you don't have that kind of feeling for what it is you are doing, you'll stop at the first giant hurdle."

George Lucas, Jr.

Ronen Abergel
Hair Stylist

"It's Better than Sex – And I Love Sex"

I had discovered my dream. I loved creating hair designs. To me it was an art form. I wanted to run my own hair salon. I had worked for my brother in his hair salons and had worked with a partner. It was my time. I just had one problem – money – a lack of it. I was down to my last $10,000. I needed seven times that amount. I had to come up with a way to get it or my dream would die.

When I was 15 years old, I told my mother that I wanted to quit school. While growing up in Israel my dream was to become a professional soccer player. I wanted to play for the Israeli national team. I didn't need school for that. Needless to say she wasn't too pleased by my proposition. When she saw how determined I was she firmly stated that I better have a job lined up before I quit. She insisted that I go to my brother's hair styling school to ensure that I had some craft that I could market.

There have always been hair stylists in my family – my father and uncle to name two. In spite of this, I never even thought about hair design as a career until that moment. After two weeks in the school that was it. I was hooked. I loved it. It brought out my creative juices. There was no turning back for me.

It motivated me because it always presented challenges. Two of the biggest challenges were creating hair designs and dealing with women. I was using my creative talents for each area. Creating hair designs brings out my inventive skills and working with women challenges my people skills. Women are complex and I go the extra mile to satisfy them.

In spite of the fact that I knew where I was going the ride along the way has been bumpy. I followed my brother to Canada and immediately had my first obstacle. My immigration papers were not in order and I regret to say that I spent my first night in this country behind bars. Thankfully that was all worked out in 24 hours.

I then went to work in my brother's hair salon for a couple of years. I was young, eager and was learning a lot about the business. After a couple of years I was ready to partner with my brother. He delivered a devastating blow to me when he selected someone else as partner. It hurt because he was my brother. I had always looked up to him. I found my dream in his school and had followed him to another country. I couldn't stand seeing someone else partnering with my brother so I left the salon altogether.

One of my clients was interested in going into business with me and together we opened our own salon shortly thereafter. She had supplied much of the financing and I brought my creative talents to the partnership. Things fell apart after one year. Her friends told her I was too fortunate because she had invested so much of the capital. They accused me of taking money from the business. It was absurd. My partner had access to the bank. She made the deposits and financial transactions, and dealt with the bank statements. But she listened to her friends and accused me of unethical business practices..

She demanded I give her $15,000 she said I took. I insisted she buy out my shares in the business for $5,000 if she wanted me out. We fought for months. I could see that my days were numbered and I began looking around for another location to take the leap and go into business for myself. On the day I closed my new lease I negotiated a deal with her – I would give back my shares in the company and we would be square. She agreed.

I was down to my last $10,000. That's all I had to invest in my new salon, which I figured would cost me about $70,000. The banks refused to lend me money because I had not built up my credit. I refused to take another partner. But these challenges were not going to stop me. I had confidence in myself. I would find a way to make it work.

I had an idea to lease everything. I would pay it back once I had positive cash flow. I leased the location, chairs, blow dryers – everything down to the pictures on the walls. I didn't own anything. I even got the contractor to take payments in monthly instalments. I was living on borrowed time and gave myself six months to build my clientele.

My timing couldn't have been worse. I opened only a few weeks before the terrorist catastrophe of September 11, 2001. People stopped coming. They stayed home and were scared to go to public places. I was starving for clients. I had a wife and young child at home, a mortgage to pay and all that debt to pay back. But I wasn't depressed. I kept showing up for work and gave my best for the clients who came.

Doing what I loved kept me going. I might have given up earlier if I didn't enjoy the process. If someone came into my salon and told me to create a beautiful new hair design, while someone else came in and wanted to go out for coffee and a good time – I would pick the hair creation. It is how I express myself. I love it. Every day I get to create and think of new ways to solve people's hair problems. I can't think of one aspect of doing hair that doesn't excite me.

The best way to market my services is to offer excellent service. Failure didn't even enter my mind. If I lost the salon, I would have bemoaned the personal loss much more than the financial one. After four months of fear people started coming out of their homes and business picked up. I went from ten clients a day to twenty five clients a day in two months. I finally turned the corner.

I learn from every experience and from my mistakes in both the creative and the business part of this industry. When I make a mistake I vow not to repeat it again. That way I continue to learn and grow as a hair stylist and businessman.

Money is not a concern for me. I would do this work for one dollar. If my salon had failed I would have worked for someone else until I built up enough capital to try again. I am only defeated when I admit defeat and I refuse to do that.

Dr. Gerstein's Comments

It is the size of the Dream
not the size of the obstacle that counts.'s

Ronen's story reminds me of a journeyman boxer who keeps getting knocked down and just keeps coming back up. It is not easy to get up after you've been knocked down for the third or fourth time. It hurts and it can be humiliating.

So why do some people get back up while others quit? One of the major factors at work here is how big your reason is for doing what you are doing. A strong will and a good business plan certainly go a long way but, if you don't have the passion for the path you are on, those will not be enough to sustain you. Think of your passion as the foundation upon which all of the other factors of success are built. If you have a weak foundation it will be hard to weather heavy storms.

Ronen was willing to do the work for one dollar. Nothing was going to keep him down and, if for some unforeseen circumstance like unreasonable rent hikes, his current salon goes under, he will turn up somewhere else and his clients will follow him because they can feel his love for his craft.

Find a WHY bigger than you and you will be able to overcome any HOW.

Myth-Diagnosis #8
Empty Pocket Stress Syndrome

✦

How *You* Can Bust This Myth

I had to include this chapter because more than any other myth, this is the most common misbelief I have encountered in the community. People believe that if only they won the big lottery they would be happy. But in my practice I have found that happiness is not an end result; it is a byproduct of doing something else.

Start doing what you love even if it is only on a part-time basis. First discover what you want to do. If you aren't sure, take time to think and then try different ideas. You will know when you are close when you find something that makes you feel good and that you want to share with others. Let your heart be your guide.

Then do it. Once a week for one hour if that is all the time you have to spare. If you are like most North Americans, you will probably be able to squeeze out a few more hours by cutting back on your TV time. It doesn't take a lot of money to start this way. And you will see opportunities that you would otherwise miss.

When you begin to feel confident in your life direction you will want to make a bigger commitment to your Dream Career. You will look at ways to transition out of your current situation. Some people I spoke with took an early retirement settlement. Some used government incentive programs to help them change. Some asked friends and family to help. Others delved into their savings or took out loans. No matter how you finance it, expect to invest more energy at the beginning to get your Dream Career moving.

Sir Isaac Newton knew this and expressed it in his first law of motion, "An object at rest tends to stay at rest and an object in motion tends to stay in motion with the same speed and in the same direction unless acted upon by an unbalanced force." You are the object at rest and if you want to get up to speed you will have to apply your force early. Once you get going, you will find that your Dream Career will stay in motion. Be prepared to put in the work early on. Living your Dream Career will not be achieved in a dream-like state.

Myth – Diagnosis #9
TooMuchToDo-osis

"I don't have the time."

"Lost time is never found again."

Benjamin Franklin

Mira Gandhi
Promotional Wear Developer

"It's very important to me to change the face of nursing."

I've been a nurse for twenty-five years and I've been thinking about going into business for myself for at least the last ten. It took a worldwide calamity to kick me into action. That's when I summoned up the courage to do it.

There's always been a part of me that wanted to go into business. Perhaps it goes to back to my youth when I did several different jobs in the summers. I worked in donut shops and offices. Selling was something I could always do – it came naturally. I'm a nurse by training, but many years ago I began selling Mary Kay Cosmetics for a bit of extra income. The selling part was easy. **I won awards for top salesperson but I felt stupid doing it because I didn't believe in it.** I am not a cosmetics person, so it didn't fit my personality. After a year, I left.

I thought to myself, "What do I want to do? What do I believe in?" I have always enjoyed nursing. My new career would need to be in addition to nursing, and not intended to replace it.

I am proud of being in the medical profession and more specifically about being a nurse.

Nurses don't get enough recognition. For quite some time we have often received more abuse than credit for what we do for our patients. Then, in 2003 the SARS epidemic hit. SARS is a highly infectious and deadly disease that spread to North America from the Far East. The media were all over it, and it is ironic that it took a devastating illness like this for both the media and the public to finally really see how much we do, and the sacrifices we make.

A similar thing happened to the firefighters in New York, albeit on a much larger scale, after the terrorist attacks of September 11, 2001. **That event was probably the turning point for me. It was a wake up call. I was determined to be proactive. I wanted to promote nurses and the medical profession in general.**

I wanted to do something to make nurses feel important. That was my purpose, and what gave me my impetus. That's where my passion came from – getting nurses to feel proud of themselves. Why not have them wear it on their sleeves? Literally.

I knew my new venture would be associated with clothing, because that was where my interest lay. I was more of a clothing person than a cosmetic person anyway, and it would allow me to be creative in my promotion. It was the ideal combination of my passion and my purpose.

I decided to create and sell medical uniforms and paraphernalia. My plan was to design and sell a line of uniforms for nurses, paramedics and doctors. In a hospital, patients sometimes have a hard time identifying who is helping them. My idea was that each garment would proudly identify the specialty or qualification of the wearer, for example REGISTERED NURSE, or the specialty unit they worked in, like EMERGENCY or ICU. The line would also include promotional attire they could wear on their off-hours.

I took a partner, Valerie Wakefield, also a nurse, as co-president. We bounced ideas off of each other and shared the financial burden of the start-up. Although we started small and decided not to carry any inventory, we still required a small bank loan. But I was afraid no bank would loan us the money. I had other fears as well. I asked myself, "Would anybody buy it?" "Would I be ridiculed by other nurses?"

But I wouldn't let my fears stop me. I acted in spite of my fears, and wouldn't give up because of them. I turned that last fear around, and used any criticisms that came up as an opportunity to watch how people reacted to our success. It became a study in human nature. We were able to each get a bank loan for $5,000. I found ready-made garments, such as draw string pants, from suppliers who allowed us to screen print them with our designs. We chose the pant leg below the right knee for the bold words that would honour each person wearing them, and began selling the clothing out of the trunks of our cars. We registered our company, *In An Absolute Heartbeat*® in 2003 and within two years had made enough revenue to pay back those two loans. As we grow, we have found that people want the garments sooner, so recently we took out a $10,000 line of credit to start building some inventory. We have to have it readily available in all sizes, so at this moment I have six hundred pairs of pants on my living room floor!

We are reaching the stage where we must consider hiring other people to help with some aspects of the business – perhaps sales, marketing, or accounting. However, in the beginning I wanted to learn everything about the business from the ground up, which included dealing with embroiderers, printers and importers. That way, when we grow large enough to hire outside professional help, I will have a good idea of what they are supposed to be doing. More importantly, I will know if they are actually doing it. I've read too many stories of people getting taken because they didn't understand what these professionals were doing.

When it came to understanding the financial matters of our business, I had a steep learning curve because in my marriage my husband takes care of that area. Now I've learned so much that it may turn out to be my biggest strength.

Although I love learning about each part of my company, it's very time consuming. My children are my number one priority, and this new career has to fit into my life and not vice versa. I have learned first hand what Einstein was hypothesizing – time is relative.

Back when I was still single and a nurse, I used to think I was busy. When I got married and had one child and then two children, I thought I was really busy. Then I had a third child – now that was busy. Now I have started a new business, I'm finding manufacturers, learning about import regulations, taxes and marketing. All this – and

I still have my family and my full-time nursing profession. Now THAT'S BUSY! One advantage of starting a business at a mature age is that my life experiences help me prioritize things a lot faster.

Using Einstein's theory again, I found a way to work everything out. I prioritized and cut out those activities that were at the bottom of the list. I gave up some of my "free time" like going for walks, or watching TV. I even learned how to compress housework. It used to take me five hours to clean my house. I now do it in two or less.

Being mature unfortunately doesn't guarantee a mistake-free ride. One of our embroidery people suggested we invest in labels. She told us they were only pennies and we could sew them on the labels of all of our promotional wear. We thought it was a great idea and quickly moved to purchasing the labels. They cost us $3,000, a good percent of our low start-up cost. It turned out that we acted in haste. The sweaters arrived before the labels did, and there was no time to put them on. And they were selling well without the labels. When we began selling our pants, the manufacturers wouldn't allow us to sew them over their label. We hadn't thought of that in our rush to act on what sounded like a good idea. I still laugh about that experience because all 10,000 labels are sitting in a box at home.

I learned a valuable lesson. There is no need to rush into any opportunity until we talk it over ourselves and with our suppliers. We must remember that even if a deal seems terrific it really isn't if it does not fit into our overall business plan.

As a nurse I have a hand in changing people's lives. As a business owner my promotional wear will never save lives, but hopefully I can help make people feel better about themselves when they wear it. Giving nurses credit for all their hard work and sacrifices is important to me, and I've only just begun with my efforts in that direction. **It's very important to me to change the face of nursing**. That alone inspires me to keep using my time wisely.

Dr. Gerstein's Comments

How much spare time do you have to begin following your dreams?

Mira realizes that she has more things on her plate now than ever before in her life yet she is still able to find the time to do them all. How does she do it? The last time I looked they have not added any more hours to our days. Her secret is that she has a larger purpose now. That allows her to prioritize her time better. And that is the key – prioritizing.

If we really wanted to we could all find an hour a week to begin our Dream. Watch one hour less of TV a week. Clean up in two hours instead of four. Limit your grocery shopping to one store instead of three. In addition, what activities can you delegate to other members of your family? What things could you begin saying "no" to that you really don't want to do anyway? By looking seriously at time as a valuable commodity instead of as an endless dimension, you could even eke out an extra hour a day.

Perhaps for you it is not cutting hours but using your time more productively. That bus ride to work can be used to read a book on one of your passions. You can use a few of your get-togethers with friends as brainstorming sessions for what they think you would love to do. (Just make sure you pick the right friends). And, instead of a movie, attend a class in an area of interest to you.

If you are dissatisfied with your work then every day you don't take action is another day wasted. Life is too short to spend it doing something you dislike. Take back your life one hour at a time.

There is an age-old adage that says that activities expand to fill the time available for them. Everyone can find an hour a week, and most people can free up an hour a day to begin their journey towards their dreams. Start now. Don't waste another minute.

"The first requisite for success is the ability to apply your physical and mental energies to one problem incessantly without growing weary."

Thomas Edison

Ginette D'Aigle
Early Childhood Educator

"I refused to let anything stop me from becoming a teacher. If I had to roll myself to get my qualification I would have done it."

As a child I was denied a lot. My mother and father were often both absent from our home, and as the oldest of seven I was forced to be the surrogate mother. Throughout my life I was constantly sick, and twice my mother said "No" to my dreams. It could have been a recipe for self-pity but I refused to let my dreams die. Just like the mythical phoenix bird, out of the ashes of my stress, rose my dream.

I've had both mental and physical challenges all of my life. When I was younger I contracted tuberculosis from my grandmother. I later contracted recurrent lung and kidney infections requiring me to take many antibiotics over the years. The different diseases and therapies would sometimes drop my weight down to eighty-five pounds in my adult life.

As the oldest of seven I was habitually expected to be the surrogate mother when my mother was out – which was a lot of the time. My dad's job took him away from the house during the week and my mother would go out and leave me alone with my sisters and brother. She expected me to take care of them, and this placed an inordinate burden on me. Truthfully, it was an abusive environment because I was always forced to abrogate my own needs for those of others. The irony was I liked taking care of people, especially children. I just didn't want to be required to do so.

I have always been a magnet for children. When I was twelve there were usually children waiting to play with me when I got to school. I would make up games and activities for them and would frequently baby-sit for their families.

My care-taking nature was easy to see. When I was eleven, a new student was transferred into my grade six class. She had epilepsy, she was developmentally challenged and she was not very pretty, to boot. The other children teased her a lot as children are apt to do. I took her under my wing and protected her, so-to-speak. It was not completely altruistic though. It felt good to have someone appreciate and need me. I've played that role much of my life.

As a teen I would come home and be responsible for my six siblings, and after they went to bed I could then sit down and study. I looked forward to my study time because I could be in my own world. I was focusing on me for a change. That was the pattern throughout my high school years. Learning was my oasis in a stormy childhood.

When summer vacation finally arrived I would collapse from exhaustion from the hectic pace I kept during the school year. I would often have to be hospitalized for bed rest and nutritional support.

Music was one of my natural talents. My teachers noticed this, and when I was fourteen they encouraged me to participate in musical festivals. At one such festival one of the judges involved suggested I attend the Conservatory of Music. My mother said, "No," because she said she didn't have the money to send me. Another door was slammed in my face. If she had allowed me to pursue my interests she would have lost a good hand at home. I was upset, but I begrudgingly accepted my fate.

When it came time to think about university, I dreamed of going to teacher's college. My mother said she didn't have the money, and in any case, she said, I was too ill to tackle such a challenge. Her response made me angry, and this time I didn't accept her decision as calmly as when she denied my pursuit of music. I was determined to find a way to make it happen, but had not yet learned to speak up for myself. It was a scenario that would repeat itself over and over until I finally found the courage to assert myself and take care of my own needs. It would also ultimately test the strength of my marriage.

Within two years I was married. We had three beautiful children. A few years later my doctor said if he had known me before I had children he would have advised me not to have any. He was concerned for my health telling me I was too weak, and raising children had put too much of a strain on me. He was correct about the energy it took to raise children, but he didn't realize my love for them. It was my destiny.

When my second daughter was eight she was in a car accident. On one of my visits to the hospital I met someone there who was an Early Childhood Educator (ECE). She said I could teach children with this certificate. When I heard this a bell suddenly went off in my head. It was an opportunity knocking on my door telling me I could become a teacher and work with children. That must have been the reason I met that lady in the hospital.

My husband, however, was less than enthusiastic. He wanted me to stay home with our children who were now eight months, five and seven. He was afraid if I took the course I would eventually leave him. In his fear he didn't support me, so I did something I had never done before.

I stood up to someone on a major issue.

I said to him: **"I will go and finish the course with or without your support."** When I said it I was so scared, I was shaking, and I wonder how I ever had the nerve to do it. I believe it was only because of how motivated I was to follow my dream. After I stood up to him he replied, "Ginette, you will never be able to do this." He said he loved me, and he was only speaking out of his own fear that our marriage would fall apart. He had seen infidelity in other couples around us when both parents worked. I understood his fear – he was afraid of the unknown.

That was a real turning point in my life. As a child I was never made to feel that I counted, and was taught to act subservient to the needs of others. As a result, I always found it very difficult to stand up for myself. Now I was thirty years old and it was not too late to begin.

If I could change anything in my life, I would have learned to stand up for myself when I was much younger. I would have looked into my mother's eyes and told her I was going to teacher's college. Period.

The ECE certification was a two-year program. I told my program supervisor that I would graduate *even if it takes me ten years to finish*. I enrolled in the program while my daughter was still recuperating in the hospital. I was determined to complete it while still raising my children by taking evening and summer courses.

During this same time I operated a day-care out of my home. One of my daughters commented to me one day, "Mommy, you are always around children. Why not try something else?" So I got a job with American Express as an authorization operator. The people I worked with sat in front of their computers all day long. They weren't sociable and it was boring. Thinking I had potential, AmEx offered me training in becoming a resource manager. It was flattering but if I didn't like the environment as an operator, I wouldn't like it as a manager. I was working evening shifts at AmEx and already feeling drained from all the schoolwork. I respectfully declined the offer. I realized I needed an interactive, social and supportive environment in which to work, or else I would stagnate. This experience further motivated me to complete my ECE training.

During this time I still suffered from recurrent bouts of pneumonia, pleurisy and kidney problems. At times I could barely drive my car while heading to school. I would get infection after infection while taking the course. My immune system was depleted because of all the medications I had to take. I suffered from recurrent kidney infections and had constant pain in my right side. But I didn't like to show my pain to anybody.

Sometimes it was convenient to drive to school with one of my daughters. One morning, she noticed how much pain I was in and said, "Mommy...I'm here with you...Hang in there." I looked at her and replied: "If I have to roll myself to get my qualification I will get it. People in wheelchairs do it. I will do it no matter what."

It took me ten years to complete my ECE certificate, the exact time I had oddly prophesied at the beginning of this long journey. What kept me going was the knowledge that once I had this I would be able to help more children and bring an income to my family.

On the night I graduated in 1991 my whole family was there. I was in so much pain I could barely walk up to receive my diploma, but I was so proud of what I had done. It was a moment I will never forget. My husband now sees that his fears were unfounded.

I have always been driven. I never wanted anyone else to know my problems so I often never told anyone when I was in pain. I just pushed through the pain. However, last year I collapsed because of pain and exhaustion, and since then I have been learning that it's okay to ask for help. Very slowly I have begun to open up to others, but I do not find it easy to switch roles and become a "receiver" once in a while. Then again, not much in my life has been easy for me but that has not stopped me.

The children at school do not question my health. They accept me even on my tough days when my energy is way down. That is one of the reasons I enjoy teaching children.

Perhaps it is because I have had so many personal challenges in my own life that I adore and embrace children with special needs. I am able to be patient with them, and give them my full attention. In my classes I had an autistic child and children with behaviour disorders. Specialists have helped me understand their needs and how I can fulfill them. They are a challenge, yet many have made so much progress in my class, and that makes me feel special.

I love what I do. What's not to love? Supportive teachers and children I adore surround me. I never lose sight of the fact that I am here to help children, not just teach them things. I may be the only person who has smiled at that child today. Knowing I have contributed to the education and growth of these children in some small way is a gift for me.

Even though I got my ECE certificate I am not finished studying. Learning is how I relax, and lifelong learning is my destiny. I'm writing a book on the ECE curriculum. My daughter says it seems like I am doing a thesis for a doctorate, and I feel the same way. When I retire I will go back to school. I don't know what I'll take, but I am looking forward to it. And it all started because one day I had the courage to stand up for myself.

Dr. Gerstein's Comments

Let go of the victim role and start playing from your strengths

As a physician, I have patients who continually replay the horrible experiences they endured when they were younger. I empathize with their suffering. As a physician I have witnessed many abusive situations; our society still has a long way to go in appreciating other people's rights. Some people, however, have difficulty in letting go of this trauma and moving on. They become stuck in the victim role and allow their lives to be defined by it. This leads to more suffering and the vicious cycle continues.

Ginette had many reasons to give up on her dreams. But instead of allowing her parents' neglectful behaviour to dominate her, she has looked at the benefits of the role that was thrust upon her early in life. She discovered her passion for children. She blossomed in the role of caretaker and decided to make it her career. She made up her mind to become a teacher. Once again her mother slammed the door in her face. She refused to support her financially or emotionally, claiming she was too ill to follow that path.

When I first saw Ginette I was struck by the apparent paradox of form and function. She has a petite frame, short hair and a soft voice, yet her passion and determination is fiery, loud and large. Like a strong tree that bends yet doesn't break, this little dynamo was undeterred. Although she lost her first opportunity to become a teacher, when she discovered she could teach with an ECE certificate she was energized to do it. It took her ten years, during which she struggled constantly with her health, but she did it. She wrote a new script for herself, and did not allow her history to control her. As Ginette put it, "I never recognized my limits, and that is why I probably achieved more than others expected."

Dr. Gerstein's Comments

I have found it is not the specific trauma that happens to people in their developing years, but rather the meaning they give it that determines whether or not they successfully move on from it. Ginette saw the tremendous benefits of being with children and made that her mission. You won't find Ginette bemoaning her ill health or her childhood woes. She has too much to look forward to.

What childhood traumas are you still holding on to? You may not have had a choice back then, but remember – you do now. You need not carry them around. Do not allow your memories to steal your life, because that is all they are. What can you do to let them go? Stand up for yourself. It may be the first time you've ever done it. Do it to help yourself. Don't do it to hurt others. If someone else is hurt, it will just add to your burden.

Write a letter to the involved parties (whether or not they are still alive) where you describe your anger and your hurts. It's a powerful tool. Go into great detail and don't leave anything out. When you are done, do not mail it. Burn it; and, as it burns, allow the smoke to carry away your anger.

Once you have done that, think of how your past has benefited you. Yes, one could look at Ginette's situation and claim she was forced to become a surrogate parent early in life. That is one side of the coin. The other side says those circumstances may have helped her nourish her love of children and develop her special talents for teaching and caring for children. No matter how thin you slice a coin it always has two sides. Admittedly this may not be easy but it may help you move away from the victim role into one of strength. And when you come from a position of strength your resolve rises and you are better able to take on the challenges that confront you.

"It's not what happens to you, it's what you do about it."

William Mitchell

Michael McGauley
Professional Speaker

"The accident probably saved my life."

I was putting in sixteen hour days building my graphic arts supply company. I was smoking two and a half packs a day, drinking fourteen cups of coffee and depending on McDonald's to satisfy my nutrition requirements. I was running at a hundred miles an hour. On weekends I would crash and burn in an attempt to catch up on sleep and rest my weary body.

I never stopped to think about whether or not I liked what I was doing, probably because deep down I already knew the answer. So I kept running. If I was to become happy, I *had* to make the business successful. My partner and I were in the third year of a five-year plan based on selling the company at the end of that period, and then repeating the process with other companies. I would keep those companies that gave me passive income, and sell those that did not. Then I would invest in real estate and live off the rental income. At twenty-two years of age I had my whole life planned out.

However, I would never make it to the fifth year. An enormous tragedy interceded, and probably also saved my life.

◇

Our edge was just-in-time inventory, but we were up against a big obstacle. Printers had brand loyalty and rarely changed brands unless something went wrong with their product. We were frustrated because like many new businesses, we were undercapitalized and lacked manpower. In our third year, we really began to feel the pinch. Our lines of credit were high, our cash flow low. In an attempt to keep our cash flow up, we didn't even draw salaries until the middle of the third year.

Add to all that, I was not being mentally challenged. I drove my beat up car from one client to the next. After discussing beautiful women and baseball scores for the fifteenth time in one day, I yearned for an intellectual conversation with someone, on just about anything. I was bored, and my heart just wasn't in the business.

I hated what I was doing and began to hate who I was becoming, but I never stopped long enough to realize it. It was tough taking care of me, when all my energy went to the business. Tired all the time, I grew short on patience. I began striking out at the people who were closest to me, and my family got the brunt of it. Dating wasn't going well either. If you want to connect with someone, you have to slow down enough to actually connect. But I was on a high-speed train and if you couldn't keep up you were off the train. I truly didn't know who I was or where I was going, but I was sure going to get there fast.

My smoking addiction exemplified my fast paced life. One night at a bar my friends hid my smokes from me, and I got a glimpse of how my life was spinning out of control. I was so drunk I don't remember what happened next, but the next day I learned I'd actually hit one of my friends over the head with an ashtray, and then physically accosted the bartender – all for a cigarette. When I got off the phone I realized that smoking owned me – I didn't own it. In that moment I made up my mind, and quit cold turkey. I haven't had a cigarette since. Having successfully given up one addiction, I had no idea I would soon be tempted to replace it with a far more insidious one, one that could swallow me up for life.

It started out as a nice Father's Day – June 18, 1989. I spent the day with my dad in the garden pulling out a hedge. Later, I went over to a friend's to watch a video. I was pretty tired, so my friend offered to let me sleep on his couch for the night. I thought it would bother my back if I did, so I declined. I'd had nothing to drink. At 11 p.m. I left. While driving home a kid in front of me ran a stop sign. There was no time to stop, and I ended up T-boning him. His head went through the side window. I was very shaken up, and it took a few minutes to clear the cobwebs from my head.

By the time I got out of my car a cop had shown up. He put barricades with flashing red lights all around the accident scene. I went over to help the kid who was only semiconscious, bleeding from a head wound, and very distressed. A lady was also there and, although I was still in shock myself, together we applied direct pressure to his wound while trying to comfort him. Then everything went blank.

The next thing I knew I was staring at a ceiling I didn't recognize. When I looked down I saw I was naked, and a woman was giving me a sponge bath. I was either in the middle of a great dream, or something was very wrong. Then I noticed tubes coming out of every orifice of my body. When I finally realized what was happening I began to scream hysterically. I was suddenly overcome with pain, and began to beg for relief.

Later, I learned that this was about forty-eight hours after the second accident. Apparently a drunk driver had driven right through the police barricades, crushed the woman and myself against the car, and then hit the cop who was trying to get into the other side of the kid's car.

My injuries were severe. I had lost a lot of blood, and my legs were badly crushed. The lady at the accident scene was confined to a wheelchair, and will probably be in one for life. The cop was not badly hurt because he was wearing a bulletproof vest, and was thrown onto a soft, freshly dug garden. The kid who was hit in the original accident went home that night with a mild concussion and ten stitches in his forehead.

It required multiple surgeries to put my legs back together. Then, one day, the surgeons came into my room and told me they would have to amputate my legs.

When I heard this, something inside me snapped and I began yelling, "Fuck you! You guys are full of shit! I am *walking*. I am going *skiing* on these legs!" They were stunned, but I guess I got their attention. After that, they said they would do everything they could to save my legs.

There were more surgeries, and after every one my surgeons told me my legs were very close to winding up in the scrap bucket. I like to believe I still have my legs today because my surgeons believed in me, and probably because *I* believed in me so strongly.

The recovery process was a long and arduous struggle. For months it hurt just to get out of bed. I used to lie praying for sleep to get relief from the agony. Surgeries followed one upon the other. Just when I was recovering from the pain of one surgery, another one had to be done. It was seven years before I could walk again without assistance.

During this time something else was developing, so insidious I almost didn't see it. I was becoming a victim all over again. I hardly noticed the transition. Society, the legal system and much of daytime television is devoted to victims. I should know – I watched a lot of it while in hospital. I could have easily gone down that road. I'd had enough terrible things happen to me that I could have played it up for years to come. Why did this happen to me? I wasn't drunk. I was hit while helping someone who caused an accident by running a stop sign. I deserved repayment. I deserved pity.

I didn't have to fight so hard, I could easily have given up. When the doctors first spoke about amputating my legs, I could have just acquiesced. There were so many points along the way when I could have given up and remained the victim. Outside forces were *obviously* working against me. I became the special one in the family, and a celebrity among my friends, at least those who remained my friends. I was the topic of conversation. People catered to me because I was physically challenged. Believe it or not, women were attracted to me – and lots of them. Further along in my recovery period when my pain was under control, I began dating like never before. Eager to hop into bed with me, women weren't shy about doing it in my hospital bed either. Whatever it was, I didn't want it to stop. I found all of this attention intoxicating, and bizarrely rewarding.

Then the real temptation arrived. When I initiated the civil suit for damages, I was told I would receive a much bigger settlement if I stayed in a wheelchair for life. It seems the legal system strangely rewards people for staying sick. My lawyers told me they could only collect for damages if I never walked again. They didn't tell me not to get better, but the temptation was there.

Before the accident I was addicted to tobacco, running fast and hard, and not taking care of myself. Now I found myself slowly slipping into another addiction – *the victim role*, and this one was more seductive and engulfing than any other I'd known. The kicker is it is so widely accepted by society. I was being forced to come face-to-face with my demons.

Part of me didn't want to give up this attention. But a stronger part kept screaming, "I just want to be normal." I said this to my doctors, my family and whoever would listen. I wanted to get back control of my life, and get to know who I really was. I wanted to make a difference in the world. I knew I hadn't come this far in physical rehab, only to lose it all by selling my soul to the highest bidder.

Fortunately I was able to see the trap being set, and continued to fight hard to regain my independence. When I became adept at handling my wheelchair, I began resenting it when people held the door open for me. For three years I intentionally stopped telling my story in order to start moving away from my victim status. I made a commitment to be true to myself. I realized that everything in life was a choice, and I was responsible for everything I did.

Despite all the attention, there were many periods when I found myself alone. Visitations began dropping off when the novelty of the accident began to pass. As I was the one keeping myself company the most, I had to decide if I liked what I saw when I looked in the mirror. I didn't. I became aware that sometimes I had been a real asshole to people, and had not treated them fairly. That realization took a long time to sink in. At first I was in denial, but eventually even I could no longer lie to the guy looking back at me. Finally, I stopped running.

I began thinking about the existential questions in life. Why was I so unhappy before the accident? What should I do now? Who was I? Before the accident I was too busy doing and didn't spend enough time thinking about whether I wanted to keep doing what I was doing. I had little time for myself. If I wasn't working for me, why was I working so hard? It was a forced period of self-reflection I badly needed.

I began reading self-improvement and motivational books. The book that really started me on this journey was *The Road Less Traveled* by M. Scott Peck. (1978, Simon and Schuster). Someone had given it to me while I was in hospital but I was not yet ready to read it. It was a good two years into the recovery process when I finally picked it up. On the first page of the first chapter Dr. Peck says, *Life is difficult. This is a great truth...Once we truly know that life is difficult – once we truly understand and accept it – then life is no longer difficult.* Those lines immediately reached out and grabbed me, and their great truth changed who I was.

I learned that happiness was not a destination, bur rather a choice I had. It was a decision I could make to be happy in whatever predicament I found myself in. I stopped complaining.

When I went for my physiotherapy rehab sessions, I was happy. Other victims would ask me what I was so happy about. "You have no reason to be happy," they'd say. I didn't fit their perception of how a victim should behave. I should be complaining and drinking my problems away – perhaps like them. Other patients, however, became inspired by my enthusiasm.

I committed to becoming the best person I could be, and try anything if I thought it might improve my life. I learned that I was worth the struggle. In taking care of me, I was now ready to help others. I reconnected with my altruistic side, always there but ignored. Zig Ziglar put it best when he said, *"If you help other people get what they want, you can get what you want."*

I realized I was living on borrowed time. I almost bled to death at the scene – most of my leg arteries had been severed. A hundred years ago I wouldn't be here. I was filled with gratitude, and I found I was ready to give back. Prior to the accident I did no charity work. Now each year I commit to giving a portion of my income to charity. I recently gave a large contribution to Etobicoke General Hospital where I spent most of my recovery time.

During this time I found a woman who liked the real me – and she married me. I had to get back to work, so I began by selling products I was familiar with from my old business. Technical products are easy to sell because you can hide behind them. I could no longer hide from myself – I was fully conscious of all of my choices now. As a result I got fired, and then went through five different jobs in five years.

There was hope though. I kept my passion alive by speaking publicly about self-empowerment. I spoke to any group that was interested in hearing me. They wanted to hear about how I recovered from such a devastating injury. The only problem was most groups weren't paying me, and I had to keep working at jobs I didn't like until my professional speaking income grew.

One day it dawned on me. If I really wanted my speaking career to take off, I had to make a choice. I had to take a leap of faith. After being laid off for the fifth time I thought perhaps God was trying to tell me something, and I decided to commit myself full time to my speaking career.

The first year was definitely financially challenging. I drew on some investments I had set aside, contributions from my wife, and my insurance claim from the accident. I would live off of my savings and build my speaking profession full time.

My biggest obstacle was not the most apparent one – my physical injury. In reality, my biggest challenge was stopping long enough to relearn who I was. I was a shy salesman. Part of my running around in the graphic design supply business may have been self-induced. I am not self-conscious now because I believe in what I am doing with my whole heart. I didn't like myself very much before the accident – I just didn't know it. I like myself a lot more now. I still have a lot of work to do, but the difference is I am now conscious when something is missing in my life.

I am doing what I love. I can now work eighteen hours a day if I want to (which I don't), but the difference is this time I love the process. I am not just doing it for the financial payoff at the end. Before, money was the goal. Now money is the byproduct of the work I love. Sometimes I speak to high-risk teens in inner city programs. I show them graphic pictures of my injuries to get their attention, and then I tell them about their own potential. I tell them they are all heroes, but as yet they have *no idea* about their potentials. "Look around the room," I say, "Statistically speaking one of you will not be here in twenty years." At that age they believe they are invincible. I show up to remind them about their mortality and why they should develop their potential before it is too late.

After one of those talks a girl came up and told me *I* was a hero. Reiterating the message from my presentation, I told her she was one too. I said, "I'm here to remind you that you count. You're precious. You have value." Two weeks later when I got my feedback forms, hers read, "Thank you Michael. What you said that day made me feel so good. It motivated me to take steps to change my life." That was really inspiring for me.

In 2001 I ran my first triathlon. I can put on skates, and I play hockey now. My friends are far superior in their hockey talent, and I know they let me score goals. But I don't care. I'm just so grateful I have the physical ability to play. I'm so wired when I come home I can't sleep. My next goal is to run in the Boston marathon.

Looking back, that accident probably saved my life. It gave me the time to look at who I was and what I had allowed myself to become. It made me face my weaknesses, and gave me time to overcome them. It allowed me the chance to be grateful for the little things in my life, the things I had once run right by.

I saw what I could do when I believed in myself, and that has inspired me to help as many other people do the same. I found what I was looking for when I finally stopped running.

Dr. Gerstein's Comments

It is important to be wary about switching addictions

Michael was on the fast road to riches, chasing the almighty dollar and killing himself to get there. For his body to keep up, he smoked, drank coffee and ate fast food. He was racing through life in the hopes of reaching an elusive destination.

After his tragic accident he became the centre of attention in many circles. These included medical treatments, legal suits, friends and family. He found himself becoming addicted to the victim role. The secondary gain and attention was very tempting. Like any addiction, he was becoming hooked, and found himself in danger of replacing one addiction with another – going from the fast-paced life to a victim-centered one.

Fortunately Michael saw what was happening and was able to extricate himself from this predicament. He began to explore who he really was and what he really wanted to do.

Have you changed addictions? Have you gone from a pursuit of money to one of power? Have you sold yourself out for dependency on someone else? It takes courage to live an authentic life. The reason it is so hard, is no one else can do it for you. Only you know what's best for you. So many of us are afraid of standing up and declaring who we really are.

But you cannot hide from yourself. Deep down you know the answer when you look in the mirror and ask yourself if you are truly happy. You may not yet be willing to admit it even to yourself, but you really do know the answer.

The reason we keep switching addictions is because of our childhood conditioning. It was based in shame, and tells us we are not good enough to stand alone. It tells us our natural gifts are not good enough.

"Whatever you can do or dream you can, begin it. Boldness has genius, power and magic in it. Begin it now."

Johann Wolfgang Von Goethe

John Robinson
Antique Reproduction Chair Maker

"I have probably the best job of anybody I know."

'Casual' was my first impression of John Robinson. He was dressed in jeans and an old flannel shirt covering a t-shirt. He had scruffy hair and a little more than a five o'clock shadow. His words were measured and his pace was slow. This is just the way he likes it now although the road that got him here was anything but smooth.

I was born in a rural community. My father owned a construction company and I began unofficially apprenticing in the business at the age of thirteen. Over the years I became a skilled contractor and began working for my father right after high school. I enjoyed the work, and within a year I was managing the office. I was able to use my organizational talents in this role and became quite adept at it.

After a while I began to struggle with the job. The industry began losing touch with people. At one time when I had a problem I would go directly to the person responsible, and talk to him about it. Eventually we would be able to iron everything out. However, advancements in technology led to distancing of relationships. I became further removed from the people who could do something about a problem. A computer transmitted the problem over the internet. Someone on the other end would pass it on, and then someone else would relay it back to his associate who would then e-mail me. The final message would have little to do with my original question. The internet became a place where the faster I worked, the less I got done. I found I couldn't trust people as much.

This got to the point where it began to wear away at my well-being. I was showing clear signs of burnout. My marriage was already shaky. I became withdrawn and short-tempered, and was accomplishing less and less at work. I hated even going to work. Then I had a nervous breakdown, which just added to the existent friction in my marriage. This ultimately led to my divorce.

I basically walked away from the industry. Although I did take some construction jobs to supplement my income over the next several years, I needed a break. I needed to get reacquainted with my true self. I sure wasn't the same person who had been doing the work I had done for the previous twenty-three years. I finally realized I had been living my father's life.

I had been living in denial for too long, often telling myself, "Tomorrow will be better." It gave me a false sense of security and ultimately led me further away from peace of mind. **I was continually giving up long-term gain to get some short-term relief from pain.**

While my life was unraveling before my eyes I started to look for a diversion from work. I needed something to keep me going. My ex-wife got our house, so I bought myself another one. Now I needed to furnish it. I wanted a special type of chair that would fit into my new home's rustic décor; however the price of antique Windsor chairs was prohibitive, so I decided to make one myself. Keep in mind I knew next to nothing about making chairs.

I found a book, which would be the turning point in my life, titled *Make a Windsor Chair With Michael Dunbar*, by Michael Dunbar (Taunton Press Inc., 1985). He is one of the preeminent Windsor Chair makers in the world. I studied it, and then using what I learned in the book, plus a little creativity of my own, I began constructing my own Windsor Chairs.

As my chairs began to take shape, so did my life. For the first time in a long time I began to relax. I became so engrossed in my new hobby that my other problems temporarily faded into the background.

I never started out thinking about what I wanted as a second career, **I just knew I wanted to slow down. I knew that I wanted a diversion.** When I found that diversion I just went with the flow. I didn't just *think* about doing something, I went out and did it.

After a couple of years of making chairs on my own, I contacted Michael Dunbar in New Hampshire and enrolled in one of his courses in making Windsor Chairs. Once we began working, my mentor recognized my talents immediately. He teased me immodestly, "You hang around me long enough and I'll make you a famous chair maker." We developed a bond right from the start. Michael often introduces me with a smile, as the second best Windsor chair maker in the world.

I now teach Windsor chair making classes in Virginia as well as my own home shop. I still love making chairs. I have made over a thousand of them, all by hand. My avocation became my vocation.

Dr. Gerstein's Comments

Taking action on your dream is as important as the dream itself.

Renowned American psychologist, Abraham Maslow, said that people need two things to become fully self-actualized: *inner exploration and action.*

John's story is typical of the people I interviewed. He *acted* on what made him feel good. He didn't just dream about it, hoping that someday he would do it.

The key is to START! Just start doing something and things will flow from there. John had no idea that making chairs was going to be his Dream Career. He just knew it interested him so he read up on it and *started* making chairs. He enjoyed it and it relaxed him, and it grew from there.

Eventually he became very good at his craft because he *did* it a lot, and was passionate about learning more. He went down to meet his mentor, who immediately recognized his talent.

If you have an itch, scratch it. Let your feelings be your guide. If it energizes you, relaxes you, or gives you a strong sense of purpose, go with it. Most of all *do* something about your feelings. If you don't, those feelings will dissipate and leave you with only painful regrets that will haunt you later in life.

Myth-Diagnosis #9
TooMuchToDo-osis

♦

How *You* Can Bust This Myth

This chapter highlights one of the biggest myths. There is no such thing as time management. We cannot directly manage time; we can only manage what we do with the time. It should be called priority management.

In my experience there are two ways we waste time: Absolutely and relatively. First, the absolute ways: We waste a lot more time than we think. According to the A.C. Nielsen Co. (1998), the average American watches three hours and forty-six minutes of TV each day. By age 65 the average American will have spent nearly NINE YEARS glued to the tube! That's simply poor priority management, whether it is a conscious choice or a subconscious one.

Continuing on the theme of scientific laws, here is one of my anthropological laws: Activity stretches to fill the available time. It is roughly based on Albert Einstein's Theory of Relativity. If you have one month to complete a small project, most people will take the whole month to get it done. If that same project was due in three days, most would find a way get it done in that time. If the project size remains constant, then it must be people's habitual behaviour patterns that cause this phenomenon. Time is relative.

We can make much better use of the time we are given. Look at your life in the following categories: Work, investments, family, friends, leisure time, fitness, personal and spiritual growth and romance. Compare how much time you currently spend in each category versus how you spent it in your young adult years. If any category has changed significantly it is because you changed your priorities and decided some areas are more valuable to you now.

If you want a more fulfilling career you have to make it a priority. You can have more than one priority but you can't have it all, all of the time. What if you were to do one thing a week – maybe one thing a day – to further your Dream? Imagine what might happen if you made this a priority in your life?

When are you going to begin to live your own dream?

After reading the true accounts of people living their dreams you may feel inspired and excited about the possibilities. It means you are ready to inspire yourself because we cannot see out in the world what we do not possess somewhere within ourselves.

People will continue to do what they always have done if they don't make a concerted effort to change old habits. It would be almost impossible to consciously be aware of every action you take in the course of a week. Personal behaviours such as grooming, eating and greeting habits are set on automatic. The same cannot be said of your career. If you are not satisfied by your current career and do little to change it you may find yourself heading in the same direction in ten years. You'll be even more frustrated by your situation and possibly suffering from the effects of work stress.

Changing any habit requires effort. One-time efforts are often forgotten in a matter of weeks. Real change comes when you apply the lessons learned from the people in *Live Your Dreams: Doctor's Orders* consistently over a number of months. Reading this book is only the beginning. Start a Dream Career journal and write down the lessons you learned from the people presented. Keep this book close by as a visual reminder of the stories that inspired you. Reread some stories over the next few weeks. If you worked on any of the exercises, that is another step. If you didn't, then do it now. Lasting change only comes through *doing*.

Keep up the momentum while it is fresh in your mind. Take time to think about your dream. It's waiting to be discovered.

Visit **www.dreamsforreal.com and:**

+ Take the **DFR Work Stress Test©**.

+ Take a look at the **DFR Dream Career Test©** to see which questions the people in Live Your Dreams: Doctor's Orders answered "yes" to and how you will respond when you are in your own Dream Career.

+ See how you score on the **Unique Dream Path Assessment Scale©**

and the **Obstacle Resilience Assessment Scale©.**

They will help you understand where you need the most help to live your own dream.

The individuals featured in this book are essentially no different than you or me. Like all of us, they have fears, lack confidence in certain areas, have families and many responsibilities. Yet, in spite of everything, they took action and debunked the myths that stop many from living their own dreams.

The number one reason most people aren't living their dream is because they don't know what they want to do. Instead, they falsely conclude that they do not have a dream. But **it's not that they don't have a dream**. It just seems that way because it has been buried so far beneath the surface under a multitude of misconceptions and fears. And fear is the second most common factor preventing people from following their dreams.

You owe it to yourself to reach your potential. Take advantage of all that is around you and let others see the gifts that you, and only you, have to offer.

When you follow your dream you will enjoy spending a good deal of your time making it a reality. Your life will have meaning, giving you a sense of purpose. More so, when you live your dream, positive aspects will carry over to the other areas of your life – your relationships and your self-esteem. You will be happier and healthier. You will have more passion and be able to give more to others. Because you will be leading by example, you will also be a remarkable role model for others.

Everyone has a dream. Your Dream Career is not a destination; it is a path and a direction. By taking the compass and using it to guide you in the right direction, your own Dream Path will unfold.

Start living your Dreams today!

Samuel M. Gerstein, M.D.

Recommended Resources:

Live Your Dreams Newsletter

Get monthly tips of how you can live your own dreams.

Sign up at:

www.dreamsforreal.com

Free Seminar - Start Your Own Dream

I am grateful to all who have helped me find my Dream Career and now would like to give something back. I want to inspire and help others to live their dreams. For that reason I am putting on a FREE seminar: Start Your Own Dream event. In it you will:

• Begin to rediscover your true self.
• Discover a method to keep you motivated on your journey.
• See where you need the most help.
• Start to dream big.
• Begin to associate with like-minded people who also want more for their lives

Discovery Your True Life Direction© Course

In reading the stories of real people in this book living their dreams I hope you now understand that living your dreams is not only possible it is being done by people in your community. The biggest obstacle stopping people from doing what they love is that they **don't know what they love**. If that describes you in any way, then this experiential course will help you to uncover your dream career.

In this workshop you will:

✦ Gain insight into yourself and how you function.
✦ Learn how to make better choices.
✦ Experience a motivational tool that will propel you to begin following your heart.
✦ Become conscious of your top values.
✦ Remember some of your passions before you stopped dreaming.
✦ Realize your unique gifts.
✦ Walk away with a sense of direction to start taking your life. **Go to**

**For full details go to www.dreamsforreal.com under "Courses"
Or call 416-221-5089 (Toronto area) or toll free at 1-877-221-5089**

Start Living Your Dreams© Course

Some people may know what they would love to do but for years have dismissed the notion as merely a fantasy, a childhood dream. The number one factor that stops them from pursuing their dream is lack of action. This life-changing seminar will teach you how to overcome your fears and obstacles to take action in the direction of your dreams.

In this workshop you will:
+ Be empowered to take action.
+ Learn how to face up to your fears.
+ Adopt a new way to look at obstacles.
+ Find out how to stay on track even when you don't feel like it.
+ Discover how to continue following your dream path even after you leave the workshop.

For full details go to www.dreamsforreal.com under "Courses"
Or call 416-221-5089 (Toronto area) or toll free at 1-877-221-5089

+ +

We Welcome Your Feedback

This project was undertaken for the specific purpose of inspiring people to follow their own dreams. If you have any comments or questions regarding the book or your own dream please send your messages to dreams@dreamsforreal.com.

Would YOU like to be featured in an upcoming book?

If you are living your Dream Career and would like to share your experiences with others, please write to **contributor@dreamsforreal.com**. Some of the stories will be chosen for future publication.

Go to http://www.dreamsforreal.com/dreamstory.html for further details of how you can submit your inspirational story.

Who is Samuel Gerstein?

Dr. Gerstein is a medical doctor who has over twenty years' experience helping people with their physical and mental challenges. Having examined over 65,000 patients as an emergency physician, Dr. Gerstein has witnessed what work stress can do to people's health. This motivated him to open his own psychotherapy practice to assist others in discovering and doing what they really want in life. A Dream Career has been proven to not only improve a person's state of mind but also physical health.

After finding a paucity of information on work satisfaction and health, Dr. Gerstein undertook his own research study in which he interviewed over 200 people who were living their dreams at work. Some of the insights gained from this innovative research is revealed in this book. The lessons learned helped him create both the, "Your Unique Life Path" Discovery System© and his Dreams into Action Program©, which he uses in his practice and his seminars. He has facilitated workshops in the U.S. and Canada.

Dr. Gerstein's speaking topics include:

Discover Your Life Direction

Start Living Your Dreams,
(Aka: Which TKA... BOOM!™ Island Are You Living On?)

Get Out of Your Own Way,
(Taking back control from your Personal Body Guard©)

Flopportunities© – A New Way to Look at Failure

Are You in the Wrong Job for You?

For further information about Dr. Gerstein's seminars and speeches please visit www.dreamsforreal.com or write to Dreams For Real Inc. 5863 Leslie Street, Suite 316 Toronto, Ontario, Canada, M2H 1J8 or Call 416-221-5089 (Toronto area) or toll free at 1-877-221-5089.

Bibliography and Suggested Reading

American Institute of Stress: General info on work stress. In a survey conducted by the Occupational Stress Research Institute in January 2001, 65% of respondents said they were not satisfied with their work. Of this 65%, 80% said it was not that there was a problem with the company they worked for – instead they just felt that they were not in a job that fit them well. 2001.

American Psychologist, Vol. 45, No. 10, October 1990. "Prevention of Work-Related Psychological Disorders": A National Strategy Proposed by the National Institute for Occupational Safety and Health (NIOSH),

Amick BC and others. *Relationship between all-cause mortality and cumulative working life course psychosocial and physical exposures in the United States labor market from 1968 to 1992.* Bored rigid: Research published last year showed that workers doing meaningless work with little opportunity for any input were more likely to die young., Psychosomatic Medicine, vol.64, pages 370-381, 2002.

Bigos SJ et al 1991. A prospective study of work perceptions and psychosocial factors affecting the report of back injury. 3020 employees at Boeing in 1991 where there were 279 reported low back injuries. Data collected on personality inventories as well as social supports, job satisfaction, strength, flexibility, aerobic capacity, height and weight. Conclusion: Psychosocial measures – specifically those related to job enjoyment – had the strongest influence of all of the variables analyzed. Those who stated that they did not enjoy their jobs were 1.85x (Odds ratio of 1.85)more likely to report a back injury. Job satisfaction counted for 15% of the variance as an injury risk factor. Spine, 16: 1-6.

Bosma H, Marmot MG, Hemingway H, Nicholson AG, Brunner E, Stansfeld A. Low job control and risk of coronary heart disease in Whitehall II (prospective cohort) study. *BMJ* 1997;Volume 314:558-65.

Duxbury, Linda, Higgins, Chris and Johnson, Karen. Survey data collected from 1991 to 1998. Exam of implications of costs of work-life conflict in Canada. June, 1999

Duxbury, L. and Higgins, C.; "Work-life balance in Saskatchewan: Realities and challenges, Saskatoon, Government of Saskatchewan. 1998.

Duxbury, L. and Higgins, C. "In Canadian organizations, conditions have declined over time: High job stress and absenteeism due to ill health have become more problematic over the past decade. Almost three times as many respondents report high job stress in 2001 (35%) than in 1991 (13%)." Work-Life Conflict in Canada in the New Millennium October, 2003.

International Archives of Occup. And Env. Health 9/2001. 7.5% of men and 6.5 % of women often/always stressed at work. Most NB job stressor was job content. Higher stress levels correlated with more health problems. N = 9,800 men and 5,600 women., aged 25 – 64.

Jenkins CD, "Psychological and social precursors of coronary artery disease". Most people below 50 yrs old who have their first heart attack have none of the major physical risk factors for CAD. NEJM 284 (1971), pp. 244-255.

Job strain related to hypercoagulable state as evidenced by increased procoagulant molecules (fibrinogen, factor VII) and by reduced fibrinolytic activity. Meta-analysis of 68 articles; Switzerland; *Psychosomatic Med, 7/2001.*

Karasek R, Brisson C, Kawakami N, Houtman I, Bongers P, Amick B. The Job Content Questionnaire (JCQ): an instrument for internationally comparative assessments of psychosocial job characteristics. *J Occup Health Psychol.* Oct;3(4):322-55. 1998

Kivimäki M and others. *Work stress and risk of cardiovascular mortality: prospective cohort study of industrial employees.* Heart stopper: Workers with stressful jobs are more than twice as likely to die from heart disease. British Medical Journal, vol.325, page 857, 19 October 2002.

Kobasa, Suzanne C., "Stressful Life Events, Personality and Health: An Inquiry into Hardiness," *Journal of Personality and Social Psychology* 37:1 (1979), pp. 1-11.

Landsbergis P and others. *Life course exposure to job strain and ambulatory blood pressure among men.* Fat chance: Long-term job strain is worse for your heart than gaining 40lbs in weight or aging 30 years (see pages 4-5). *American Journal of Epidemiology,* vol.157 (11), pages 998-1006, 2003.

Lown B: Sudden cardiac death: Biobehavioral perspective. The epidemiologic and biological data, taken together, indicate that the stress of work after a weekend of respite may precipitate acute cardiac events among working patients. *Circulation* 76 Suppl I:I186-I195, 1987.

Muller, James E. et al., "Circadian variation in the frequency of sudden death". More fatal heart attacks occur on Monday than on any other day of the week. *Circulation* 75, p. 131, Jan 1987

Marmot MG, Bosma H, Hemingway H, Brunner E, Stansfeld S. Contribution of job control and other risk factors to social variations in coronary heart disease incidence. *Lancet* 1997;350:235-39.

Marmot MG, Smith GD, Stansfeld S, Patel C, North F, Head J, White I, Brunner E, Feeney A. Health inequalities among British civil servants: the Whitehall II study. *The Lancet* 1991; 337:1397-93.

North FM, Syme LS, Feeney A, Shipley M, Marmot M. Psychosocial Work Environment and Sickness Absence among British Civil Servants: The Whitehall II Study. *Am J Public Health* 1996;86:332-340.

Northwestern National Life Insurance Company. Employee burnout: causes and cures. One-fourth of employees view their jobs as the number one stressor in their lives. Minneapolis, MN: 1992.

Peter RW, McQuillan S, Resnick SK, Gold MR: Increased Monday incidence of life-threatening ventricular arrhythmias: Experience with a third-generation implantable defibrillator. *Circulation* 94:1346-1349, 1996.

Rabkin SW, Mathewson FAL, Tate RB: Chronobiology of cardiac sudden death in men. There is some empirical evidence of a septadian overrepresentation of Mondays vis-à-vis cardiac events. (53,77). 53. *JAMA* 44:1357-1358, 1980.

Robbins, "Organizational Behavior", New Jersey, Prentice Hall. "Employees who are satisfied with their job live longer and are less prone to illness." 1993.

St. Paul Fire and Marine Insurance Co. "Problems at work are more strongly associated with health complaints than are any other life stressor-more so than even financial problems or family problems."

Salvatore R. Maddi and Suzanne C. Kobasa, *The Hardy Executive:* Health Under Stress (Homewood, Il.: Dow Jones-Irwin, 1984.

Schnall PL, Landsbergis PA, Baker D. Job strain and cardiovascular disease. *Annual Review of Public Health*; 15:381-411, 1994.

Spengler, DM et al, "Back injuries in industry: A retrospective study. Overview and cost analysis, injury factors and employee-related factors. Analyzed 4645 injuries of which 900 were to the lower back, at Boeing plant in Washington State from 1979 – 1980. Found correlation between incidence of back injury and poor appraisal rating by supervisor within 6 month of the injury. *Spine*, 11:3 (1986) pp. 241-256)

Willich SN, Lowel H, Lewis M, et al: Weekly variation of acute myocardial infarction: Increased Monday risk in the working population. *Circulation* 90:87-93, 1994.

Work in America: Report of a special task force to the Secretary of Health, Education and Welfare. The best predictor for heart disease was not any of the major physical risk factors (smoking, high blood pressure, high cholesterol, and diabetes mellitus) but job dissatisfaction. And the second best predictor was what the researchers called "overall happiness." Canbridge, MA: MIT Press, 1973.

Books

Awaken The Giant Within by Anthony Robbins. New York: Simon & Shuster, 1992.
Billionaire Secrets to Success by Bill Bartmann. Dallas, Texas: Brown Books Publishing Group, 2005.
Chicken Soup for the Soul at Work by Jack Canfield, Mark Victor Hansen, Maida Rogerson, Martin Rutte & Tim Clauss. Deerfield Beach: Health Communications Inc., 1996.
Chicken Soup for the Soul: Living Your Dreams by Jack Canfield & Mark Victor Hansen Deerfield Beach, Florida: Health Communications Inc., 2003.
Creating the Work You Love by Rick Jarow. Rochester, Vermont: Destiny Books, 1995.
Finding Your Perfect Work by Paul and Sarah Edwards. New York: Jeremy P. Tarcher/Putnam, 1996.
Flow: The Psychology of Optimal Experience by Mihaly Csikszentmihalyi. New York: Harper Collins Publishers, 1990.
Frames of Mind: The Theory of Multiple Intelligences by Howard Gardner. New York: Basic Books, 1983.
Gesundheit! by Patch Adams M.D. Rochester, Vermont: Healing Arts Press, 1998.
How To Live Between Office Visits: A Guide to Life, Love an Health by Bernie Siegel M.D. New York: Harper Collins Publishers Ltd., 1993.
It's Not What Happens to You, It's What You Do About It by W. Mitchell. Partners

Publisher's Group, 1997.

Live The Life You Love In Ten Easy Step-By-Step Lessons by Barbara Sher. New York: Delacorte Press, 1996.

Living In The Light by Shakti Gawain. Novato, California: Nataraj Publishing, 1986.

Love, Medicine & Miracles by Bernie Siegel M.D. New York: Harper Perennial, 1986.

Meaning & Medicine by Larry Dossey, M.D. New York: Bantam Books, 1991.

On Becoming a Person: A Therapist's View of Psychotherapy by Carl Rogers. New York: Houghton Mifflin Company, 1989.

Passionate Longevity – The Ten Secrets to Growing Younger by Elaine Dembe. Toronto, Canada: Macmillan Canada, 1995.

Secrets of the Millionaire Mind by T. Harv Eker. Toronto, Canada: Harper Collins Publishers Ltd., 2005.

Stedman's Medical Dictionary 23rd Edition. Baltimore, Maryland: The Williams & Wilkins Company, 1976.

The Celestine Prophecy – An Adventure by James Redfield. New York: Warner Books, 1993

The Dance by Oriah Mountain Dreamer. Toronto, Canada: Harper Collins Publishers Ltd., 2001.

The 5 Patterns of Extraordinary Careers by James M. Citrin and Richard A. Smith. New York: Crown Business, 2003.

The Inner Game of Tennis by W. Timothy Gallwey. New York: Random House, 1997.

The Inner Game of Work, by W. Timothy Gallwey. New York: Random House Trade Paperbacks, 2000.

The Monk who sold his Ferrari by Robin S. Sharma. Toronto, Canada: Harper Collins Publishers Ltd., 1997.

The One Minute Millionaire: The Enlightened Way to Wealth by Mark Victor Hansen and Robert G. Allen. New York: Harmony Books, 2002.

The Pathfinder by Nicholas Lore. New York: Simon & Schuster, 1998.

The Pursuit of Happiness by David G. Myers. New York: Avon Books, Inc., 1992.

The Seat of the Soul by Gary Zukav. New York: Simon & Schuster, 1989.

The Stress of Life by Hans Selye. McGraw-Hill; 2nd edition, 1978.

The Tipping Point – How Little things can make a Big Difference by Malcolm Gladwell. New York: Little Brown and Company, 2002.

This Time I Dance! Creating the Work You Love by Tama J. Kieves. New York: Jeremy P. Tarcher/Penguin, 2002.

To Build the Life You Want, Create the Work You Love by Marsha Sinetar. New York: St. Martin's Press, 1995.

Toward a Psychology of Being, 3rd Edition (Hardcover) by Abraham H. Maslow. New York: John Wiley & Sons, Inc., 1999.

You'll See It When You Believe It: The Way to Your Personal Transformation by Wayne W. Dyer. New York: Harper Collins Publishers Inc., 1989.

What Color is you Parachute? By Richard Nelson Bolles. Berkeley, California: Ten Speed Press, 1980.

What Should I Do with My Life? by Po Bronson. New York: Random House, 2002.

When The Body Says No – The Cost of Hidden Stress by Gabor Maté, M.D. Toronto: Alfred A. Knopf Canada, 2003.

Zen and the Art of Motorcycle Maintenance by Robert M. Pirsig. New York: Bantam Books, 1974.

Dream Careers in Alphabetical Order

Small Business Owners

Profiles of the People featured in this Book

(in alphabetical order)

Ronen Abergel
Ronen Abergel Hair Artist. 8138 Yonge St. – 2nd floor, Thornhill, Ontario, L4J 1W5. 905-771-1084

Brenda Barnes
Owner, Operator and Principal of Martingrove Montessori School, 35 Hedges Blvd, Etobicoke, ON M9B 3C3. Phone: 416-626-8176. Our Mission Statement: Martingrove Montessori School is dedicated to the Montessori philosophy of unlocking the promise inherent in each child in an encouraging, safe, joyful and enriched environment, providing programs for children. ages 3 yrs. to 6 yrs. and Grades 1–3. martingrovemontessori@bellnet.ca. www.martingrovemontessorischool.ca

Joan Barrington
Joan Barrington is the Senior Program Manager, The Therapeutic Clown Program at SickKids. The Therapeutic Clown Program at SickKids eases the stress and anxiety of hospitalization and treatment for seriously ill and injured children and is made possible by generous donations from individuals, corporations and foundations. 555 University Avenue, Toronto, Ontario, M5G 1X8. 416-813-6629 Joan.barrington@sickkids.ca. www.sickkids.ca/therapeuticclownprogram

Jennifer Beale
Although shy as a teenager, Jennifer Beale became enthusiastic whenever she met an expert. Her enthusiasm compelled her to come out of her shell and tell the world about their expertise. After years as a freelance writer and editor, she turned her natural compulsion to promote and connect people into a successful career as a publicist. To promote and connect small business owners, she publishes BizNetworkNews.com, a free weekly newsletter of business networking events in every region of North America. You can sign up at www.BizNetworkNews.com and contact Jennifer at editor@BizNetworkNews.com

Orlando Bowen
Gameday Training and Consulting Inc. 8-400 Steeles Avenue East Suite 321, Brampton, ON L6W 4T4. Call toll free - 1-866-562-GAME (4263). Direct: (905) 487-0150. Fax (905) 487-0151. info@gamedaycamps.com

Normand Bouliane
Streetcar Operator

Greg Brophy
President and Chairman of Shred It. International Head Office, 2794 S. Sheridan Way, Oakville, Ontario, Canada L6J 7T4. tel: 905.829.2794. fax: 905.829.1999 Toll free: United States: 1-800-69 SHRED (74733). Canada: 1-800-69 SHRED (74733)

Ginette D'aigle
I would like to dedicate this to my children, so they never forget that you can live your dreams no matter how old you are or whatever obstacles might appear on your path. Never let anyone say you can't do it.

Mark Diamond
Co-director/owner of Camp Manitou
Camp Manitou is a residential camp for children age 7-16. We attract campers and

staff from the world over and offer fun, friends and fulfillment for each and every camper. With over 160 staff, for approximately 400 campers, we offer mature dedicated staff that act as excellent role models and mentors for our campers. Situated on the majestic Lake Manitouwabing, 2.5 hours from Toronto, Manitou offers over 32 activities, in visual and theatre arts, land and water sports, outdoor recreation, canoe tripping and climbing. www.manitoucamp.com

Cathleen Fillmore

Cathleen Fillmore is President of Speakers Gold – the boutique bureau. She founded and is past president of CAPS Halifax. Cathleen has written three books and more than 300 articles. She leads seminars across the country called 'The Seven Figure Speaker' and has a coaching program for professional speakers. To subscribe to her free Speakers Gold newsletter, email Cathleen@speakersgold.com or call 416-532-9886

Mira Gandhi

Promotional Wear Developer - In An Absolute Heartbeat 905-840-0597

Mark Gelgor

To my beloved wife Carmella, without her strength, skill and absolute commitment, this would not have been possible. To my two boys Gabriel-Sam and Dru who teach me daily about being a Dad. I love them deeply. Sportball to date: Spring 2006: Teaching 4000 kids across the GTA with just over 40 coaches. We have expanded to 127 locations and have opened 4 franchises. Currently running in B.C. (Vancouver and Victoria)

Noel Gordon

I operate a West Indian restaurant located at the corner of Derry and Goreway (3417 Derry Road E. Unit 102, Mississauga Ont. L4T 1A8 Tel. 905-673-5627). The menu consists of Jerk Pork, Jerk Chicken, Curried Goat, Curried Chicken, Oxtail beef, Cows Foot, Fish, Rice and Peas, Festivals and Dumplings. The name of the restaurant is Mr. Jerk which emphasizes our main dish. Our hours are Mon-Thurs 11 a.m.-11 p.m., Fri 11 a.m.-midnight., Sat 12 noon-11p.m. We cater for parties if you want to experience the best food of the Caribbean without going there. Mr. Jerk is the place to go.

Gregory Kaminsky

At Gregory Signs, companies of all sizes find the advertising expertise and talent they need to help differentiate their company in today's competitive market. Created in 1981 as an engraving shop, Gregory Signs has expanded over the years due to customer demands. We recently moved into a new 14,000 square foot facility. We now design, consult, manufacture, service and install custom signage, sign systems, sign programs and outdoor advertising packages. You can find our clients all across North America. Gregory Signs, 672 Petrolia Rd, Toronto, Ontario, M3J 2V2. 416-684-8025

Shirley Koch

Specializing in Hostas and Day Lilies over 400 varieties of each offered for sale. Ornamental grasses, both lilies and other perennials also available. Display gardens contain thousands of perennials including many unusual varieties for the gardener's viewing pleasure. Riverbend Gardens and Nursery, 43846 C-Line Rd., RR#2, Wroxeter, Ont., N0G 2X0

Laura Koot
News Presentation Editor, National Post. t: 416.383.2396. f: 416.442.2209

Janice Lindsay
Janice Lindsay, PINK, Colour + Design, is Canada's leading colour designer and an out-of-the-box design coach. She believes people know what they want but not how to get there. One short on-site consultation solves all colour and design conundrums and lays out a path for clients tailored to who they are, where they are and where they want to go. With an open mind and a wealth of experience she helps clients build on the good ideas and eliminate bad ones. Besides saving them time and heart ache, she often save them more money than they spend. [www.janicelindsay.com]

Charles Marcus
Charles is a best selling author, success strategist and a highly sought after motivational keynote speaker. For more information on how Charles can impact your organization and on his learning materials, please visit his website at http://www.cmarcus.com or call toll free at (800) 837-0629.

John McAuley
President/CEO Muskoka Woods. 200-20 Bamburgh Circle., Scarborough, Ont., M1W 3Y5 416-495-6960. www.muskokawoods.com

Scott McDiarmid
I work as a residential renovator for my own contracting and renovation business. The services that I offer are complete home renovations for any and all rooms of a house of condominium. My target market is a home owner in the Greater Toronto Area. Contact cell phone no.: 416-587-4129.

Michael McGauley
Michael McGauley is an inspiring speaker, and trauma recovery. He works with people all over North America to help them discover their inner strength when faced with adversity. http://www.thedreambuildersinc.com or mike@thedreambuildersinc.com, 1-866-878-8289.

Kim Mitchell
I would like to dedicate this story to my two daughters, Lauren Michelle Mitchell and Nicole Leigh Mitchell. I have always stressed to them that learning is a life long process and that they could achieve anything they dreamed for, with hard work and a dedicated effort. Also, this is dedicated to all of my very talented, successful adult students who helped to make my dream job a reality. Co-operative Education Instructor, Dufferin-Peel Adult Learning Centre-St.Gabriel School Telephone (905)362-0705 Ext.354. email:Kim.Mitchell@dpcdsb.org

Elaine Morton
Aesthetic Salon owner at the Nottawasaga Inn Resort in Alliston, Ont.
I live in Aurora, Ont. My Art Studio is in Aurora. I paint in multi media.
E-mail: Elaine.morgan073@sympatico.ca Salon Services: Full aesthetic services including manicures, pedicures, specialty facials, body treatments, make-up, medical camouflage, waxing, lash and brow tinting, spa days.
Email: Elaineskincare@sympatico.ca or www.Nottawasagaresort.com

Elaine Overholt
Elaine Overholt's voice techniques and passionate teachings are available in her Big Voice DVD and Vocal Warm-Up – The Step by Step Guide to Finding Your Most Powerful Authentic Voice! (CD) If you are an aspiring singer, someone who loves to sing, or even if you simply wish to speak with more confidence and intention, this easy-to-use step by step DVD and CD set is for you. It will show you how to develop the voice you always knew was there. Elaine's unique series of exercises will teach you how to warm up, develop, and experience your voice in ways you never thought possible. Visit www.elaineoverholt.com or Call 416-466-1816.

Avraham E. Plotkin
Rabbi at Chabad Lubavitch. 83 Green Lane, Thornhill, L3T 6K6. 905-886-0420

Jeffrey Prosserman
During the four years before launching Instinct Pictures (http://www.instinctpictures.ca), Jeffrey Prosserman was the president and co-founder of the multimedia-advertising firm, Twisted Cow Productions (http://www.twistedcow.com). In 2004, Prosserman co-directed and produced Snapped, a straight-to-video horror film internationally distributed by Velocity Home Entertainment and American World Pictures. In 2005, he produced and directed Unlearn, a short documentary distributed by the National Film Board of Canada focusing on the stigmatization faced by those who live with mental illness. At 22, Prosserman is currently producing a coming-of-age, camp comedy and a feature-length documentary on mental illness. Contact: jeff@instinctpictures.ca Instinct Pictures: http://www.instinctpictures.ca

Ricky Ramos
First I would like to thank Sam for allowing me to share my story. Secondly I would like to thank my parents for everything they did for me and for still loving me from above. Los amo por spempre. Ricky Ricardo Ramos Rodriguez, 105 La Rose Ave., Etobicoke, Ont., M9P 3S9

Susan Regenstreif
Music Specialist and Teacher. I presently run music programming for newborn up to preschool age children. My classes are both entertaining and educational. Instruments, props, puppets and movement are excellent tools in fostering a child's creativity, expression, and natural rhythmic ability. I also work for the City of Vaughan Recreation and Culture Department as well as at United Synagogue Day Schools. I can be contacted at: musicwithsusan@rogers.com

John Robinson
I still continue to make hand made Windsor chairs for sale to private and historical institutions. I also continue to teach chair making classes at my home shop in Virginia, Welland and Walkerton Ont. I have become quite involved with Lee Valley Tools as an instructor for a number of different working projects and seminars.

Brent Rogers
Principal, Strategic Advisory. Toronto, Canada. Phone: 416-527-2045; brogers@strategicadvisory.ca
Knowledge + Experience + Execution = Results
Business management coaching and advisory services for small and medium size business owners/managers including all aspects of business management,

marketing, finance and financial planning, business law, human resources and process improvement; Commercial banking and credit advisory services to obtain and/or optimize commercial credit and banking facilities, all aspects of commercial banking and finance; Business "rescue" expertise for businesses facing distress situations; General aviation consulting and light aircraft management; Over 30 years professional experience.

Daniella Santana

Penny Simmons

President and Founder of Penny Loafers Shoe Shine Company Inc. This old-fashioned shoe-shine stand provides complete care for women's and men's dress and casual footwear. 416.203.7496 E-mail: penny.simmons@pennyloafersshoeshine.com. www.pennyloafersshoeshine.com

Doug Sole

As co- owner of Soul Drums Ltd. I am the director of our outreach programs and training sessions. I am booked actively as a professional speaker and combine into my presentation the application of multi-cultural and values integration based drumming circles. My clients range from senior management teams with the federal government to many international corporations. Classroom applications are also included as I train teachers to apply my program as a multi-level character based social integration program. Soul Drums Ltd., 5295 Yonge Street, Toronto, Ontario, M2N 5R3. 416-225-5295; 800-305-SOUL (7685). Author of The Soul of Hand Drumming and The Soul of Circle Drumming. www.souldrums.com. sales@souldrums.com

Phil Solomon

I would like to thank former Attorney General David Young for changing my life forever by appointing me as a Justice of the Peace. This once in a lifetime opportunity has allowed me to grow in a positive and challenging environment.

Judy Suke

Judy is a motivational humorist, presentation skills coach, and author. Through her keynote speeches, workshops, retreats, and books, she dedicates her time to bringing humour and hope to people around the world. She was named "Mississauga Woman of the Year", for volunteer efforts; District 60 "Toastmaster of the Year" for leadership; and the "Pinnacle Business Woman of Distinction" for excellence in education and training. Judy is the President of the Hamilton-Niagara Region Chapter of the Canadian Association of Professional Speakers. Judy Suke, Motivational Humorist, Triangle Seminars. www.triangleseminars.com.

Robin Tapley

rtapley@deltahotels.com. Tel: (705) 789-1871 ext. 3478. Fax: (705) 789-1674
Nature Trails continues to evolve on a regular basis, therefore, we have a variety of new programs offered on a seasonal basis including everything from astronomy to fisheries research where the client becomes the scientist for the day helping us collect useable fisheries data. Our newest program (Spring 2006) is our Living Off the Land program. Designed in partnership with First Nations and Nature Trails we offer a hands-on experience on how to live in harmony with the forces of nature through demonstration and participation.

Shavey Tishler
Mother Nature Day Care is the name of our facility. We are licensed by the Ministry of Community and Social Services and are allowed 24 children from 2 1/2 to 5 years old. We are situated in mid-town Toronto and all the employees are early childhood educators. We serve only whole grain, natural food and provide a warm home away form home environment. Mother Nature Day Care, 124 Belsize Drive, Toronto, Ontario, M4S 1L8, 416-487-7345.

Tsufit
Tsufit coaches entrepreneurs and keynote speakers to sparkle in the spotlight! She's in demand as a coach, keynote speaker, singer, TV show guest, seminar leader and mom (although TSUFIT points out that she's not currently taking on any new clients in the last category!) Tom Peters says TSUFIT's new book, Step Into The Spotlight! is "necessary and delightful." Check it out or listen to her music CD at www.followthatdream.ca & www.tsufit.com.

Ila Faye Turley
I never much thought about getting older (don't feel it), much less living my dream now, much less a dream that values and nurtures youth. Feel free to contact me at my email address for film, TV or theater roles you may need filled, ila_faye_turley@yahoo.ca, 403-284-2556

Jeff Wilson
Director, Camp Manitou, Canada. 2660 Yonge St., Toronto, Ont., M4P 2J5. Jeff@manitourcamp.com

Order Copies of
Live Your Dreams: Doctor's Orders
by Dr. Samuel Gerstein, M.D.

Buy this book if you are serious about
living your dreams or as a gift for friends,
family and colleagues.

Order Form
(Please print clearly)

Full Name _____

Mailing address _____

City _____

Prov./State _____Country _____Postal Code _____

Phone number_____Email_____

Live Your Dreams - Doctor's Orders

Pricing		Quantity	Unit Price	Total
1-4	$22.95 Cdn			
5-49	$20 Cdn			
50-99	$18 Cdn			
100-499	$16 Cdn			
500+	$14 Cdn			
*single copy shipping. For multiple books you will be notified of your shipping charges prior to processing.		Subtotal		
		Shipping & Handling within Canada*		$7.00
		Shipping & Handling within USA*		$12.00
		6% GST (Canada only)		
		Total		

❏ Cheque payable to: **Dreams For Real Inc.**
Mail to 5863 Leslie Street, Suite 316 Toronto, Ontario, Canada M2H 1J8
❏ Visa # _____-_____-_____-_____ exp ___/___
❏ M/C # _____-_____-_____-_____ exp ___/___

Authorization Signature: _____ Date: _____